THE AWAKENED WARRIOR

For books written by the editor, see the last page of this book.

A NEW
CONSCIOUSNESS
READER

This *New Consciousness Reader* is part of a new series of original and classic writing by renowned experts on leading-edge concepts in personal development, psychology, spiritual growth, and healing. Other books in this series include:

Dreamtime and Dreamwork
EDITED BY STANLEY KRIPPNER, PH.D.

The Erotic Impulse
EDITED BY DAVID STEINBERG

Fathers, Sons, and Daughters
EDITED BY CHARLES SCULL, PH.D.

Healers on Healing
EDITED BY RICHARD CARLSON, PH.D., AND BENJAMIN SHIELD

In the Company of Others
EDITED BY CLAUDE WHITMYER

Meeting the Shadow
EDITED BY CONNIE ZWEIG
AND JEREMIAH ABRAMS

Mirrors of the Self
EDITED BY CHRISTINE DOWNING

The New Paradigm in Business
EDITED BY MICHAEL RAY AND ALAN RINZLER
FOR THE WORLD BUSINESS ACADEMY

Paths Beyond Ego
EDITED BY ROGER WALSH, M.D., PH.D., AND FRANCES VAUGHAN, PH.D.

Reclaiming the Inner Child
EDITED BY JEREMIAH ABRAMS

Spiritual Emergency
EDITED BY STANISLAV GROF, M.D., AND CHRISTINA GROF

To Be a Man
EDITED BY KEITH THOMPSON

To Be a Woman
EDITED BY CONNIE ZWEIG

What Survives?
EDITED BY GARY DOORE, PH.D.

Who Am I?
EDITED BY ROBERT FRAGER

SERIES EDITOR: CONNIE ZWEIG

THE AWAKENED WARRIOR

LIVING WITH COURAGE, COMPASSION & DISCIPLINE

Edited by Rick Fields

A JEREMY P. TARCHER / PUTNAM BOOK
Published by G. P. Putnam's Sons
New York

A Jeremy P. Tarcher/Putnam Book
Published by G. P. Putnam's Sons
Publishers Since 1838
200 Madison Avenue
New York, NY 10016

Permissions and copyrights are listed on pages 263–67.

Library of Congress Cataloging-in-Publication Data

The Awakened warrior : living with courage, compassion & discipline /
edited by Rick Fields.
p.   cm.
A Jeremy P. Tarcher/Putnam book.
ISBN 0-87477-775-5 (pbk.)
1. Conduct of life.   2. Courage.   3. Caring.   4. Self-control.
I. Fields, Rick.
BJ1533.C8A92   1994   93-50875 CIP
158'.1—dc20

Design by Irving Perkins Associates

Printed in the United States of America
1   2   3   4   5   6   7   8   9   10

This book is printed on acid-free paper.

To Kanjuro Shibata Sensei,
Zen archer and teacher —
"Mind is target."

And Frederick Douglass,
liberator —
"Whence came the spirit
I do not know."

And Crazy Horse,
Tashunka-Witko —
"One does not sell
the earth upon which the people walk."

Contents

PART II

THE WARRIOR IN EVERYDAY LIFE:
LOVING, FIGHTING, WORKING

PART III

MARTIAL ARTS: FIGHTING FOR LIFE
ON AND OFF THE MAT

PART IV

THE OUTER WARRIOR:
ACTIVISM IN THE REAL WORLD

PART V

SPIRITUAL COMBAT: THE BATTLE WITHIN

Acknowledgments

Many people contributed to this anthology over the years it has taken shape. For suggestions and encouragement, I would particularly like to thank Eve Wallace, Robert Moore, Jude Blitz and Tom Daly, Bob Wing, Richard Heckler, Ron Myer, John McClellan, John White, Donna Zerner, and the gently persistent editor of this series, Connie Zweig.

Introduction

The warrior is by definition a fighter, a man or woman of action, who meets and resolves the challenges of life. But the warrior is also more than a fighter. Like the thorn on the rose, the warrior is pledged to protect whatever is lovely, vulnerable, and truly precious. This may include the warrior's own life, but it does not stop with self-interest. The warrior's care and protection extends outward in an ever-widening circle, from family, tribe, king, nation, and now to earth herself.

In order to meet this challenge, warriors throughout the world always have cultivated certain qualities and values: courage and bravery in facing both life and death; discipline in training both body and mind; strategy in keeping and restoring peace, as well as in battle; knowledge of one's own weakness and strength, as well as of the opponent's; and loyalty to comrades, as well as to a transcendent value.

These noble ideals are part of the warrior spirit that is our evolutionary heritage. This warrior spirit is one of the patterns of our deep psychic structure, archetypal and innate. As William James wrote, "Ancestral evolution has made us all warriors."

This archetypal warrior energy is one of the most powerful forces of the human psyche. When it goes astray, it can cause tremendous destruction and suffering. But when it is properly honored, honed, and disciplined, when we know how to work with it, the warrior within can be the source of tremendous good. Without a well-developed warrior spirit, it is difficult to accomplish anything worthwhile.

There is, in fact, an ancient tradition, a lineage, of "awakened warriors," who serve rather than ravage humanity and the earth. The awakened warrior follows the Buddha, who taught that "the man who conquers himself is the greatest of conquerers." For this reason, as Buddhist scholar Lobsang Lhalungpa tells us, the way of the bodhisattva, an "awakened being" dedicated to helping others, is "popularly called in Tibetan 'the way of the warrior,' since a practicing bodhisattva conquers formidable enemies—his egoistic delusions and all its forces—and then seeks to liberate others enslaved by similar adversaries."

The awakened warrior is not a person who makes war, but a person who relates to himself and the world with courage, in order to end war and violence. "The key to warriorship," says Chögyam Trungpa, "is not being afraid of who you are. Ultimately, that is the definition of bravery: not being afraid of yourself." Such bravery involves discipline and training, of course, but it also involves being kind and vulnerable, both to ourselves and others.

The path of the awakened warrior has existed in many cultures and traditions, and taken many different forms. Among the Sioux, for example, as elder Matthew King tells us, "The warrior only fights to protect the people. The warrior is always the first to help and the last to eat." In feudal Europe, the knights vowed to defend widows and orphans. In Taoist China, the great general Sun Tzu wrote in *The Art of War*, "To win one hundred victories in one hundred battles is not the acme of skill. To subdue the enemy without fighting is the acme of skill." And in Japan, the martial arts evolved into a spiritual training leading to, in the words of the founder of aikido, "a life of loving protection of all beings with a spirit of reconciliation."

Now more than ever, we need the fierce compassion of the awakened warrior to inspire and guide us in our daily lives, as well as in our social and environmental struggles. We also need the bravery and determination of the warrior in our spiritual search. For the awakened warrior recognizes that our first and deepest struggle, the struggle which informs all our other battles, is to wake up to the precious life that is ours to live, to serve, to protect, and—if need be—to defend as well.

The ancient and varied lineage of the awakened warrior is very much alive in the world today. In fact, as this anthology makes clear, we are in the midst of both a revisioning and renewal of this enduring ideal.

PART I

WHO IS A WARRIOR?

SURVEYING THE TERRAIN

Warrior's Creed

I have no parents: I make the heavens and earth my parents.

I have no home: I make awareness my home.

I have no life or death: I make the tides of breathing my life and death.

I have no divine power: I make honesty my divine power.

I have no means: I make understanding my means.

I have no magic secrets: I make character my magic secret.

I have no body: I make endurance my body.

I have no eyes: I make the flash of lightning my eyes.

I have no ears: I make sensibility my ears.

I have no limbs: I make promptness my limbs.

I have no strategy: I make "unshadowed by thought" my strategy.

I have no designs: I make "seizing opportunity by the forelock" my design.

I have no miracles: I make "right action" my miracles.

I have no principles: I make adaptability to all circumstances my principles.

I have no tactics: I make emptiness and fullness my tactics.

I have no talents: I make ready wit my talent.

I have no friends: I make my mind my friend.

I have no enemy: I make carelessness my enemy.

I have no armor: I make benevolence and righteousness my armor.

I have no castle: I make immovable-mind my castle.

I have no sword: I make absence of self my sword.

—ANONYMOUS SAMURAI, FOURTEENTH CENTURY

Introduction

The contemporary awakened warrior draws inspiration from many different traditions and approaches: Perhaps the most influential are the Shambhala warrior tradition of Tibet; the Native American shaman-warrior, Don Juan; the peaceful warrior presented by gymnast Dan Millman; a new appreciation of the importance of the woman warrior; the tradition of the knights; the mythopoeic studies of the Jungians; and the aikido-inspired Modern or New Warrior trainings conducted by George Leonard and others.

In Part I, we examine the question "What Is a Warrior?" with essays and interviews by some of these major contemporary exponents of the way of the awakened warrior. In "Confidence and Compassion," Chögyam Trungpa, the late Tibetan meditation master who introduced the teachings of the Shambhala warrior to the West, writes that "warriorship refers to realizing the power, dignity, and wakefulness that is inherent in all of us as human beings." The Shambhala teachings owe much to the Buddhist teachings, but they also include elements drawn from the shamanistic Tibetan Bon tradition, as well as the Chinese Taoists and Japanese samurai.

This is followed by an excerpt from Sam Keen's interview with Carlos Castaneda, whose 1967 bestseller, *The Teachings of Don Juan*, introduced readers to an indigenous Amerindian tradition of warriorship as taught by the wily warrior-sorcerer Don Juan. "The basic difference between an ordinary man and a warrior," Don Juan says, "is that a warrior takes everything as a challenge while an ordinary man takes everything as either a blessing or a curse."

Chapter 3 presents an interview with Dan Millman, the author of the underground classic *The Way of the Peaceful Warrior*. According to Millman, the peaceful warrior "combines courage and love—a warrior's spirit with a peaceful heart." This is followed by Ambrose Redmoon's impassioned article, "There Are No Peaceful Warriors,"

3

which argues that the trendy term "peaceful warrior" is an "insult to those who have placed themselves between innocence and evil."

Chapter 5, "The Warrior in His Fullness," by Robert Moore and Douglas Gillette, represents the deconstruction and revisioning of the warrior that has come out of the mythopoeic men's movement. According to their analysis, "The masculine developmental trajectory floods young males with instinctual aggressive energy ... before life experience can provide wisdom for the modulation of these energies." This wisdom, they say, was once provided by tribal initiations. But the loss of these traditions "has left us in a situation in which the immature expression of male aggression terrorizes the global community, including the world of women and children."

The fully developed or mature warrior, however, has gained the wisdom to modulate aggression, and so becomes "energetic, decisive, courageous, enduring, persevering, and loyal to some greater good beyond our personal gain." This is a psychological profile of the awakened warrior.

Moore and Gillette's work on the immature (or shadow) warrior and the mature warrior is an important contribution to the discussion of male violence. But it must be remembered that the close identification between the warrior and the masculine may be traced to an early human adaptive strategy in which women gathered and cared for infants while men hunted. This mutually beneficial arrangement resulted in certain physical divergencies. On the whole, men developed greater musculature and upper body strength, qualities easily adaptable to hand-to-hand combat between humans.

Yet the evolutionary selection of men as warrior-soldiers does not mean women lack an innate warrior spirit. This spirit is expressed in mythological figures like Inanna, the Amazon queen Penthesilea, and Kali; in heroines like Joan of Arc or the Chinese swordswomen; and in contemporary anti-war and eco-warriors.

In "Warrioring: Male and Female," psychologist Carol Pearson compares the male and female expressions of the warrior archetype. "Men are socialized practically from birth to be warriors," she writes, "so their issue is whether they can develop other sides of themselves. For women, the issue is whether they will have the audacity even to enter a contest culturally defined as male. . . ."

Most recently, the feminine warrior spirit has found a voice in the work of Clarissa Pinkola Estés. While her "wild woman" is not necessarily a warrior, it is also true that the wolf, which inspires her work, is a traditional totem-figure for the warrior among Native Americans and ancient Indo-Europeans. In an interview with Peggy Taylor, Estés gives voice to the women's warrior spirit when she speaks of the "fierceness of the wolf, and its ability to survive—but also to thrive, to love its children, to choose lifelong mates, to live together in a group, and to have its own kind of music and joyfulness."

This is followed by two mythological approaches to the theme of the woman warrior. Gloria Steinem writes about the inspiration she drew from the comic-book Amazon, Wonder Woman, while the heroine of Maxine Hong Kingston's memoir, "The Woman Warrior," becomes a Chinese swordswoman in a faraway land.

In "Soldiers of Christ," Charles A. Coulombe explores the mixed Christian and pagan origin of the knights and their chivalric code. He suggests that the time may be ripe for a revival of "the original Western 'way of the warrior.' "

Renowned mythologist Joseph Campbell's contribution knits together stories from Siberia, Sumeria, medieval France, and the Blackfoot Indians to lay bare the archetypal structure of the warrior-hero: "The sword edge of the hero-warrior flashes with the energy of the creative Source: before it fall the shells of the Outworn. . . . The dragon to be slain by him is precisely the monster of the status quo: Holdfast, the keeper of the past."

In a work of erudition and insight, "Wars, Arms, Rams, Mars," Jungian analyst James Hillman delves deeply into the warrior archetype, reminding us "it was an ancient custom and is still a modern psychological technique to turn for aid to the same principle that causes an affliction. The cure of the Mars we fear is the God himself."

We end this section with two manifestos: "The Warrioress Creed" by Mirtha Vega, leader of warrioress retreats; and "The Modern Warrior" by George Leonard, author and black belt in aikido. Leonard developed his points in the Modern Warrior trainings conducted at Esalen Institute with Jack Cirie. Leonard calls on the Modern Warrior to create a "more vivid peace . . . make every moment intense. Live each day as though a fire is raging. Expect nothing. Be ready for anything."

1

Confidence and Compassion

by Chögyam Trungpa

By warriorship we are not particularly talking about the skills necessary to wage war in the conventional sense. We are not talking about learning how to handle lethal weapons and crank up our aggression and territoriality so that we can burst forth and conquer all our enemies. Warriorship here refers to realizing the power, dignity and wakefulness that is inherent in all of us as human beings. It is awakening our basic human confidence, which allows us to cheer up, develop a sense of vision and succeed in what we are doing.

Because warriorship is innate in human beings, the way to become a warrior—or the warrior's path—is to see who and what we are as human beings and cultivate that. If we look at ourselves directly, without hesitation or embarrassment, we find that we have a lot of strength and a lot of resources available constantly. From that point of view, if we feel we are without resources, if we feel incompetent or as if we were running out of ideas, it is said that we are being attacked by the enemy of warriorship: our own cowardice. The idea of warriorship is that because of our human potential we can go beyond that, step over the enemy of cowardly mind and discover further banks of resources and inspiration within ourselves.

Cowardly mind is based on the fear of death. Ordinarily we try to ward off any reminders that we are going to die. We constantly produce artificial environments to shield ourselves from any harsh edges. We weave ourselves warm cocoons in which we can live and feel comfortable and sleepy all the time. We try to keep everything under control so that nothing unexpected will pop up and give us a nasty shock, reminding us of our impermanence, our mortality. By doing this we are trying to defend ourselves from death, which we could say is the opposite of celebrating life. By maintaining our defensive attitude, we keep ourselves surrounded by a familiar fog. We wind up breeding depression and general unhappiness. In fact, that unceasing atmosphere of depression is what makes our little created environments feel so familiar and nestlike. But because it is based on struggle, this cowardly approach of ours is very far from the sense of real joy and playfulness that is associated with warrior-ship.

Becoming a warrior means that we can look directly at ourselves, see the nature of our cowardly mind, and step out of it. We can trade our small-minded struggle for security for a much vaster vision, one of fearlessness, openness and genuine heroism. This doesn't happen all at once but is a gradual process. Our first inkling of that possibility comes when we begin to sense the claustrophobia and stuffiness of our self-imposed cocoon. At that point our safe home begins to feel like a trap and we begin to sense that an alternative is possible. We begin to have tremendous longing for some kind of ventilation, and finally we actually experience a delightful breath of fresh air coming into our stale nest.

At this point we realize that it has been our choice all along to live in this restrictive, and by now somewhat revolting, mentality of defensiveness and cowardice. Simultaneously, we realize that we could just as easily switch our allegiance. We could break out of our dark, stuffy prison into the fresh air where it is possible for us to stretch our legs, to walk, run, or even dance and play. We realize that we could drop the oppressive struggle it takes to maintain our cowardice, and relax instead in the greater space of confidence.

It is important to understand what we mean by the confidence of the warrior. The warrior is not developing confidence *in* anything. He is not simply learning one skill, such as swordsmanship, in which he feels he could always take refuge. Nor is he falling back on some mentality of choicelessness, a sense that if only he can hold out long enough and keep a stiff upper lip, then he is bound to come out all right. Those conventional ideas of confidence would simply be further cocoons, based once again on yet further styles of defensiveness and fundamental aggression.

In this case we say the warrior has self-existing confidence. This means that he remains in a *state* of confidence free from competition and any notion of struggle. The warrior's confidence is unconditional. In other words, because he is undistracted by any cowardly thoughts the warrior can rest in an unwavering and wakeful state of mind, which needs no reference points whatsoever.

On the other hand, we do not mean to say that once the warrior has uncovered his innate confidence there is nothing left for him to do. In many ways, the path of the warrior is very similar to the Buddhist notion of the bodhisattva path of selfless action. The bodhisattva is a practitioner who isn't satisfied with the possibility of liberating himself from the pain of samsara but heroically commits himself not to rest until he has helped save all sentient beings. In the same way, the confident warrior does not simply feel proud of having seen the nature of his cocoon and stepped out of it. He cannot rest in any sense of smugness at his achievement, or even in the sense of freedom and relief itself. Rather his understanding and personal experience of the claustrophobia of cowardly mind serve as an inspiration for the warrior to free others as well as himself. He actually cannot ignore the suffering and depression he sees in those around him. So from his unconditional confidence, spontaneous compassion naturally arises.

The warrior's compassion manifests in different qualities, which all arise from the nature of his basic confidence. Because the warrior's confident state of mind is self-existing, unmanufactured by aggression, he is not bloated or arrogant. Instead he is humble, kind and self-contained in relating with others. The warrior is not captured by doubts; therefore he is humorous, uplifted and perky in his dealings. He is not trapped by the pettiness of hope and fear, so his vision becomes vast and he is not afraid of making mistakes. Finally his mind itself becomes as fathomless as space, so he attains complete mastery over the phenomenal world. With all of these qualities, the warrior has a tremendous sense of forward vision. In other words, he is not deterred or depressed by obstacles, but with genuine inquisitiveness and cheerfulness he includes all of them as part of his path.

The confident warrior conducts himself with gentleness, fearlessness and intelligence. Gentleness is the warm quality of the human heart. Because of the warmth of his heart, the warrior's confidence is not too hard or brittle. Rather it has a vulnerable, open and soft quality. It is our gentleness which allows us to feel warmth and kindness and to fall in love. But at the same time we are not completely tender. We are tough as well as soft. We are fearless as well as gentle. The warrior meets the world with a slight sense of detachment, a sense of distance and precision. This aspect of confidence is the natural instinct of fearlessness which allows the warrior to meet challenges without losing his integrity. Finally our confidence expresses itself as innate intelligence, which raises ordinary gentleness and fearlessness to the level of warriorship. In other words, it is intelligence that prevents gentleness from becoming cheap romanticism without any vision, and fearlessness from becoming purely macho. Intelligence is our sense of wakeful inquisitiveness toward the world. It is what allows us to appreciate and take delight in the vivid qualities of the world around us.

We have already called cowardice the warrior's enemy. Cowardice is the seductive and distracting quality of our wandering or neurotic minds which prevents us from resting in our natural state, the state of unwavering wakefulness which we have called the warrior's confidence. Cowardice is actually the force of evil which obstructs what we could call our basic goodness, our inherent state of confidence which is by nature devoid of cowardice and aggression, free from evil. From that point of view, the purpose of warriorship is to conquer the enemy, to subjugate the evil of our cowardly minds and uncover our basic goodness, our confidence.

When we talk here about conquering the enemy, it is important to understand that we are not talking about aggression. The genuine warrior does not become resentful or arrogant. Such ambition or arrogance would be simply another aspect of cowardly mind, another enemy of warriorship in itself. So it is absolutely necessary for the warrior to subjugate his own ambition to conquer at the same time that he is subjugating his other more obvious enemies. Thus the idea of warriorship altogether is that by facing all our enemies fearlessly, with gentleness and intelligence, we can develop ourselves and thereby attain self-realization.

2

A Path with Heart: An Interview with Carlos Castaneda

by Sam Keen

KEEN: Rumors flourish in an information vacuum. We know something about Don Juan but too little about Castaneda.

CASTANEDA: That is a deliberate part of the life of a warrior. To weasel in and out of different worlds you have to remain inconspicuous. The more you are known and identified, the more your freedom is curtailed. When people have definite ideas about who you are and how you will act, then you can't move. One of the earliest things Don Juan taught me was that I must erase my personal history. If little by little you create a fog around yourself then you will not be taken for granted and you will have more room for change. That is the reason I avoid tape recordings when I lecture, and photographs.

KEEN: Maybe we can be personal without being historical. You now minimize the importance of the psychedelic experience connected with your apprenticeship. And you don't seem to go around doing the kind of tricks you describe as the sorcerer's stock-in-trade. What are the elements of Don Juan's teachings that are important for you? How have you been changed by them?

CASTANEDA: For me, the ideas of being a warrior and a man of knowledge, with the eventual hope of being able to stop the world and see, have been most applicable. They have given me peace and confidence in my ability to control my life. At the time I met Don Juan, I had very little personal power. My life had been very erratic. I had come a long way from my birthplace in Brazil. Outwardly I was aggressive and cocky, but within I was indecisive and unsure of myself. I was always making excuses for myself. Don Juan once accused me of being a professional child because I was so full of self-pity. I felt like a leaf in the wind. Like most intellectuals, my back was against the wall. I had no place to go. I couldn't see any way of life that really excited me. I thought all I could do was make a mature adjustment to a life of boredom or find ever more complex forms of entertainment such as the use of psychedelics and pot and sexual adventures. All of this was exaggerated by my habit of introspection. I was always looking within and talking to myself. The inner dialogue seldom stopped. Don Juan turned my eyes outward and taught me how to see the magnificence of the world and how to accumulate personal power.

I don't think there is any other way to live if one wants to be exuberant.

KEEN: He seems to have hooked you with the old philosopher's trick of holding death before your eyes. I was struck with how classical Don Juan's approach was. I heard echoes of Plato's idea that a philosopher must study death before he can gain any access to the real world and of Martin Heidegger's definition of man as being-toward-death.

CASTANEDA: Yes, but Don Juan's approach has a strange twist because it comes from the tradition in sorcery that death is a physical presence that can be felt and seen. One of the glosses in sorcery is: death stands to your left. Death is an impartial judge who will speak truth to you and give you accurate advice. After all, death is in no hurry. He will get you tomorrow or next week or in fifty years. It makes no difference to him. The moment you remember you must eventually die, you are cut down to the right size.

I think I haven't made this idea vivid enough. The gloss—"death to your left"—isn't an intellectual matter in sorcery; it is a perception. When your body is properly tuned to the world and you turn your eyes to your left, you can witness an extraordinary event, the shadowlike presence of death.

KEEN: In the existential tradition, discussions of responsibility usually follow discussions of death.

CASTANEDA: Then Don Juan is a good existentialist. When there is no way of knowing whether I have one more minute of life, I must live as if this is my last moment. Each act is the warrior's last battle. So everything must be done impeccably. Nothing can be left pending. This idea has been very freeing for me. I don't have any more loose ends; nothing is waiting for me. I am here talking to you and I may never return to Los Angeles. But that wouldn't matter because I took care of everything before I came.

KEEN: This world of death and decisiveness is a long way from psychedelic utopias, in which the vision of endless time destroys the tragic quality of choice.

CASTANEDA: When death stands to your left, you must create your world by a series of decisions. There are no large or small decisions, only decisions that must be made now.

And there is no time for doubts or remorse. If I spend my time regretting what I did yesterday, I avoid the decisions I need to make today.

KEEN: How did Don Juan teach you to be decisive?

CASTANEDA: He spoke to my body with his acts. My old way was to leave everything pending and never to decide anything. To me, decisions were ugly. It seemed unfair for a sensitive man to have to decide. One day Don Juan asked me: "Do you think you and I are equals?" I was a university student and an intellectual and he was an old Indian, but I condescended and said: "Of course we are equals." He said: "I don't think we are. I am a hunter and a warrior and you are a pimp. I am ready to sum up my life at any moment. Your feeble world of indecision and sadness is not equal to mine." Well, I was very insulted and would have left, but we were in the middle of the wilderness. So I sat down and got trapped in my own ego involvement. I was going to wait until he decided to go home. After many hours I saw that Don Juan would stay there forever if he had to. Why not? For a man with no pending business, that is his power. I finally realized that this man was not like my father who would make twenty New Year's resolutions and cancel them all out. Don Juan's decisions were irrevocable as far as he was concerned. They could be canceled out only by other decisions. So I went over and touched him and he got up and we went home. The impact of that act was tremendous. It convinced me that the way of the warrior is an exuberant and powerful way to live.

KEEN: It isn't the content of decision that is important so much as the act of being decisive.

CASTANEDA: That is what Don Juan means by having a gesture. A gesture is a deliberate act which is undertaken for the power that comes from making a decision. For instance, if a warrior found a snake that was numb and cold, he might struggle to invent a way to take the snake to a warm place without being bitten. The warrior would make the gesture just for the hell of it. But he would perform it perfectly.

KEEN: There seem to be many parallels between existential philosophy and Don Juan's teachings. What you have said about decision and gesture suggests that Don Juan, like Nietzsche or Sartre, believes that will rather than reason is the most fundamental faculty of man.

CASTANEDA: I think that's right. Let me speak for myself. What I want to do, and maybe I can accomplish it, is to take the control away from my reason. My mind has been in control all of my life, and it would kill me rather than relinquish control. At one point in my apprenticeship, I became profoundly depressed. I was overwhelmed with terror and gloom and thoughts about suicide. Then Don Juan warned me this was one of reason's tricks to retain control. He said my reason was making my body feel that there was no meaning to life. Once my mind waged this last battle and lost, reason began to assume its proper place as a tool of the body.

KEEN: "The heart has its reasons that reason knows nothing of" and so does the rest of the body.

CASTANEDA: That is the point. The body has a will of its own. Or rather, the will is the voice of the body. That is why Don Juan consistently put his teachings in dramatic form. My intellect could easily dismiss his world of sorcery as nonsense. But my body was attracted to his world and his way of life. And once the body took over, a new and healthier reign was established.

KEEN: Don Juan's techniques for dealing with dreams engaged me because they suggest the possibility of voluntary control of dream images. It is as though he proposes to establish a permanent, stable observatory within inner space. Tell me about Don Juan's dream training.

CASTANEDA: The trick in dreaming is to sustain dream images long enough to look at them carefully. To gain this kind of control you need to pick one thing in advance and learn to find it in your dreams. Don Juan suggested that I use my hands as a steady point and go back and forth between them and the images. After some months I learned to find my hands and to stop the dream. I became so fascinated with the technique that I could hardly wait to go to sleep.

KEEN: Is stopping the images in dreams anything like stopping the world?

CASTANEDA: It is similar. But there are differences. Once you are capable of finding your hands at will, you realize that it is only a technique. What you are after is control. A man of knowledge must accumulate personal power. But that is not enough to stop the world. Some abandon also is necessary. You must silence the chatter that is going on inside your mind and surrender yourself to the outside world.

KEEN: Of the many techniques that Don Juan taught you for stopping the world, which do you still practice?

CASTANEDA: My major discipline now is to disrupt my routines. I was always a very routinary person. I ate and slept on schedule. In 1965 I began to change my habits. I wrote in the quiet hours of the night and slept and ate when I felt the need. Now I have dismantled so many of my habitual ways of acting that before long I may become unpredictable and surprising to myself.

KEEN: Your discipline reminds me of the Zen story of two disciples bragging about miraculous powers. One disciple claimed the founder of the sect to which he belonged could stand on one side of a river and write the name of Buddha on a piece of paper held by his assistant on the opposite shore. The second disciple replied that such a miracle was unimpressive. "My miracle," he said, "is that when I feel hungry I eat, and when I feel thirsty I drink."

CASTANEDA: It has been this element of engagement in the world that has kept me following the path which Don Juan showed me. There is no need to transcend the world. Everything we need to know is right in front of us, if we pay attention. If you enter a state of nonordinary reality, as you do when you use psychotropic plants, it is only to draw from it what you need in order to see the miraculous character of ordinary reality. For me the way to live— the path with heart—is not introspection or mystical transcendence but presence in the world. This world is the warrior's hunting ground.

KEEN: The world you and Don Juan have pictured is full of magical coyotes, enchanted crows and a beautiful sorceress. It's easy to see how it could engage you. But what about the world of the modern urban person? Where is the magic there? If we could all live in the mountains, we might keep wonder alive. But how is it possible when we are half a zoom from the freeway?

CASTANEDA: I once asked Don Juan the same question. We were sitting in a café in Yuma and I suggested that I might be able to learn to stop the world and to see, if I could come and live in the wilderness with him. He looked out the window at the passing cars and said: "That, out there, is your world. You cannot refuse it. You are a hunter of that world." I live in Los Angeles now and I find I can use that world to accommodate my needs. It is a challenge to live with no set routines in a routinary world. But it can be done.

KEEN: The noise level and the constant pressure of masses of people seem to destroy the silence and solitude that would be essential for stopping the world.

CASTANEDA: Not at all. In fact, the noise can be used. You can use the buzzing of the freeway to teach yourself to listen to the outside world. When we stop the world, the world we stop is the one we usually maintain by our continual inner dialogue. Once you can stop the internal babble, you stop maintaining your old world. The descriptions collapse. That is when personality change begins. When you concentrate on sounds, you realize it is difficult for the brain to categorize all the sounds, and in a short while you stop trying. This is unlike visual perception which keeps us forming categories and thinking. It is so restful when you can turn off the talking, categorizing, and judging.

KEEN: The internal world changes, but what about the external one? We may revolutionize individual consciousness but still not touch the social structures that create our alienation. Is there any place for social or political reform in your thinking?

CASTANEDA: I came from Latin America where intellectuals were always talking about political and social revolution and where a lot of bombs were thrown. But revolution hasn't changed much. It takes little daring to bomb a building, but in order to give up cigarettes or to stop being anxious or to stop internal chattering, you have to remake yourself. This is where real reform begins.

Don Juan and I were in Tucson not long ago when they were having Earth Week. Some man was lecturing on ecology and the evils of the war in Vietnam. All the while he was smoking. Don Juan said, "I cannot imagine that he is concerned with other people's bodies when he doesn't like his own." Our first concern should be with ourselves. I can like my fellow men only when I am at my peak of vigor and am not depressed. To be in this condition I must keep my body trimmed. Any revolution must begin here in this body. I can alter my culture but only from within a body that is impeccably tuned in to this weird world. For me, the real accomplishment is the art of being a warrior, which, as Don Juan says, is the only way to balance the terror of being a man with the wonder of being a man.

3

The Way of the Peaceful Warrior: An Interview with Dan Millman

by Rick Fields

RICK FIELDS: Dan, what exactly do you mean by the term "peaceful warrior"? It sounds like a contradiction.

DAN MILLMAN: You mean, how can we be both peaceful and a warrior? Famous warriors from every culture, in spite of their violent image, have demonstrated qualities of courage, commitment, and inner strength; yet few of these warriors have had a peaceful heart. On the other hand, the peacemakers of history have shown qualities of loving-kindness and compassion, yet few of these peacemakers possessed a warrior's spirit. The peaceful warrior combines courage and love—a warrior's spirit with a peaceful heart.

RF: But do peaceful warriors fight? Do peaceful warriors go to war?

DM: Well, this is a cliché, obviously, it's been said so many times—but the first war we have to deal with is within ourselves. People who like themselves and care about themselves are not naturally going to want to go out and hurt anybody else. For example, I'll state publicly: I will not go to war. Period. I will not kill people. I will not go to some foreign country and defend an ideology. I will not do it. I'll go to jail. I'll go to Canada. On the other hand, if our country is attacked, our shores, then I'll do what I can to defend this country.

And if a brother comes up to me on the street, temporarily insane and suffering, and attacks me, he doesn't have a right to do that and I will defend myself. And I'll inflict the least possible harm. I want to become good enough at the martial arts where I can control them without having to hurt them. So I'm going to do the minimal damage I can, but I will stop that person. I have a right to do that, not because they're my enemy, but because I'm going to be giving them valuable feedback about life, about the inappropriateness of their action. I can love them at the same time, but I won't allow them to do that.

I do see light and dark forces in life. I'm not saying they're good and bad. I'm just saying they manifest as light and darkness. There's a certain element in society, in life, that is negative and pulling toward death. And there's another element that is strong and valiant, which is light and expansive. It's being vulnerable, and opening up to life. That interplay is happening inside us, too. It's not just out there. And what happens to each one of us inside determines what is reflected outside.

RF: But isn't there also a place for action in the outer world, for political action, for example?

DM: Of course. There's a scene in the screenplay I've been writing for "The Peaceful Warrior," where Socrates and I are walking down the street and somebody hands me a flyer about saving the whales and the dolphins. I say, "Last week, Socrates, I got a flyer about saving starving children and oppressed peoples. I feel guilty doing all this work on myself . . . sitting and meditating and doing these funny exercises, and there's so many people in crying need out there." And he doesn't say anything. He just walks on. Then suddenly, he stops and says, "Take a swing at me."

I don't want to do it, but he finally goads me into it, and I suddenly find myself on the ground in a painful wrist lock, and he says, "You notice a little leverage at the right place at the right time is very effective." And I say, "Yeah, I noticed," shaking my wrist out. And he says, "Well, you want to help people, that's wonderful. But you can't help people unless you can understand them. And you can't understand them unless you can understand yourself. So you work on that first. Then you'll have the clarity and the compassion to know where to exert the right leverage."

I believe in action, but action from the lowest chakra is one kind of action, just sheer survival, which is where I see Rambo coming from. Action from the sexual chakra, simply seeking pleasure and amusements, is another kind of action. Action from the power center, overcoming others and conquering, that's another kind of action. And there's action of the heart chakra. So, yes, I believe in action, but it depends on where it's coming from.

And I'm not judging it. Some people need to strengthen their survival instincts. Some people need to strengthen power and have more pleasure in life, so I am not saying one's better than the other. In my own life, I've been gifted by being able to feel my own power in gymnastics and in other things I've done.

But many people are very frustrated, you know. They haven't had a coming of age, male or female. They say, "Okay, so now you're an adult." But how do they know? One very important part of education is really testing youngsters, putting stretch marks on their soul, letting them see they can go beyond what they think they can do, like they did in many native societies. This is so important. So people need to see the warrior, the power. People need to experience it themselves. People need to face their own moment of truth.

Because society is so complex, we don't have much power. We don't feel like it on an individual basis. Everything's big. When people lived in small towns they could have an influence. They could speak up at their town meeting. There's not as many opportunities for that. That's why we will see more trainings like "The Peaceful Warrior Training."

RF: But there is a paradox here. Doesn't there have to be a real element of danger? For example, in one of your trainings, participants practice defending themselves against an attacker with a knife, but it's a rubber knife.

DM: That's right, we don't want to kill anybody, so we use rubber knives. But I suggest that if I had had a real knife, sure it would have been a little different, but I don't know how different. You still would have had to come in and stop me. The consequences would have been different, though. Instead of my touching you, you would have had blood all over your belly, and maybe you would have gotten killed. But that's not the point of the training. It's not a macho training. There's no need to do that if you can access what you need to without it. To me, when you're closest to death, you know you're really alive. And by facing fear you break through to new limits. That's the moment of truth.

4

There Are No Peaceful Warriors

by Ambrose Redmoon

As a real, live, initiated, trained, experienced, traditional, hereditary warrior with thirty-seven body scars and a trophy or two on my belt, I find such expressions as "peaceful warrior" offensive, trivializing, and insulting.

"Peaceful warrior" is far more than a contradiction in terms. The function of a warrior is to eliminate an exterior enemy presence. A warrior is an antitoxin, a protector. The warrior does combat where and when necessary and not otherwise. This is not a philosophical or in any way abstract subject; the warrior cannot be discussed or even comprehended in an ivory tower.

This is not relative reality, dear gentle reader; this is empirical reality—that which is, with or without the existence of human consciousness. It will sustain or trample you, depending on how realistic you are. It can be known only by personal experience, not by principle or logic. Experience is the only teacher.

The warrior protects the innocent, weak, and vulnerable; the home; the sovereignty of the individual; the Mother. These are the four sacred directions of the way of the warrior. To protect in spite of danger, fear, difficulty, pain, and personal cost is the condition.

Destroy the enemy. My oh my! Violence! Hostility! Unpleasantness! Yes, dear gentle reader. Most people on this planet have not the luxury of abstract philosophy or of living out fantasies. Possibly you have never interfered with the activities of a bully or with physical abuse of any kind. Possibly you have never interfered with conscious, determined evil at all. Possibly you have never felt fear so intense you think it will pull the skin off your face—but gone on anyhow to protect the weak, the home, the individual, the Mother.

It is possible that interference with abuse is not everyone's style. And it is possible that you live mainly in the mental world and just don't relate much to physical reality. It is even possible that you give fear your first priority. I suppose that's OK as long as you are honest about it. If you pretend you are not afraid but instead are being righteous and conscientious and wise, or that some deity has told you to scamper off and seek inner transformation when you see someone being raped or molested or killed, that is not OK.

Maybe you've never been in the presence of conscious, willful evil. Maybe you do not know such people. If not, you may think you are not missing anything. And so you are not, unless of course you care to know life in its fullness. Unless you care to know what you are talking about when you bandy the term "warrior" about in pink-cheeked philosophizings as you play peekaboo with the real world.

"Peaceful warrior" indeed. An unnecessary abuse of language and a foul insult to all those who have placed themselves between innocence and evil and attacked the evil. It is especially insulting to those who do so physically, where the money meets the mouth. I don't know how many "spiritual warriors" I've rescued from the bad guys, and how glad they are to see me when warriorhood gets to basics. Nothing piled higher and deeper can save them then. So do not pickpocket a fundamental term of a reality of which you know little or nothing to dangle on the charm bracelet of New Age thought.

As for reward, besides knowing you have saved good at the expense of evil, there is something inexpressible that can be known only by experience. To call it "divine recognition" is only poetry. Nor is reward the incentive anyway. "You have never lived until you have been almost killed; and for those who fight for it, life has a savor the protected can never know." This was found scratched on a mess kit in Vietnam in the early sixties.

Nor is even that savor the incentive. Have you ever heard the roar of the crowd or the silence in ranks—all for you? If so, you know that all glory is fleeting. That is not the incentive of the warrior either. Glory will do for the soldier but not for the warrior. (On the other hand, don't sell glory short if you have never been there. There is something to it which, if not gulped but lightly tasted, is surely part of life's elixir.)

Warrior? Soldier? Is there a distinction? Yes, and a most important one, which most civilized intellects seem unable to understand. A few soldiers are warriors; many do not need to be. All warriors can soldier; most do not. The warrior is a protector, a preserver, and a destroyer, not a conqueror. He destroys the invader, the raper, the killer—the enemy. When there is no enemy, a soldier might contrive one; never the warrior. The warrior may be a rogue or a rowdy; he may have many vices, but he is ever-discriminating and never insincere. Only an enemy has anything to fear from a warrior.

This last is an important point. It is misplaced fear of the warrior that is largely responsible for this timid dilution of the term, this attempt to soften and sweeten it. Yet it seems to me at best a bit addle-brained, at worst a short-circuit in the instincts, to fear a protector.

The warrior's quest is for the throat of the enemy. If it were not the warrior's quest it would have to be someone else's. For there are those, dear gentle reader, who with a clear consciousness and immense power enjoy the full exercise of their will at the expense of others. Sadistic greed is combined with a clear, intelligent mind and a tough, powerful, fast physique, all in a person who is quite beyond the reach of "consciousness lifting." Such people are not confused, they are not victims, they are not seeking. They are not cowards, most of them. They are going to abuse, terrify, and possess because they find it efficient and enjoyable. There is also another type, an unpredictable idiot fringe, where most of the weirdos, exhibitionists, sneaks, and thrill-seekers are to be found. These latter squabble over the leavings after the previous types eat a few "peaceful warriors" for breakfast. I have seen New Age philosophers turn to shivering tofu in the mere presence of such hairy and muscular evil.

It is one thing, while smoothing skirts and stroking chins, to assemble new-sounding legitimizations for intellectual laziness and physical cowardice. It is quite another to stand eye-to-eye with a large enemy when the talk is done and the action is about to commence.

To recognize a hostile intent, to plan a defensive strategy, within that strategy a tactic, within that tactic a combat—a blood and iron, muscle and bone contact with high risk to one's physical vehicle—that is what a warrior does. The situation does not always get all the way to physical contact. It is often resolved at some point along the way. Sometimes merely recognizing the hostile intent is enough to discourage its development. The warrior does not desire pretexts. Diplomacy is the first move of a response to conflict: even the imperial Roman legions always offered the olive branch first. After that a still-persistent enemy can often be dislocated and defeated by maneuver alone.

But dear, gentle reader, the true warrior is ready to decide the issue by direct physical violence if the enemy refuses to desist otherwise. This means being skilled in physical violence. Whether one ever needs to use it or not, without being so skilled and twice-tested, nobody is a warrior.

Like all paths of initiation, that of the warrior begins on that level claimed by some ignorant ones to be only an illusion, and by others, equally ignorant, to be the only reality: the plane of dense matter, the world of form, where the vibrations are slowest and strongest and where life is most complicated. This is not to suggest there are no spiritual warriors, only that one must first be a physical warrior, twice-tested in the present incarnation. Why twice-tested? Because of the great difference between the known and the unknown—the danger of physical encounter with an enemy. There is no mystic or spiritual warrior who is not a physical warrior first.

Assuming one has the necessary physical courage, there is also the matter of skill. Those who think physical combat is all strength and recklessness have a brief career. Even more often overlooked is the need to be in shape, to have the reflexes and endurance as well as that explosive energy to execute the skills one does have. More disastrous than the bluff is the commitment to an act one cannot complete.

The physical is stressed because it is the most obvious and the most difficult to fake. It requires more commitment and preparation than the other planes of existence. It is the best test of awareness and sincerity. It is not like a seminar or a book-signing party. You cannot be posturing or naive. You cannot pretend it is happening, as can be done with the spiritual or mental or psychic (and often is). The risks, both physical and emotional, are immediate. Something outside yourself has to be destroyed or you—or what you are protecting—will be. You cannot make a wrong move and transform it into a right move by saying so. You cannot agree to disagree; you cannot "create" reality. You are within the context, not vice versa.

Only an enemy can initiate a warrior.

Hmm . . . perhaps there is more to this warriorhood than one first thought.

In the Western (meaning European and some North American) secret traditions, the capabilities of any given phase or degree of initiation generally cannot be wielded until one passes the next phase. Full experience is required before the powers can be applied. This means that anyone with capabilities beyond the physical is also adept on the physical plane of existence. To be in a physical vehicle and to be physically incompetent, while claiming to be "beyond the physical," might sound like an adolescent excuse for being a screwup. Yet it is popular with the adult "transformation" set.

The warrior is the protector. The warrior can handle himself on all planes of existence. The warrior does not collapse in fear and ineptitude when an enemy shows up in physical form. Nor does a warrior spin out into insanity when the physical form happens to be alien to some previously held doctrine or presumption about reality.

The first test is physical. By "test" I do not mean something arranged, but rather the real thing. Part of the test is the warrior's ability to recognize the real thing. As Colonel Frank Rood, a combat infantry commander in Korea, once said, "The first rule of war is to know it when you're in one." Then comes the courage to act. And then the judgment to act appropriately. Whatever you do must be effective and not excessive. Finally the action must be thorough and decisive so it does not have to be repeated, locally or elsewhere.

Judgment, restraint, courage, and skill. You'd better be good at it, whatever it is you do; knowing what to do and being able to do it are not the same. And you have to do it well, and while under mortal pressure. The warrior has to satisfy all these conditions at once.

There are people who do have all these skills and can apply them in a physical emergency or disaster—but not in front of an enemy. They can cope with any danger, including animals, but not with another person. Heroic and necessary though they are, such people are not warriors.

The enemy is what separates the warrior from everyone else. The physical courage of search-and-rescue people, for example, is un-surpassable. Yet anyone with experience will agree that the addition of the enemy factor screens out half to three-fourths of even these people.

The sheer existence of a conscious, intelligent intent by another person to injure or kill you brings a shock to the psyche that few can survive intact. Which returns us to that essential fact of life: the empirical reality of conscious, willful evil.

Respect, as primitive people usually understand it, is the recogni-tion of the validity of the existence of a being, thing, idea, or activity. Evil is the absence of respect. Respect is not admiration or even agreement. It is not fear. One does not respect evil, one respects all that is not evil. Respect is not an act; one can show a respect that one does not feel, thereby fooling people who go by externals. Whereas evil can abide love, evil cannot abide respect. Permitters of evil are evil.

The warrior is not someone dealing with the buffets and knocks of life, doing battle within; everyone does that, dear gentle reader. The term is being usurped by certain whispery types who couldn't qualify as a pimple on a real warrior's ass. The image of a "peaceful warrior" thrown into the warrior situation may arouse guffaws, but this abuse of language is a serious insult to the real warriors who have gone before.

Now about anger. The same semantic acrobats who are trying to soften and sweeten warriorhood are all aflutter over anger. "Oh, what can I do with my anger?" What a morally limp question! Anger is energetic disapproval. That is it. Anger is not a tantrum, nor is it sublimated fear, cruelty, envy, frustration, competition, or discipline. Anger is innocence invaded, beauty ravished, truth scorned, reality denied, weakness bullied. Possibly you have never been angry. Maybe you have only lost your temper, or felt affronted, or have been denied a desire. Do not confuse that with the wrath of a protector. Anger is not triggered, it is inspired.

Watch out also for glib slogans such as "two wrongs don't make a right." OK . . . I'm not trying to "make a right"; I'm trying to stop abuse. Another lie is "violence only begets violence and never settles anything." I have witnessed violence halting violence too many times since my childhood to even begin to accept that flippancy.

Fortunate enough to have been country-raised, I attended a little grammar school with two grades to a room and a ten-acre playground of natural turf, on which we played tackle football with no gear but the ball. On that field we learned certain fundamentals of life. I learned the best way to attract a fight is to act as if you don't want one and are unready for one. I learned about bullies who will stop only if forced or scared. Since then, life has not come up with any significant exceptions.

I for one have never struck as an expression of anger. While angry, yes, but not because of anger. None of this wild-eyed crap. No grabbing at a weapon out of frustration. All my life I've had weapons, including loaded firearms, around me in my home. No matter how incensed I was, I have never reached for a weapon. It would be abnormal of me to go from verbal to physical violence except in defense. Restraint is the key to effective violence of any kind, including the use of weapons. And except with an enemy, what I cannot accomplish without a weapon I do not accomplish. This is not a moral decision on my part, it's merely my nature.

On the other hand, part of the profile of the wife beater is a fondness for weapons (which should caution us in our use of profiles). I have no tolerance for wife beating; this is a crime second only to rape, which is a capital offense in my book. Men who beat women do so because they can. There is no good reason, there is no excuse. It is the responsibility of the protectors, both female and male, to prevent this and to help women become physically too dangerous for men to even try. Although batterers (along with the shrinks who study them) claim they "cannot help it," they "cannot stop," nevertheless, when confronted by a court order with an arrest clause, or with physical force, these guys are suddenly able to stop after all. Court orders are extremely difficult for women to obtain in most areas. Physical force is considerably more available. *And it works.*

Yes, dear gentle reader, more of that gritty empirical reality. Most males are not going to stop dominating and abusing females any other way. And stopping them is the thing of first importance. Then study them and treat them if you want to. As with rape, the crisis is prior to and during the action. If you prefer not to stop them, stay out of the way of those who do.

Metaphysically speaking, diddling with the notion of the "peaceful warrior" is just as dishonorable and inept. One of the functions of astrology, for example, is to show what is natural and valid in life. Mars is a warrior, not a soul-searcher or a Peace Corps worker or a pissed-off poet. Mars rules Aries, the sign of initiative, without which no battle was ever won. In all the pantheons and occult sciences, the warrior is fundamental. The warrior is not the soldier; the god of war is not the god of the warrior. Soldiers marching in anonymous masses into the obscene maw; individual warriors seated at vast round celebration tables, each attired and adorned (or not) as they choose, all seated on chairs inscribed with their names. Which of these scenes have you attended—if any?

Even among the flashes and shadows of occult tradition, the nagging suggestion arises that the warriorhood of the "peaceful warrior" is all coffee-table chatter and papers for Ph.D.s and their dupes. Such people are, for the most part, not even occultists in the first place. Study of the occult is like the study of woodcraft: mere knowledge is of no worth—only application has meaning. You have to go out to apply the craft, not in the park or campground, but in the wilderness, which is indifferent to humanity and where woodcraft means survival.

Aries is red, and everywhere but in a few plastic towers, red is warrior. The red ray is the ray of will, as all know who have actually stood in it. The Furies, the three red ones of the Mother's bodyguard, follow the miasma, the spiritual stink given off by violators of the Mother, and tear them to pieces. Sweet justice.

Another term bandied about by New Age glibness is "coward." It's quite the thing to breezily admit to being a coward as though that's merely a quirk, more than atoned for by its admission and even regarded as mildly charming. Notice also the current popularity of the Hansel and Gretel word "scary," which in current usage refers to "cute fear." This is not only a childish word, it is trivializing. Cowardice is a serious vice. Courage is not the absence of fear, but rather the judgment that something else is more important than one's fear. The timid presume it is lack of fear that allows the brave to act when the timid do not. But to take action when one is not afraid is easy. To refrain when afraid is also easy. To take action regardless of fear is brave. Courage, of course, is not restricted to the warrior; anyone can be brave. Courage in the presence of an enemy is a warrior's courage.

It may have been noticed that I have applied no gender to the warrior. You may have assumed that I presume a warrior is masculine. Not so. There is no gender. I have fought shoulder-to-shoulder and back-to-back with women, and I am here to tell you that women and men are equally effective in combat. Men excel at packing ammo and bearing wounded. Women have a higher pain threshold. And most of the women warriors I have known are heterosexual and are not promiscuous. They are in fact too female for most modern men.

As a protector, the warrior's purpose is outside the self, thus ensuring that warriorhood will not be popular. So with all due respect for the spiritual and mystical seekers, and for those who serve, counsel, study, and treat—however important these are, they do not constitute warriorhood. My suggestion is that they respect whatever they *are* enough to call themselves what they are. They should not usurp the name of that which they neither care nor dare to be.

The worst offenders, in my experience, are in the field of psychology. They presume that human consciousness is the creator and container of all superphysical events. At the very least, this is inept. The peril for such people is that of the sorcerer's apprentice; the difficulty is that it often does not come until late in their career. Something then comes to them from the outside. In the case of the pretend warrior, this can be especially unpleasant. And consider the fate of the one being protected by a pretend warrior. Do you want a bodyguard who communicates and relates and counsels while you are being destroyed? Of course not. You're no nitwit.

The supreme protection is, of course, to provide someone with self-defense. This requires respect, which is no problem for the true warrior. But how many men would, if they could, coach or provide their wives or daughters with self-defense? It would diminish their false *machismo*, which is the only kind they have. This aside from the fact that most males are not really qualified to coach anyone in realistic self-defense. Even among professional male instructors, how many adjust their techniques to the female physique?

Physical courage and combat, restraint, the reality of willful evil, the priority of a purpose outside the self—these are the facts of warriorhood that keep it esoteric, that keep it for the few.

One obvious question remains. You may have noticed that I have used the term "warrior" as referring not to an image but to a practical function. What is the function of a civilian warrior in modern civilized society?

The police are not the citizen's bodyguard; they cannot be and do not pretend to be. The reason for warriors today is to infuse society with protectors. I happen to be an enemy of bullies, especially abusers of women: he who abuses any woman abuses my mother. I am not a politician, a sympathetic male, or a counselor. I am a warrior. I use whatever works. Only a male might be surprised to hear I've had plenty of opportunity to function.

The way of the wandering champion, the free lance, is not an easy one in modern society. A romantic throwback maybe? In civilized society it's much more difficult to live by principle than by expediency. The last time the itinerant champion was a recognized component of mainstream society was the so-called Old West. A complete example today is the Guardian Angels: pure and simple, dear gentle reader, warriors true and real.

Respect is the cardinal virtue,
Courage comes next, as it should.
For you need not be good to be brave.
But you have to be brave to be good.

5

The Warrior in His Fullness

by Robert Moore and Douglas Gillette

The characteristics of the warrior in his fullness amount to a total way of life, what the samurai called a *do*. These characteristics constitute the warrior's dharma, Ma'at, or Tao, a spiritual or psychological path through life.

We have already mentioned aggressiveness as one of the warrior's characteristics. Aggressiveness is a stance toward life that rouses, energizes, and motivates. It pushes us to take the offensive and to move out of a defensive, or "holding" position, about life's tasks and problems. The samurai advice was always to "leap" into battle with the full potential of *ki*, or "vital energy," at your disposal. The Japanese warrior tradition claimed that there is only one position in which to face the battle of life: frontally. And it also proclaimed that there was only one direction: forward.

How does the warrior know what aggressiveness is appropriate under the circumstances? He knows through clarity of thinking, through discernment. The warrior is always alert. He is always awake. He is never sleeping through life. He knows how to focus his mind and his body. He is what the samurai called "mindful." He is a "hunter" in the Native American tradition. As Don Juan, the

Yaqui Indian warrior-sorcerer in Carlos Castaneda's *Journey to Ixtlan*, says, a warrior knows what he wants, and he knows how to get it. As a function of his clarity of mind, he is a strategist and a tactician. He can evaluate his circumstances accurately and then adapt himself to the "situation on the ground," as we say.

An example of this is the phenomenon of guerrilla warfare, an ancient tradition but one that has come into increasing use since the eighteenth century. The rebellious colonists adopted this technique in the American Revolutionary War. The Communists in China and later in Vietnam, under the guidance of the master strategist Ho Chi Minh, used it with stunning success to defeat the more cumbersome military operations of his enemies. Most recently, the Afghan resistance fighters used this strategy to drive the Soviet army out of their country. The warrior knows when he has the force to defeat his opponent by conventional means and when he must adopt an unconventional strategy. He accurately assesses his own strength and skill. If he finds that a frontal assault will not work, he deflects his opponent's assault, spots the weakness in his flank, then "leaps" into battle. Here is a difference between the warrior and the hero. The hero, as we've said, does not know his limitations; he is romantic about his invulnerability. The warrior, however, through his clarity of thinking realistically, assesses his capacities and his limitations in any given situation.

In the Bible, King David, up against the superior force of the armies of Saul, at first avoided direct confrontation with Saul's troops, allowing Saul to wear himself out pursuing him. David and his ragtag band were guerrillas, living off the land and moving fast. Then David, evaluating his situation clearly, fled Saul's kingdom and went over to the Philistine king. From this position, he had the force of thousands of Philistine soldiers behind him. He had put himself into position to checkmate Saul. Then, again through his accurate assessment of the situation at the time, David reentered Saul's kingdom, gathered his own troops, and waited for Saul's collapse. Sometimes, the maxim "Forward, always forward!" means shifting tactics. It means a flexibility of strategy that comes from razor-sharp evaluation.

The warrior traditions all affirm that, in addition to training, what enables a warrior to reach clarity of thought is living with the awareness of his own imminent death. The warrior knows the shortness of life and how fragile it is. A man under the guidance of the warrior knows how few his days are. Rather than depressing him, this awareness leads him to an outpouring of life force and to an intense experience of his life that is unknown to others. Every act counts. Each deed is done as if it were the last. The samurai swordsmen were taught to live their lives as if they were already dead. Castaneda's Don Juan taught that there is "no time" for anything but meaningful acts if we live with death as "our eternal companion."

There is no time for hesitation. This sense of the imminence of death energizes the man accessing the warrior energy to take decisive action. This means that he engages life. He never withdraws from it. He doesn't "think too much," because thinking too much can lead to doubt, and doubt to hesitation, and hesitation to inaction. Inaction can lead to losing the battle. The man who is a warrior avoids self-consciousness, as we usually define it. His actions become second nature. They become unconscious reflex actions. But they are actions he has trained for through the exercise of enormous self-discipline. This is how Marines are made. A good Marine is one who can make split-second decisions and then act decisively.

Part of what goes into acting decisively in any life situation, along with aggressiveness, clarity of thinking, the awareness of one's own death, is training. The warrior energy is concerned with skill, power, and accuracy, and with control, both inner and outer, psychological and physical. The warrior energy is concerned with training men to be "all that they can be"—in their thoughts, feelings, speech, and actions. Unlike the hero's actions, the warrior's actions are never overdone, never dramatic for the sake of drama; the warrior never acts to reassure himself that he is as potent as he hopes he is. The warrior never spends more energy than he absolutely has to. And he doesn't talk too much. Yul Brenner's character in the movie *The Magnificent Seven* is a study in trained self-control. He says little, moves with the physical control of a predator, attacks only the enemy, and has absolute mastery over the technology of his trade. That is another aspect of the warrior's interest in skill, his mastery of the technology that enables him to reach his goal. He has developed skill with the "weapons" he uses to implement his decisions.

His control is, first of all, over his mind and his attitudes; if these are right, the body will follow. A man accessing the warrior archetype has "a positive mental attitude," as they say in sales training. This means that he has an unconquerable spirit, that he has great courage, that he is fearless, that he takes responsibility for his actions, and that he has self-discipline. Discipline means that he has the rigor to develop control and mastery over his mind and over his body, and that he has the capacity to withstand pain, both psychological and physical. He is willing to suffer to achieve what he wants to achieve. "No pain, no gain," we say. Whether you are literally a hunter, crouched for hours in the same position in the chill early morning of the Kalahari waiting for your prey to come within range, or whether you're a triathlon trainee, a medical school student, an executive enduring the misguided attacks of your board members, or a husband trying to work out difficulties with your wife, you know that discipline of your mind and perhaps your body is essential.

The warrior energy also shows what we can call a transpersonal commitment. His loyalty is to something—a cause, a god, a people, a task, a nation—larger than individuals, though that transpersonal loyalty may be focused through some important person, like a king. In the Arthurian stories, Lancelot, though fiercely devoted to Arthur and to Guinevere, is ultimately committed to the ideal of chivalry and to the God who lies behind such things as noble quests, "might for right," and the lifting up of the oppressed. Of course, because of his love for Guinevere, Lancelot unwittingly acts to destroy the object of his transpersonal commitment, Camelot. But he does so because he has encountered the paradoxically personal and transpersonal goal of romantic love. By then, he has already lost his access to the warrior energies and has ceased being a knight.

This transpersonal commitment reveals a number of other characteristics of the warrior energy. First, it makes all personal relationships relative, that is, it makes them less central than the transpersonal commitment. Thus the psyche of the man who is adequately accessing the warrior is organized around his central commitment. This commitment eliminates a great deal of human pettiness. Living in the light of lofty ideals and spiritual realities such as God, democracy, communism, freedom, or any other worthy transpersonal commitment, so alters the focus of a man's life that petty squabbling and personal ego concerns no longer matter much.

There is a story about a samurai attached to the household of a great lord. His lord had been murdered by a man from a rival house, and the samurai was sworn to avenge his lord's death. After tracking the assassin for some time, after great personal sacrifice and hardship, and after braving many dangers, the samurai found the murderer. He drew his sword to kill the man. But in that instant the assassin spit in his face. The samurai stepped back, sheathed his sword, and turned and walked away. Why?

He walked away because he was angry that he'd been spat on. He would have killed the assassin, in that moment, out of his own personal anger, not out of his commitment to the ideal his lord represented. His execution of the man would have been out of his ego and his own feelings, not out of the warrior within. So in order to be true to his warrior calling, he had to walk away and let the murderer live.

The warrior's loyalty, then, and his sense of duty are to something beyond and other than himself and his own concerns. The hero's loyalty, as we have seen, is really to himself—to impressing himself *with* himself and to impressing others. In this connection, too, the man accessing the warrior is ascetic. He lives a life exactly the opposite of most human lives. He lives not to gratify his personal needs and wishes or his physical appetites but to hone himself into an efficient spiritual machine, trained to bear the unbearable in the service of the transpersonal goal. We know the legends of the founders of the great faiths Christianity and Buddhism. Jesus had to resist the temptations Satan pictured to him in the wilderness, and the Buddha had to endure his three temptations under the Bo Tree. These men were spiritual warriors.

Spiritual warriors abound in human history. The religion of Islam as a whole is built on warrior energy. Mohammed was a warrior. His followers are, to this day, still drawing on warrior energy as they wage *jihad* against the powers of evil as they define them. The God of Islam, even though he is addressed as "the Merciful" and "the Compassionate," is a warrior God.

We see this same warrior energy manifested in the Jesuit Order in

Christianity, which for centuries taught self-negation for the sake of carrying God's message into the most hostile and dangerous areas of the world. The man who is a warrior is devoted to his cause, his God, his civilization, even unto death.

This devotion to the transpersonal ideal or goal even to the point of personal annihilation leads a man to another of the warrior's characteristics. He is emotionally distant as long as he is in the warrior. This does not mean that the man accessing the warrior in his fullness is cruel, just that he does not make his decisions and implement them out of emotional relatedness to anyone or anything except his ideal. He is, as Don Juan says, "unavailable," or "inaccessible." As he says, "To be inaccessible means that you touch the world around you sparingly," with emotional detachment. This attitude is part of the clarity of the warrior's thinking, too. He looks at his tasks, his decisions, and his actions dispassionately and unemotionally. Samurai training involved the following kind of psychological exercise. Whenever, the teaching went, you feel yourself frightened or despairing, don't say to yourself, "I am afraid," or "I am despairing." Say, "There is someone who is afraid," or "There is someone who is despairing. Now, what can he do about this?" This detached way of experiencing a threatening situation objectifies the situation and allows for a clearer and more strategically advantageous view of it. The warrior is then able to act with less regard for his personal feelings; he will act more forcefully, swiftly, and efficiently with himself out of the way.

Often, in life, we need to "step back," we say, from a situation in order to gain perspective, so that we can act. The warrior needs room to swing his sword. He needs separation from his opponents in the outer world and from his own inner opponents in the form of negative emotions. Boxers in the ring are separated by the referee when they get too close to each other and engage each other in body locks.

The warrior is often a destroyer. But the positive warrior energy destroys only what needs to be destroyed in order for something new and fresh, more alive and more virtuous to appear. Many things in our world need destroying—corruption, tyranny, oppression, injustice, obsolete and despotic systems of government, corporate hierarchies that get in the way of the company's performance, unfulfilling lifestyles and job situations, bad marriages. And in the very act of destroying, often the warrior energy is building new civilizations, new commercial, artistic, and spiritual ventures for humankind, new relationships.

When the warrior energy is connected with the other mature masculine energies something truly splendid emerges. When the warrior is connected with the King, he is consciously stewarding the "realm," and his decisive actions, clarity of thinking, discipline, and courage are, in fact, creative and generative.

The warrior's interface with the Magician archetype is what enables him to achieve such mastery and control over himself and his "weapons." It is what allows him to channel and direct power to accomplish his goals.

His admixture with the Lover energy gives the warrior compassion and a sense of connectedness with all things. The Lover is the masculine energy that brings him back into relatedness with human beings, in all their frailty and vulnerability. The Lover makes the man under the influence of the warrior compassionate at the same time that he is doing his duty.

6

Warrioring: Male and Female

by Carol Pearson

Male and female experiences with the warrior archetype differ significantly. Men are socialized practically from birth to be warriors, so their issue is whether they can develop other sides of themselves or even deepen and grow in their experience of the archetype insofar as doing so is dependent upon their satisfactory resolution of Orphan,

Wanderer, and Martyr dilemmas. For women, the issue is whether they will have the audacity even to enter a contest culturally defined as male, and, if they do, whether they will learn to speak in their own voices, to express their own wisdom. Because women usually enter the Warrior after the Martyr stage, moreover, they often enter at a higher and more complex level.

Books such as Betty Harragan's *Games Mother Never Taught You: Corporate Gamesmanship for Women* explain the rules of male culture to women, for although one can say generally that the warrior's consciousness informs our culture, that is only because it is a patriarchal culture. Women have been discouraged from doing battle. These kinds of books teach women to enter the contest and to learn men's rules for doing so. Books such as Anne Wilson Schaef's *Women's Reality: The Emerging Female System in a White Male Society* or Carol Gilligan's *In a Different Voice: Psychological Theory and Women's Development* go further to challenge the notion that male culture *is* reality by defining, respectively, an emerging women's culture and the stages of women's moral development. Male culture, as defined in each case, is equivalent to what I call the warrioring modality.

The hero/villain/victim plot is the characteristically macho way of making meaning of the world. Accordingly, there is a certain alienation for women when they first confront it. This follows naturally from male culture's exclusivity. Indeed, both the military and football—the institutions that dramatize the myth in its most primitive and basic forms—have been defined as male-only preserves. Although there are now women in the military (though not in professional football), neither women themselves nor the society as a whole have viewed warrioring as an attribute of womanliness.

But I do not think this alienation means that women do not or should not learn warrioring. Women need to learn to struggle, to fight for themselves and others, and it is this archetypal pattern that teaches them how to do it. Because it has been defined as for men only, the warrioring archetype is the new frontier for women. The real issue for them and for all warriors is to learn to come from their core and to fight for what they truly believe in and care for. Men are so strongly socialized to be warriors that it not only prevents them from developing other aspects of themselves but also tends to foster a confusion that sees the battle or contest as justified *for its own sake.*

The contest seems so important to men because it has defined their *identity* as males: Man the hunter lives on through all these pseudo battles. In our culture, mastery and nurturance have been defined in opposition. Women have been charged with nurturance, men with mastery. Women fear achievement, agency, and mastery precisely because the world that has honored these qualities—the male world—is profoundly painful to them, not only because it does not value women but because it often does not value care.

Women are offended by the male world because they see little love there. Indeed, too often men even have forgotten that the point of the battle or the contest is to make the world a better place. On the other hand, men are horrified by the female world because they see the sacrifice there and fear being swallowed up in it. Because women are more apt to explore care and sacrifice before agency, they are likely to deplore the killing, the defeating of others—all the aspects of the battle that hurt other people. Women, therefore, often are seduced into the fray only to save others. It was women who lent most of the energy to the nineteenth-century reform movements, and today they provide much of it to the environmental and peace movements. Conversely, many men move into warrioring prematurely when they really still are at the narcissistic Orphan stage, and only later begin to see the importance of caring for others.

When agency is separated from care, it becomes will, domination. This is the primary danger of warrioring for men. In Ursula Le Guin's *A Wizard of Earthsea*, Sparrowhawk, as a young student of magic, looses something horrid and evil upon the world when, merely to show off, he summons the dead. His sin, the typical male one, is pride. In his egocentrism, Sparrowhawk does powerful magic just for his own glory, even though he knows that to do so threatens the equilibrium of the world and can have unforeseen effects on everyone. He is so engaged with proving himself, however, that he does not care about the outcome, which is that a Shadow emerges from the underworld that threatens to possess his body and terrorize the world.

Women's socialization to receptivity poses analogous difficulty for them. They may be able to fight for others and not for themselves because they think doing so is selfish. In this case, the fray may be simply another form of martyrdom. So, too, for some men. Those who *have* integrated care and sacrifice into their lives can fight for their country, their company, or their family, but sometimes not truly for themselves. Indeed, that the hero traditionally has been cast as male and the victim as female holds dangers for both men and women. While women may fear the presumption of stepping into the heroic role, men may identify their heroism solely in terms of protecting and rescuing others—especially women and children—while they neglect the captive victim in themselves: men, they believe, are not supposed to need rescue! Neither men nor women can fight intelligently for themselves unless they have taken the time, as Wanderers, to find out who they are and what they want.

In a ground-breaking work on moral development in men and women, *In a Different Voice*, Gilligan argues that men and women solve moral dilemmas differently because they view the world differently. One example she gives is Lawrence Kohlberg's famous Heinz dilemma, in which men and women were given a hypothetical dilemma to solve: Heinz's wife is very ill and will die if she is not given a specific drug. However, the drug is extremely expensive, and Heinz does not have enough money to buy it. He has tried unsuccessfully to borrow the money, and the druggist is not willing to give it to him for less. Should he steal the drug? According to Lawrence Kohlberg, at the highest stage of moral development people resolve this problem by arguing from universal moral principles: specifically, they will argue the relative merits of property rights versus human life. If life is more important, he should steal the drug. If property rights are more important, he should not, and presumably he then should allow his wife to die. Now, notice that this moral reasoning is not only hierarchical—which value is more important—but dualistic. It is, in fact, the equivalent in moral reasoning to the shoot-out at the O.K. Corral. May the best value win.

Gilligan notes that women rarely scored at Kohlberg's highest levels. Moreover, from a moral development point of view, women seemed to be avoiding the questions, asking for more information

(Has he really explained to the druggist that his wife will die, and did anyone try talking with the neighbors or collecting money?) or even, to the annoyance of the interviewers, making pronouncements like, "He shouldn't steal the drug and he shouldn't let his wife die." Gilligan realizes that Kohlberg's formulation of the question—and thus his resulting scale of moral development—was predicated on a male way of thinking. Women think about moral questions differently, and, hence, these women were answering another question: Instead of "*Should* Heinz steal the drug?" they were asking "Should Heinz *steal* the drug?" The women assumed the necessity of action to save the wife's life. Their questions were designed to determine the most effective action.

Beyond the practicality and narrative quality of women's responses (If he stole the drug, he might be sent to jail. If she got sick again, who would steal it for her?) was a different way of envisioning problems. Instead of seeing the world hierarchically as a ladder, the women reenvisioned it as a net or web of human interconnectedness. Accordingly, rather than defining the basis of most problems as an irreconcilable difference between two people / countries / values, women saw the problems as arising from a breakdown in the network of human connection. The solution when that web was broken was communication: Has anybody talked to the neighbors? Has he explained to the druggist? The other approach was to critique the problem: What kind of world is it where a druggist can have a drug, yet let a woman die?

Although it probably is true that more women than men negotiate in the "female system" mode, it also is true that many men learn to do so when they move through the more primitive us/them understanding of the warrior's legacy into more sophisticated (i.e., cognitively and affectively integrated) approaches to problem solving. When Gilligan traced the development of male and female moral reasoning over time and through many levels of understanding reality, she discovered that although men and women still have recognizable differences in the language and metaphors used, they began to sound more and more alike as the thinking of each became more complex and subtle.

I have come to understand that while the emphasis on affiliation and nets of connectedness keeps women overlong in the Martyr mentality, women often are able to maintain an affiliative way of thinking about the world—especially in defining just what they are looking for—even as they choose independence from the net of connectedness to find themselves and to slay dragons. They go through the same stages as men do even though their rhetoric and their basic belief systems may conflict with the us/them mentality of the Wanderer and warrior. They move quickly, then, pushed by a need to reconcile the discrepancy between their beliefs and the action motivated by the urgency of their own development. Hence they quickly redefine warrioring and learn to have an impact on the world through bridging and communication rather than by slaying dragons or winning contests.

The most important challenge to women's assertiveness today is not entering the male-defined contest but their willingness to speak in their own voices and with their own wisdom. Men appropriately have asserted their own truths in the world, but the suppression of the female voice leaves the culture dangerously lopsided.

Further, the overreinforcement of the warrioring voice in men retards their development in other areas and leaves them and the culture at a more primitive level of thinking and assertion than is good for many of us. I cannot help noting, however, how many men find this macho level of functioning limiting and inappropriate to their lives. For such men, the issue is analogous to women's: the challenge to become clear enough to speak in a voice that is not yet fully validated and articulated in the culture as a whole, and that may confuse, alienate, or mystify more conventional people around them. As we have seen, men may avoid the lessons of the Martyr and consequently have great difficulty moving on to the more subtle, complex, and affiliative levels of warrioring. For many it takes a crisis to propel them to move on—such as a heart attack, ulcers, or recognition that the cost of their stoic struggle has been the loss of a wife, lover, or children. This crisis usually requires an acknowledgment of the need to care—for oneself and for others. For other men, movement into the hero/hero/hero mode from the hero/villain/victim merely requires that they have so completely experienced the warrior mentality that their inner need for growth propels them onward.

7

Women Fierce and Loving: An Interview with Clarissa Pinkola Estés

by Peggy Taylor

With regard to your book, how did you come to relate to wolves, vis-à-vis women?

My first encounter with wolves happened when I was seven years old and living for a time far up in the north woods, a bit beyond the Michigan peninsula. One day I was washing a little metal tea set in a stream when a wolf pup staggered up to me—the way they do when they cannot walk very well—and licked my elbow. Then it hopped back into the woods that funny way they do when they're so young. I had the sensation that there were other wolves in the brush, but I could not see them. I was so taken. I thought it was so wonderful. I made my way back to the cabin and told everyone that a wolf had come and licked my arm. They said it wasn't a wolf—it must have been a dog, a mongrel of some sort. But I knew who and what it was.

Then, as a young adult, I lived up in the Rocky Mountains and had a team of huskies that I loved very much. I came to know "wolfness" through my dogs. We lived at the edge of a rocky precipice, and I could let the children go out onto the mesa because the dogs watched over them and gently grabbed them by the diapers and pulled them back from the edge if they went too close. I was very taken with how maternal the dogs were, how much they cared about life—not only their own lives, but the lives of others.

Then, in 1973, as I was beginning this work, I had a dream in which beautiful creatures—I could not tell if they were wolves or women—were running in between the staves of trees in a forest. It was dusk and they were so, so *fuerte*, strong and beautiful. Suddenly I realized that it was not wolves or women, it was women and wolves together. And when I awakened, I realized that this should be the title of my book. It felt like the dream had filled me with all the seeds necessary for the subsequent work.

Wolves were generally thought to be very terrible, violent creatures.

Yes, and they had been tarred with a great black brush in fairy tales also. This was in part due to the Christian overlay of the older Earth religions in which the wolf was a god. In ancient Greece, the wolf was the consort of Artemis, the huntress, and also of young girls, who belonged to a kind of religious order that revolved around the life-cycles of the wolf. They wore the aegis of the wolf, and there was also a festival, later named the wild hunt, in which all the people who were identified with the wolf as totem and god ran together and held a celebration in the forest.

What did the wolf, as totem, mean for those people?

It is hard for me to imagine that ancient people were as dim as some anthropologists surmise them to be. I feel strongly that ancient people were able to observe the wolf and be amazed by its humanity, its fierceness, and its ability to survive—but also to thrive, to love its children, to choose lifelong mates, to live together in a group, and to have its own kind of music and joyfulness and also its own kind of sorrow and repair. I believe the meaning ultimately was one of kinship and even emulation.

How did your study of wolves relate to your understanding of women?

I began thinking that women had been treated in a similar manner psychologically—that they had been routed out of their own territory and told that they could not coexist with "the other"; that in order for "civilization" to occur, a woman in her right natural mind was not an asset but a fearsome revolting thing, a deficit in the worst sense. Even though that sort of thinking was absolutely erroneous and deleterious to the soulfulness of all women's lives, it became accepted as a cultural mean.

So what's a woman to do?

One thing that can help is to decide right now to not be a well-behaved dog anymore and to begin to repair and reassert the instinctual nature that knows when is the right time to do all things: time to live, time to die, time to rest, time to love, time to have sex, time to have babies, time to not have babies, time to have a lover, time to be alone. Following the natural cycles of one's body, one's psyche, one's feminine nature comprises a spiritual practice in and of itself.

And how can the metaphor of the Wild Woman help women do that?

The Wild Woman is an archetype—a universal idea that emerges spontaneously in the consciousness of many people across all cultures, across all economic spheres. There are many archetypal images. The archetype of the Divine Child, for instance, which represents at its base a new potential waiting to grow into fullness, is found in the mythos, fairy tales, and night dreams of all cultures. In Christianity, of course, it's represented as the Christ Child, and in fairy tales it's often represented as the child in the woods. In mythos, its birth is often unconventional—from the thigh, the forehead, the hat, the ear. There is something so important about that image, something so revivifying or helpful in understanding a mystery of life, that it comes to us suddenly—it just erupts in the psyche. And we are most often refreshed, enlivened, or deepened by it. It is like a message from the great Self to us humans. The Self broadcasts many vital messages wrapped in images of the Virgin, the Great Mother, the Wise Old Woman, the Shadow, and so forth.

I chose the Wild Woman archetype because I think she is Nature herself, because the instinctual nature is basic to all women and absolutely necessary to their development. The Wild Woman was the greatest divisible image I could imagine. In my years of research in mythos and folklore, I found many, many tales that spoke of the great instinctual nature, of such as she. Also, I felt all other feminine archetypes fit under her great umbrella, so to speak. In rather the same way that a family tree is constructed, I felt that within the embrace of the Wild Woman were the archetypes of the Mother, the Child, the Maiden, the Crone, the Hag, the Sister, the Widow, and so on—all the beautiful shards of the greater archetype.

The Wild Woman archetype has to do with the ability to discern what is needed in both our inner and outer lives at any given moment. It is the aspect of women's psyches that knows. It knows, it knows, and it knows, and no matter what you do to a woman, it still knows. She may be distanced from that voice—which I would call the voice of the "soulSelf"—but eventually, and most likely through her suffering, she will be brought back to that center. She will begin by hook or by crook to listen again to what it says to her, because it broadcasts to her what she should do next, what is in her interest, what she should beware of. The wildish instinctual nature not only strengthens her but also, through breathtaking intuitions, insights, images, and thoughts, gives her explicit maps and instructions.

How can we access that part of ourselves?

Thankfully, there are many ways. You can access the wildish nature through expressive arts, such as dance, painting, sculpture, weaving, or pottery. You can do this by letting your hands make what they wish to make and then looking to see what it is they have made. You proceed by letting that artwork be the harbinger or the message about what is trying to surface. One of my close friends, for example, recently made a whole series of artworks in which young women are holding old women in their arms. So her psychic task is to understand. Why this image, why now? What meaning and instruction does this image hold for her now at this time in her life?

Another way is through prayer—talking to one's God. Another way is through active imagination, which is a form of trance or altered consciousness that Jung talks about at length in his essay called "The Transcendent Function." A fourth way is to record and begin to work to understand your night dreams. The night dreams speak Wild Woman's language. She is there broadcasting. All we have to do is take dictation.

Are there any women in the public eye who you feel particularly exemplify one who has reclaimed her instinctual nature?

I wouldn't put it quite that way, but let me just speak of some of the women whom I admire: Jean Shinoda Bolen, because of her unshakable interest in justice. Audre Lorde—she is a black woman poet—

for speaking out. Also Gwendolyn Brooks, the black poet laureate of Illinois who's now in her seventies, who wrote a poem years ago on abortion that begins "To all the children I got that I did not get." I admire Georgia O'Keeffe, who told me when I was nineteen years old that there was a certain advantage to wrapping oneself in mystery. Everyone said she was a very mean old woman and that it was futile for me to try to talk to her, because she would, you know, cook me for dinner and eat me. And so I wrote her a letter to that effect and she wrote back and said—and you could tell in the letter she was laughing—"You can come see me any time, girl." Also, Dorothy Day, whom I met when I was in high school, who was the head of the Catholic Worker movement. And Eleanor Roosevelt, who came out to the farms to talk to the migrant people in the early fifties. She was truly kind; she truly loved people. And other people: Bella Abzug, again, for speaking. And I think also Jean Harris, the woman who is in prison for killing Herman Tarnower, the so-called "diet doctor."

Now why do you admire her?

She petitioned for a program in the prison to help minority women maintain contact with their children while incarcerated. She was turned down many times, but she stayed with it and the mother-child visitation program became a reality. There are so many other women as well. Rigoberta Menchu, a Guatemalan-Kich woman who has in fact been nominated for the Nobel Peace Prize this year. I truly hope it is bestowed upon her. She has traveled all over the world from her tiny Indian village in her *trajes típicos*, Indian garb, and she has spoken out about the death squads, the *desaparecidos*, in Guatemala, and about how people can help. For obvious reasons, she is very brave.

It seems that the women you most admire are those who speak out.

Yes, people who speak. When you see a woman who is silent, deathly silent, there is a strange deadness in her eyes where there should be a glow. You know that something is wrong. Sometimes thinking too hard is hardly thinking.

Whoopi Goldberg speaks out, Oprah Winfrey speaks out. There

are many, many women who do, and I think they are excellent models for those who are injured in instinct. Most of the women whom I have described to you have had their sorrows in life—and those sorrows are well documented—whether it's child abuse, sexual abuse, having a philandering mate, being ostracized by her religion, being laughed at, tortured by senseless gossip, being ridiculed. I have always loved something that Thomas Merton once said: that eccentricity might be the first sign of a person being a saint. These women have a certain quality that is like that, and it always makes me feel very joyful.

8

The Amazon Princess

by Gloria Steinem

Comic books were not quite respectable, which was a large part of the reason I read them: under the covers with a flashlight, in the car while my parents told me I was ruining my eyes, in a tree or some other inaccessible spot; any place that provided sweet privacy and independence. Along with cereal boxes and ketchup labels, they were the primers that taught me how to read. They were even cheap enough to be the first items I could buy on my own; a customer whose head didn't quite reach the counter but whose dignity was greatly enhanced by making a selection (usually after much agonizing) and offering up money of her own.

If, as I have always suspected, children are simply short people—ancient spirits who happen to be locked up in bodies that aren't big enough or skillful enough to cope with the world—then the superhuman feats in comic books and fairy tales become logical and necessary. It's satisfying for anyone to have heroes who can see through walls or leap over skyscrapers in a single bound, but it's especially satisfying if our worldview consists mostly of knees and tying our shoes is still an exercise in frustration.

The trouble is that the comic book performers of such superhuman feats—and even of only dimly competent ones—are almost always heroes. Literally. The female child is left to believe that, even when her body is as grown-up as her spirit, she will still be in the childlike role of helping with minor tasks, appreciating men's accomplishments, and being so incompetent and passive that she can only hope some man will come to her rescue. Of course, rescue and protection are comforting, even exhilarating, experiences that should be and often are shared by men and boys. Even in comic books, the hero is frequently called on to protect his own kind in addition to helpless women. But dependency and zero accomplishments get very dull as a steady diet. The only option for a girl reader is to identify with the male characters—pretty difficult, even in the androgynous years of childhood. If she can't do that, she faces limited prospects: an "ideal" life of sitting around like a technicolor clothes horse, getting into jams with villains, and saying things like, "Oh, Superman! I'll always be grateful to you," even as her hero goes off to bigger and better adventures. It hardly seems worth learning to tie our shoes.

I'm happy to say that I was rescued from this plight at about the age of seven or eight, rescued (great Hera!) by a woman. Not only was she as wise as Athena and as lovely as Aphrodite, she had the speed of Mercury and the strength of Hercules. Of course, being an Amazon, she had a head start on such accomplishments, but she had earned them in a human way by training in Greek-style contests of dexterity and speed with her Amazon sisters. (Somehow it always seemed boring to me that Superman was a creature from another planet, and, therefore, had bullet-proof skin, x-ray vision, and the power to fly. Where was the contest?) This beautiful Amazon did have some fantastic gadgets to help her: an invisible plane that carried her through dimensions of time and space, a golden, magic lasso, and bullet-proof bracelets. But she still had to get to the plane, throw the lasso with accuracy, and be agile enough to catch bullets on the steel-enclosed wrists.

Her creator had also seen straight into my heart and understood the secret fears of violence hidden there. No longer did I have to pretend to like the "pow!" and "crunch!" style of Captain Marvel or the Green Hornet. No longer did I have nightmares after reading ghoulish comics filled with torture and mayhem, comics made all the more horrifying by their real-life setting in World War II. (It was a time when leather-clad Nazis were marching in the newsreels *and* in the comics, and the blood on the pages seemed frighteningly real.) Here was a heroic person who might conquer with force, but only a force that was tempered by love and justice. She converted her enemies more often than not. And if they were destroyed, they did it to themselves, usually in some unbloody accident.

She was beautiful, brave, and explicitly out to change "a world torn by the hatreds and wars of men."

She was Wonder Woman.

Looking back now at these Wonder Woman stories from the forties, I am amazed by the strength of their feminist message. One typical story centers on Prudence, a young pioneer in the days of the American frontier. (Wonder Woman is transported there by her invisible plane, of course, which also served as a time machine.) Rescued by Wonder Woman, Prudence realizes her own worth and the worth of all women: "I've learned my lesson," she says proudly in the final scene. "From now on, I'll rely on myself, not on a man." In yet another episode, Wonder Woman herself says, "I can never love a dominant man who is stronger than I am." And throughout the strips, it is only the destructive, criminal woman—the woman who has bought the whole idea that male means aggression and female means submitting—who says, "Girls want superior men to boss them around."

Many of the plots revolve around evil men who treat women as inferior beings. In the end, all are brought to their knees and made to recognize women's strength and value. Some of the stories focus on weak women who are destructive and confused. These misled females are converted to self-reliance and self-respect through the example of Wonder Woman. The message of the strips is sometimes inconsistent and always oversimplified (these are, after all, comics), but it is still a passable version of the truisms that women are rediscovering today: that women are full human beings; that we cannot love others until we love ourselves; that love and respect can only exist between equals.

Wonder Woman's family of Amazons on Paradise Island, her band of college girls in America, and her efforts to save individual women are all welcome examples of women working together and caring about each other's welfare. The idea of such cooperation may not seem particularly revolutionary to the male reader: Men are routinely depicted as working well together. But women know how rare and, therefore, exhilarating the idea of sisterhood really is.

Wonder Woman's mother, Queen Hippolyte, offers yet another welcome example to young girls in search of a strong identity. Queen Hippolyte founds nations, wages war to protect Paradise Island, and sends her daughter off to fight the forces of evil in the world. Perhaps most impressive in an age fraught with Freudian shibboleths, she also marshals her queenly strength to protect her daughter in bad times. How many girl children grew to adulthood with no experience of a courageous and worldly mother, except in these slender stories? How many adult women disdain the birth of a female child, believe it is "better" to bear male children, and fear the competition and jealousy they have been conditioned to believe is "natural" to a mother and daughter? Feminism is just beginning to uncover the sense of anger and loss in girls whose mothers had no power to protect them in the world, and so trained them to be victims, or left them to identify with their fathers if they had any ambitions outside the traditional female role.

Wonder Woman symbolizes many of the values of the women's culture that feminists are now trying to introduce into the mainstream: strength and self-reliance for women, sisterhood and mutual support among women, peacefulness and esteem for human life, a diminishment both of "masculine" aggression and of the belief that violence is the only way of solving conflicts.

*   *   *

Of course, the Wonder Woman stories are not admirable in all ways. Many feminist principles are distorted or ignored. Thus, women are converted and saved. Mad scientists, foreign spies, criminals, and other male villains are regularly brought to the point of renouncing violence and, more often, of saying, "You're right, Wonder Woman. I'll never make the mistake of thinking women are inferior again." Is the reader supposed to conclude women are superior? The Wonder Woman stories not only depict women as culturally different (in ways that are sometimes constructive and sometimes not), they also hint that women are biologically, and, therefore, immutably, superior to men.

Few modern feminists would agree. There are as yet no perfectly culture-free tests to prove to us which traits come from conditioning and which do not, but the consensus seems to be that society, not biology, assigns some human traits to males and others to females. Women have suffered from being taught to develop what society considers the less-valued traits of humanity, but this doesn't mean we want to switch to a sole claim on the "more valuable" ones either. That might accomplish nothing more than changing places with men in the hierarchy. Most feminist philosophy supposes that the hierarchy itself must be eliminated, that individuals who are free of roles assigned because of sex or race will also be free to develop the full range of human qualities. It's the multitudinous differences in individuals that count, not the localized differences of sex or race.

For psychologist William Moulton Marston—who, under the pen name of "Charles Moulton," created Wonder Woman—females were sometimes romanticized as biologically and unchangeably superior. "Women," he wrote, "represent love; men represent force. Man's use of force without love brings evil and unhappiness. Wonder Woman proves that women are superior to men because they have love in addition to force." If that's the case, then we're stuck with yet another social order based on birth.

For the purposes of most Wonder Woman stories, however, the classic argument of nature versus nurture is a mere intellectual quibble. Just helping women to respect themselves, to use their strength and refuse domination by men is time-consuming enough:

Wonder Woman rarely has the leisure to hint at what the future social order ought to be. As for men, we do get the idea that they have some hope—even if vague—of collective redemption. "This man's world of yours," explains Wonder Woman, "will never be without pain and suffering until it learns respect for human rights." Put in more positive terms, this does seem to indicate that humanized men will have full membership in the new society.

Some of the Wonder Woman stories preach patriotism in a false way, but much of the blame rests with history. Wonder Woman was born in 1941, just about the time that World War II became a reality for most Americans, and she, therefore, had to spend much of her time protecting this country from foreign threats. Usually, that task boiled down to proving that women could be just as brave and loyal as men in the service of their country. Even when her adventures took place in other countries or at other times, they still invariably ended with simplistic commercials about democracy. Although Wonder Woman was shocked by America's unjust patriarchal system—a shock she recorded on her arrival here from Paradise Island—she never had much opportunity to follow up on it; a nation mobilized for war is not a nation prepared to accept criticism. In fact, her costume was patterned after the American flag, and her wartime adventures sometimes had highly jingoistic and even racist overtones, especially when she was dealing with Japanese and Germans.

Compared to the other comic book characters of the period, however, Wonder Woman is still a relief. Marston invented her as a counter to the violence and "bloodcurdling masculinity" that pervaded most comic books, and he remained true to his purpose. Wonder Woman and her sisters were allowed to use violence, but only in self-defense and only if it stopped short of actually killing someone. Most group conflicts between men and women were set not in America, but in a mythological past. Thus Mars, the God of War, periodically endangered the Amazon community and sometimes tried to disarm Queen Hippolyte through the ruses of love. Mars, of course, was the "heavy." He preached that women "are the natural spoils of war" and must remain at home, the helpless slaves of the male victors. Marston used Mars as the symbol of everything Wonder Woman must fight against, but he also gave

the God of War a rationale for his beliefs that was really the female superiority argument all over again: If women were allowed to become Warriors like the Amazons, they would grow
stronger than men and put an end to war. What future for an
unemployed god?

The inconsistencies in Wonder Woman's philosophy are especially apparent in her love life. It is confused, to say the least.
Sometimes her adventures with Steve, the pilot she is supposedly
"in love" with, bear a feminist message. And sometimes they
simper and go conventional in a way that contradicts everything
that has gone before. In her American disguise as mild-mannered
Diana Prince (a clear steal from Superman), she plays the classic
feminine role: secretary, nurse, and worshipful, unrequited side-
kick to Steve. The implicit moral is that, at least as Wonder
Woman, she can love only an equal. But an equal never turns up,
and sometimes she loses her grip on herself and falls for the
masculine notion that there must be a permanent winner and a
permanent loser, a conqueror and a conquered. "Some girls love to
have a man stronger than they are to make them do things," she
muses aloud. "Do I like it? I don't know, it's sort of thrilling. But
isn't it more fun to make a man obey?"

I remember being worried by these contradictions. How could
Wonder Woman be interested in Steve, who seemed so weak and so
boring? Did women really have to live in a community by themselves—a separate country like Paradise Island—in order to be
both happy and courageous? The very fact that the ideal was an
island—insular, isolated, self-contained, cut-off—both pleased and
bothered me. And why, when she chose an earthly disguise, did
Wonder Woman have to pick such a loser? How could she bear to be
like Diana Prince? Did that mean that all women really had to
disguise their true selves in weak, feminine stereotypes in order to
survive?

But all these doubts paled beside the relief, the sweet vengeance,
the toe-wriggling pleasure of reading about a woman who was
strong, beautiful, courageous, and a fighter for social justice. A
woman who strode forth, stopping wars and killing with one hand,
distributing largesse and compassionate aid with the other. A
Wonder Woman.

Wonder Woman may be just one small, isolated outcropping of a larger human memory. And perhaps the girl children who love her are responding to one small echo of dreams and capabilities in their own forgotten past.

9

The Woman Warrior

by Maxine Hong Kingston

The door opened, and an old man and an old woman came out carrying bowls of rice and soup and a leafy branch of peaches.

"Have you eaten rice today, little girl?" they greeted me.

"Yes, I have," I said out of politeness. "Thank you."

("No I haven't," I would have said in real life, mad at the Chinese for lying so much. "I'm starved. Do you have any cookies? I like chocolate chip cookies.")

"We were about to sit down to another meal," the old woman said. "Why don't you eat with us?"

They just happened to be bringing three rice bowls and three pairs of silver chopsticks out to the plank table under the pines. They gave me an egg, as if it were my birthday, and tea, though they were older than I, but I poured for them. The teapot and the ricepot seemed bottomless, but perhaps not; the old couple ate very little except for the peaches.

When the mountains and the pines turned into blue oxen, blue dogs, and blue people standing, the old couple asked me to spend the night in the hut. I thought about the long way down in the ghostly dark and decided yes. The inside of the hut seemed as large as the outdoors. Pine needles covered the floor in thick patterns;

someone had carefully arranged the yellow, green, and brown pine needles according to age. When I stepped carelessly and mussed a line, my feet picked up new blends of earth colors, but the old man and old woman walked so lightly that their feet never stirred the designs by a needle.

A rock grew in the middle of the house, and that was their table. The benches were fallen trees. Ferns and shade flowers grew out of one wall, the mountainside itself. The old couple tucked me into a bed just my width. "Breathe evenly, or you'll lose your balance and fall out," said the old woman, covering me with a silk bag stuffed with feathers and herbs. "Opera singers, who begin their training at age five, sleep in beds like this." Then the two of them went outside, and through the window I could see them pull on a rope looped over a branch. The rope was tied to the roof, and the roof opened up like a basket lid. I would sleep with the moon and the stars. I did not see whether the old people slept, so quickly did I drop off, but they would be there waking me with food in the morning.

"Little girl, you have now spent almost a day and a night with us," the old woman said. In the morning light I could see her earlobes pierced with gold. "Do you think you can bear to stay with us for fifteen years? We can train you to become a warrior."

"What about my father and mother?" I asked.

The old man untied the drinking gourd slung across his back. He lifted the lid by its stem and looked for something in the water. "Ah, there," he said.

At first I saw only water so clear it magnified the fibers in the walls of the gourd. On the surface, I saw only my own round reflection. The old man encircled the neck of the gourd with his thumb and index finger and gave it a shake. As the water shook, then settled, the colors and lights shimmered into a picture, not reflecting anything I could see around me. There at the bottom of the gourd were my mother and father scanning the sky, which was where I was. "It has happened already, then," I could hear my mother say. "I didn't expect it so soon." "You knew from her birth that she would be taken," my father answered. "We'll have to harvest potatoes without her help this year," my mother said, and they turned away toward the fields, straw baskets in their arms. The water shook and became just water again. "Mama. Papa," I called, but they were in the valley and could not hear me.

"What do you want to do?" the old man asked. "You can go back now if you like. You can go pull sweet potatoes, or you can stay with us and learn how to fight barbarians and bandits."

"You can avenge your village," said the old woman. "You can recapture the harvests the thieves have taken. You can be remembered by the Han people for your dutifulness."

"I'll stay with you," I said.

So the hut became my home, and I found out that the old woman did not arrange the pine needles by hand. She opened the roof; an autumn wind would come up, and the needles fell in braids—brown strands, green strands, yellow strands. The old woman waved her arms in conducting motions; she blew softly with her mouth. I thought nature certainly works differently on mountains than in valleys.

"The first thing you have to learn," the old woman told me, "is how to be quiet." They left me by streams to watch for animals. "If you're noisy, you'll make the deer go without water."

When I could kneel all day without my legs cramping and my breathing became even, the squirrels would bury their hoardings at the hem of my shirt and then bend their tails in a celebration dance. At night, the mice and toads looked at me, their eyes quick stars and slow stars. Not once would I see a three-legged toad, though; you need strings of cash to bait them.

The two old people led me in exercises that began at dawn and ended at sunset so that I could watch our shadows grow and shrink and grow again, rooted to the earth. I learned to move my fingers, hands, feet, head, and entire body in circles. I walked putting heel down first, toes pointing outward thirty to forty degrees, making the ideograph "eight," making the ideograph "human." Knees bent, I would swing into the slow, measured "square step," the powerful walk into battle. After five years my body became so strong that I could control even the dilations of the pupils inside my irises. I could copy owls and bats, the words for "bat" and "blessing" homonyms. After six years the deer let me run beside them. I could jump twenty feet into the air from a standstill, leaping like a monkey over the hut. Every creature has a hiding skill and a fighting skill a warrior can use. When birds alighted on my palm, I could yield my muscles under their feet and give them no base from which to fly away.

But I could not fly like the bird that led me here, except in large, free dreams.

During the seventh year (I would be fourteen), the two old people led me blindfolded to the mountains of the white tigers. They held me by either elbow and shouted into my ears, "Run. Run. Run." I ran and, not stepping off a cliff at the edge of my toes and not hitting my forehead against a wall, ran faster. A wind buoyed me up over the roots, the rocks, the little hills. We reached the tiger place in no time—a mountain peak three feet from the sky. We had to bend over.

The old people waved once, slid down the mountain, and disappeared around a tree. The old woman, good with the bow and arrow, took them with her; the old man took the water gourd. I would have to survive barehanded. Snow lay on the ground, and snow fell in loose gusts—another way the dragon breathes. I walked in the direction from which we had come, and when I reached the timberline, I collected wood broken from the cherry tree, the peony, and the walnut, which is the tree of life. Fire, the old people had taught me, is stored in trees that grow red flowers or red berries in the spring or whose leaves turn red in the fall. I took the wood from the protected spots beneath the trees and wrapped it in my scarf to keep dry. I dug where squirrels might have come, stealing one or two nuts at each place. These I also wrapped in my scarf. It is possible, the old people said, for a human being to live for fifty days on water. I would save the roots and nuts for hard climbs, the places where nothing grew, the emergency should I not find the hut. This time there would be no bird to follow.

10

Soldiers of Christ

by Charles A. Coulombe

To begin with, it is important to bear in mind that the modern picture of Christ as a teacher preaching love alone is a relatively recent one. While love and peace were perhaps His ultimate objectives, they were certainly not His methodology: "Do not think that I came to send peace upon earth: I came not to send peace, but the sword"; He then goes on to describe the various relatives that would object to the believer's profession of Him. His parables are filled with military symbolism.

This ought not to be too surprising, for the Jewish people among whom Christ had arisen had proved their military prowess over and over again, and would continue to do so. The greater part of the history of the Old Testament is filled with accounts of their battles and wars; the very settling of the Holy Land required the attempted annihilation of the Canaanites. Yet they were sure they were doing this, not on their own behalf, but at the behest of Yahweh. All the wars of the Hebrews were holy wars, and this they bequeathed to Christianity.

The interior life of the Christian has always been portrayed as spiritual combat against the world, the flesh, and the devil. So it was natural for early Christian converts like St. Paul to say things like, "Let us, who are of the day, be sober, having on the breastplate of faith and charity, and for a helmet the hope of salvation." Martyrdom was likened to victory in war, and the idea of the nascent Church as a sort of army of God was very popular among early Christian writers.

It was of course the conversion of the Roman emperor Constantine in A.D. 312 that made the greatest impact in this regard. In one of the most epochal events in the history of Christianity, Constantine, about to face his brother-in-law and rival Maxentius in a battle for control of the empire, saw the Christian monogram ☧ in the sky along with the words "*In hoc signo vinces*" ("In this sign thou shalt conquer"). For the rest of his life, Constantine was to ascribe his victory in this battle to the help of the Christian God.

The following year Constantine issued the Edict of Milan, granting official toleration to Christianity and beginning a complete reorientation in the relations between Church and empire. From being enemies, they became close, if sometimes bickering, allies. Prelates preached loyalty to the emperor; emperors demanded conformity to whatever versions of the faith they themselves held. The term *miles Christi*, "soldier of Christ," formerly applied to Christians in general and to martyrs in particular, came to be used as a special title for soldiers of the now-Christian empire, particularly when they were engaged in combat with the pagan barbarians on the imperial frontiers. "War is bad: but since it is inevitable, one must justify those who make war honestly, and simply for the advancement of the right," St. Augustine wrote in the late fourth century.

When those same barbarians not only breached the empire's frontier but set up their own nations on Roman soil, yet another element would be added to the concept of soldiering for Christ. Like many other nomadic peoples, the Germanic tribes prized warfare for its own sake. Intertribal conflicts provided the means for establishing one's manhood and acquiring prestige. When the newly settled tribes were converted, the Church strove to moderate and channel their warlike ardor. Apart from forbidding combat during Lent, Advent, Sundays, and holy days (the *Treuga Dei*, or Truce of God), and declaring priests, religious, noncombatants, monasteries, and churches to be immune from warfare (the *Pax Dei*, or Peace of God), the Church attempted to spiritualize and ritualize the profession of arms itself. The process was speeded by the appearance of the Muslim threat in the seventh century, and was brought to fruition by the Crusades in Palestine in the eleventh through the thirteenth centuries. This Christianization of soldiering was what we call chivalry.

"Chivalry," says Leon Gautier in his work on the subject, "may be considered an eighth sacrament, and this is perhaps the name that suits it best. . . . It is the sacrament, it is the baptism of the warrior. But we must also regard it as a corporation, like a college, of which every member is a responsible individual."

The "corporation" of chivalry was endowed with definite codes, which were quite similar despite regional variations. Gautier enumerates the "ten commandments of chivalry," as they were known in France:

I. Thou shalt believe all that the Church teaches, and shalt observe all its directions.

II. Thou shalt defend the Church.

III. Thou shalt defend all weaknesses, and constitute thyself the defender of them.

IV. Thou shalt love the country in which thou wast born.

V. Thou shalt not recoil from thine enemy.

VI. Thou shalt make war against the Infidel without cessation, and without mercy.

VII. Thou shalt perform scrupulously thy feudal duties, if they be not contrary to the laws of God.

VIII. Thou shalt never lie, and shalt remain faithful to thy pledged word.

IX. Thou shalt be generous, and give *largesse* to everyone.

X. Thou shalt be everywhere and always the champion of the Right and the Good against Injustice and Evil.

While the earliest knights went through a relatively simple accolade ceremony to receive their knighthood, the ritual of dubbing would eventually be transformed through the influence of the Church. The night previous to the ceremony, the squire to be knighted would place his armor on the high altar of the church wherein the ceremony was to take place. All night he watched it, in emulation of the liturgical vigils of Easter and Pentecost. In the morning, he was placed in a bath; the consecrating knight said, "Even as the infant emerges without spot of sin from the font after baptism, so do you emerge from this bath spotless and without blemish." The squire was then taken to a couch. As he lay upon it, his mentor told him, "Win a resting place in heaven; such is the aim of chivalry!"

Rising, the squire was dressed in a white garment reminiscent of the baptismal garment and told, "It is necessary that those who desire to reach heaven should be pure in mind as in body." Then the knight performing the dubbing placed a vermilion robe around the aspirant's shoulders with the words, "Remember: you must not hesitate to shed every drop of your blood in defense of Holy Church!" A girdle was tied around the knight-to-be, and he was reminded again of the importance of chastity. He was then given a pair of dark shoes with golden spurs, which were to remind him to be "in future as obedient to the spur of the Divine Will as the charger is to material spurs."

Then came the presentation of the two-edged sword. In the order we have been following (for there were many variations), the aspirant was told, "With one side thou must strike the rich who oppress the poor, with the other punish the strong who persecute the weak!" The Roman Pontifical has at the same point: "Receive this sword in the name of the Father and the Son and the Holy Ghost; use it in defense of thyself and of the holy Church of God, for the confusion of the enemies of the cross of Christ and of the Christian faith, and never unjustly to the injury of any man, so far as human frailty will permit."

A white cap was then placed on the aspirant's head to remind him of the necessity of possessing an unspotted soul that was either protected by innocence or cleansed by penitence. Then at last arrived the accolade, which consisted in earlier centuries of a light blow to the head, and in later times of the threefold tapping with the sword with which we are familiar.

While any knight could admit any man to the order of chivalry, kings and bishops took particular pleasure in doing so. The knighting ceremony remained in the Roman Pontifical until Pope John XXIII took it out (along with many other interesting and beautiful things) in 1962.

In this sacred ritual, with its rich symbolism, we see a sort of active lay spirituality, distinct from, although dependent on and connected to, that of the clergy. While students of the esoteric will find in it resemblances to other initiatory rites, its influence was also felt elsewhere in the liturgy. Until Vatican II, the rite of confirmation included a light blow to the confirmand's face; the sacrament was said to make one a "soldier of Christ." Most Western coronation rites came to include presentations of spurs and other chivalric touches.

Armed with the essence of this chivalric spirituality (though its form would continue to evolve), the knights embarked upon the Crusades. These wars remain among the most controversial episodes in history. Much ink has been spilled to prove the crusaders bloody butchers, whose cruelty and greed were exceeded only by their hypocrisy. The noted English historian Kenelm Digby provides an alternative voice:

> When St. Bernard and the Popes called upon the princes of Christendom to take the Cross, it was to save Europe, and to prevent the Crescent from dispossessing the Cross. There is not a point of history more clearly established than this by the concurrent testimony of all real historians. Hence has the memory of the Crusaders been ever dear to all great men who loved Christianity. Thus Dante sees the Cross placed in the planet Mars, to denote the glory of those who fought in the Crusades.

However that may be, chivalry regarded the defense of the Church, its buildings, and its communicants as a holy responsibility. By the time Pope Urban II launched his appeal for the First Crusade in 1095, the Muslims had long been considered a threat. In 732 the Frankish hero Charles Martel only narrowly stopped the Saracen invasion of Gaul at Poitiers; three and a half centuries of hard combat had not dislodged them from southern Spain. Indeed, they would not be pushed out completely until 1492.

At the other end of the Mediterranean, the Byzantines had held the frontier in Asia Minor against the Saracens for four hundred years. This static but bloody combat "was chronicled in Byzantine ballads, and the song of 'Digenis Akritas' shows us what this border country was, the country where the great feudal lords, heroes of chivalry, maintained an endless struggle against the infidel in the name of the Emperor." The Byzantines were defeated, however, at Manzikert in 1071, resulting in the Muslim conquest of virtually all of Asia Minor. The Byzantine emperor's call for help, the sufferings of his erstwhile subjects and of Christians elsewhere in the Muslim domains, and above all the destruction of the Holy Sepulcher by the Turks, impelled Pope Urban II to issue his famous summons for the First Crusade.

Sworn to defend the Church, the weak, and the holy places, the knighthood of Europe rallied to the call. As the "Crusader's Song" from the *Chronicles of the Dukes of Normandy* (1145) puts it:

> *Help me God, in this my pleading!*
> *Tardy we have been to free*
> *That Thy Cross and that Thy country*
> *Where the infidels mock Thee.*
> *'Tis our sins that have delayed us*
> *Let us cast them and be free,*
> *Leaving everything behind us,*
> *Finding Paradise with Thee.*

For the knightly crusader, combat with the Saracen was almost a sacramental act.

Unlike the Muslim, however, who would go straight to paradise if he died fighting unbelievers in a *jihad*, the Christian crusader had no such assurance, but merely a hope. Like indulgences and the sacraments themselves, combat in a crusade was of no effect unless the individual was in a state of grace already. If a crusader died in his sins, it was believed that he would go to hell, no matter what deeds of prowess he performed. Of all the independent knights to take the cross and travel to Outremer (the crusaders' name for the Holy Land), only one was canonized after dying in battle—St. Matthew of Beauvais. Even such crusader kings as St. Louis and St. Ferdinand were canonized for their personal holiness rather than for military prowess.

Temptations were great for the individual knight on crusade. To combat these, and to render the "order" of knighthood more "conducive to salvation," there arose in the Holy Land that peculiar institution known as the military orders. Organized originally to defend pilgrims and to staff hospitals for their welfare, they maintained the familiar organizations of other religious orders: priest-chaplains, nuns, and brothers. All took the three vows of poverty, chastity, and obedience; unlike the other orders, however, these required postulants to be of noble birth.

Inspired by their example, various European rulers formed personal orders of knights; able to marry, these knights were nevertheless required to spend certain days together in prayer, in special chapels, or in churches dedicated to the order. Among these were the Burgundian (later Austrian and Spanish) Golden Fleece, the English Garter, and the French Holy Ghost orders. Less organized were the chivalrous confraternities, which were formed by several knights joining together, generally under the patronage of a saint.

Although the Reformation took away much of the spiritual backing behind knighthood, and many of its proponents began the Crusade-debunking which has survived even to our own time, both chivalry and the crusading impulse have retained much of their hold on the popular imagination.

From the French Revolution until the present century, Catholics fighting the modern centralized state have invoked the memory of the Crusades. So it was with the fighters of the Vendée, the Carlists of Spain, the Miguelists of Portugal, the Cristeros of Mexico, and even the Nationalists in the Spanish Civil War. Today the ultraconservative Catholic lay organization, Tradition, Family, Property, is modeled to a degree on the old military orders.

Outside of Catholic circles the mystique is no less compelling. The nineteenth-century Romantics were attracted by the spirituality of knighthood. Evangelical activists in the same period invoked the crusader spirit in their various campaigns against slavery, child labor, and demon rum. During World War I, both Britain and Germany used the image of St. George fighting the dragon in their propaganda posters, and Churchill and Roosevelt employed chivalric imagery in the Second World War when they performed their famous duet of "Onward, Christian Soldiers." Such organizations as the Salvation Army and the Boy Scouts were consciously formed along chivalric lines.

The knight was called upon to wage never-ending war against darkness. Precisely because this war is never-ending, knighthood and the Crusades will, for the foreseeable future, continue to maintain their hold on the human heart.

Today, when innumerable new "ways of the warrior" are offered, perhaps there will be a revival of the original Western "way of the warrior."

11

The Hero as Warrior

by Joseph Campbell

The place of the hero's birth, or the remote land of exile from which he returns to perform his adult deeds among men, is the mid-point or navel of the world. Just as ripples go out from an underwater spring, so the forms of the universe expand in circles from this source.

"Above the broad, unmoving depths, beneath the nine spheres and the seven floors of heaven, at the central point, the World Navel, the quietest place on the earth, where the moon does not wane, nor the sun go down, where eternal summer rules and the cuckoo everlastingly calls, there the White Youth came to consciousness." So begins a hero myth of the Yakuts of Siberia. The White Youth went forth to learn where he was and what his dwelling place was like. Eastward of him lay stretching a broad, fallow field, in the middle of which arose a mighty hill, and on the summit of the hill a gigantic tree. The resin of that tree was transparent and sweet scented, the bark never dried or cracked, the sap shone silver, the luxuriant leaves never wilted, and the catkins resembled a cluster of reversed cups. The summit of the tree rose over the seven heaven-floors and served as a tethering post for the High God, Yryn-ai-tojon; while the roots penetrated into subterranean abysses, where they formed the pillars of the dwellings of the mythical creatures proper to that zone. The tree held conversation, through its foliage, with the beings of the sky.

When the White Youth turned to face south, he perceived in the midst of a green, grassy plain the quiet Lake of Milk that no breath of wind ever stirs; and around the shores of the lake were swamps of curdle. To the north of him a somber forest stood with trees that rustled day and night; and therein was moving every kind of beast. Tall mountains were lifting beyond it, and appeared to be wearing caps of white rabbit fur; they leaned against the sky and protected this middle place from the northern wind. A thicket of scrub stretched out to the west, and beyond it stood a forest of tall firs; behind the forest gleamed a number of blunt-headed solitary peaks.

This was the manner, then, of the world in which the White Youth beheld the light of day. Presently tired, however, of being alone, he went over to the gigantic tree of life. "Honored High Mistress, Mother of my Tree and my Dwelling Place," he prayed; "everything that lives exists in pairs and propagates descendants, but I am alone. I want now to travel and to seek a wife of my own kind; I wish to measure my strength against my kind; I want to become acquainted with men—to live according to the manner of men. Do not deny me thy blessing, I do humbly pray. I bow my head and bend my knee."

Then the leaves of the tree began murmuring, and a fine, milk-white rain descended from them upon the White Youth. A warm breath of wind could be felt. The tree began to groan, and out of its roots a female figure emerged to the waist: a woman of middle age, with earnest regard, hair flowing free, and bosom bare. The goddess offered her milk to the youth from a sumptuous breast, and after partaking of it he felt his strength increase a hundred-fold. At the same time, the goddess promised the youth every happiness and blessed him in such a way that neither water, nor fire, iron, nor anything else should ever do him harm.[1]

From the umbilical spot the hero departs to realize his destiny. His adult deeds pour creative power into the world.

> *Sang the aged Väinämöinen;*
> *Lakes swelled up, and earth was shaken,*
> *And the coppery mountains trembled,*
> *And the mighty rocks resounded.*
> *And the mountains clove asunder;*
> *On the shore the stones were shattered.*[2]

The stanza of the hero-bard resounds with the magic of the word of power; similarly, the sword edge of the hero-warrior flashes with the energy of the creative Source: before it fall the shells of the Outworn.

For the mythological hero is the champion not of things become but of things becoming; the dragon to be slain by him is precisely the monster of the status quo: Holdfast, the keeper of the past. From obscurity the hero emerges, but the enemy is great and conspicuous in the seat of power; he is enemy, dragon, tyrant, because he turns to his own advantage the authority of his position. He is Holdfast not because he keeps the *past* but because he *keeps.*

The tyrant is proud, and therein resides his doom. He is proud because he thinks of his strength as his own; thus he is in the Clown role, as a mistaker of shadow for substance; it is his destiny to be tricked. The mythological hero, reappearing from the darkness that is the source of the shapes of the day, brings a knowledge of the secret of the tyrant's doom. With a gesture as simple as the pressing of a button, he annihilates the impressive configuration. The hero-deed is a continuous shattering of the crystallizations of the moment. The cycle rolls: mythology focuses on the growing-point. Transformation, fluidity, not stubborn ponderosity, is the characteristic of the living God. The great figure of the moment exists only to be broken, cut into chunks, and scattered abroad. Briefly: the ogre-tyrant is the champion of the prodigious fact, the hero the champion of creative life.

The world period of the hero in *human* form begins only when villages and cities have expanded over the land. Many monsters remaining from primeval times still lurk in the outlying regions, and through malice or desperation these set themselves against the human community. They have to be cleared away. Furthermore, tyrants of human breed, usurping to themselves the goods of their neighbors, arise, and are the cause of widespread misery. These have to be suppressed. The elementary deeds of the Hero are those of the clearing of the field.[3]

Kut-o-yis, or "Blood Clot Boy," when he had been taken from the pot and had grown to manhood in a day, slew the murderous son-in-law of his foster parents, then proceeded against the ogres of the countryside. He exterminated a tribe of cruel bears, with the exception of one female who was about to become a mother. "She pleaded so pitifully for her life, that he spared her. If he had not done this, there would have been no bears in the world." Then he slaughtered a tribe of snakes, but again with the exception of one "who was about to become a mother." Next he deliberately walked along a road which he had been told was dangerous. "As he was going along, a great windstorm struck him and at last carried him into the mouth of a great fish. This was a sucker-fish and the wind was its sucking. When he got into the stomach of the fish, he saw a great many people. Many of them were dead, but some were still alive. He said to the people, 'Ah, there must be a heart somewhere here. We will have a dance.' So he painted his face white, his eyes and mouth with black circles, and tied a white rock knife on his head, so that the point stuck up. Some rattles made of hoofs were also brought. Then the people started in to dance. For a while, Blood Clot sat making wing-motions with his hands, and singing songs. Then he stood up and danced, jumping up and down until the knife on his head struck the heart. Then he cut the heart down. Next he cut through between the ribs of the fish, and let all the people out.

"Again Blood Clot said he must go on his travels. Before starting, the people warned him, saying that after a while he would see a woman who was always challenging people to wrestle with her, but that he must not speak to her. He gave no heed to what they said, and, after he had gone a little way, he saw a woman who called him to come over. 'No,' said Blood Clot. 'I am in a hurry.' However, at the fourth time the woman asked him to come over, he said, "Yes, but you must wait a little while, for I am tired. I wish to rest. When I have rested, I will come over and wrestle with you.' Now, while he was resting, he saw many large knives sticking up from the ground almost hidden by straw. Then he knew that the woman killed the people she wrestled with by throwing them down on the knives. When he was rested, he went on. The woman asked him to stand up in the place where he had seen the knives; but he said, 'No, I am not quite ready. Let us play a little, before we begin.' So he began to play with the woman, but quickly caught hold of her, threw her upon the knives, and cut her in two.

"Blood Clot took up his travels again, and after a while came to a camp where there were some old women. The old women told him that a little farther on he would come to a woman with a swing, but on no account must he ride with her. After a time he came to a place where he saw a swing on the bank of a swift stream. There was a woman swinging on it. He watched her awhile, and saw that she killed people by swinging them out and dropping them into the water. When he found this out, he came up to the woman. 'You have a swing here; let me see you swing,' he said. 'No,' said the woman, 'I want to see you swing.' 'Well,' said Blood Clot, 'but you must swing first.' 'Well,' said the woman, 'now I shall swing. Watch me. Then I shall see you do it.' So the woman swung out over the stream. As she did this, he saw how it worked. Then he said to the woman, 'You swing again while I am getting ready,' but as the woman swung out this time, he cut the vine and let her drop into the water. This happened on Cut Bank Creek."[4]

We are familiar with such deeds from our Jack-the-Giant-Killer nursery tales and the classical accounts of the labors of such heroes as Herakles and Theseus. They abound also in the legends of the Christian saints, as in the following charming French tale of Saint Martha.

"There was at that time on the banks of the Rhône, in a forest situated between Avignon and Arles, a dragon, half animal, half fish, larger than an ox, longer than a horse, with teeth as sharp as horns, and great wings at either side of its body; and this monster slew all the travelers and sank all the boats. It had arrived by sea from Galatia. Its parents were the Leviathan—a monster in the form of a serpent that dwelt in the sea—and the Onager—a terrible beast bred in Galatia, which burns with fire everything it touches.

"Now Saint Martha, at the earnest request of the people, went against the dragon. Having found it in the forest, in the act of devouring a man, she sprinkled holy water on it and exhibited a crucifix. Immediately, the monster, vanquished, came like a lamb to the side of the saint, who passed her belt around its neck and conducted it to the neighboring village. There the populace slew it with stones and staffs.

"And since the dragon had been known to the people under the name of Tarasque, the town took the name of Tarascon, in remembrance. Up to then it had been called Nerluc, which is to say, Black Lake, on account of the somber forests which there bordered the stream.[5]

The warrior-kings of antiquity regarded their work in the spirit of the monster-slayer. This formula, indeed, of the shining hero going against the dragon has been the great device of self-justification for all crusades. Numberless memorial tablets have been composed with the grandiose complacency of the following cuneiform of Sargon of Agade, destroyer of the ancient cities of the Sumerians, from whom his own people had derived their civilization.

"Sargon, king of Agade, viceregent of the goddess Ishtar, king of Kish, *pashishu*[6] of the god Anu, King of the Land, great *ishakku*[7] of the god Enlil: the city of Uruk he smote and its wall he destroyed. With the people of Uruk, he battled and he captured him and in fetters led him through the gate of Enlil. Sargon, king of Agade, battled with the man of Ur and vanquished him; his city he smote and its wall he destroyed. E-Ninmar he smote and its wall he destroyed, and its entire territory, from Lagash to the sea, he smote. His weapons he washed in the sea. . . ."

12

Wars, Arms, Rams, Mars: On the Love of War

by James Hillman

You will recall, if you saw the film *Patton*, the scene in which the American General, who commanded the Third Army in the 1944–45 drive across France into Germany, walks the field after a battle: churned earth, burnt tanks, dead men. The General takes up a dying officer, kisses him, surveys the havoc, and says: "I love it. God help me, I do love it so. I love it more than my life."

This scene gives focus to my theme—the love of war, the love in war and for war that is more than "my" life, a love that calls up a God, that is helped by a God and on a battlefield, a devastated piece of earth that is made sacred by that devastation.

I believe we can never speak sensibly of peace or disarmament unless we enter into this love of war. Unless we enter into the martial state of soul, we cannot comprehend its pull. This special state must be ritualistically entered. We must be "inducted," and war must be "declared"—as one is declared insane, declared married or bankrupt. So we shall try now to "go to war" and this because it is a principle of psychological method that any phenomenon to be understood must be empathically imagined. To know war we must enter its love. No psychic phenomenon can be truly dislodged from its fixity unless we first move the imagination into its heart.

War is a psychological task, which Freud recognized and addressed in several papers. It is especially a psychological task because philosophy and theology have failed its overriding importance. War has been set aside as history, where it then becomes a sub-chapter called military history. Or war has been placed outside the mainstream of thought into think tanks. So we need to lift this general repression, attempting to bring to war an imagination that respects its primordial significance.

My method of heading right in, of penetrating rather than circumambulating or reflecting, is itself martial. So we shall be invoking the God of the topic by this approach to the topic.

During the 5,600 years of written history, there have been at least 14,600 recorded wars. Two or three wars each year of human history. Since Edward Creasy's *Fifteen Decisive Battles* (1851), we have been taught that the turning points of Western civilization occur in such battles as Salamis and Marathon, Carthage, Tours, Lepanto, Constantinople, Waterloo, Midway, Stalingrad. . . . The ultimate determination of historical fate, we have been taught, depends upon battle, whose outcome in turn depends upon an invisible genius in a leader or hero through whom a transcendent spirit is manifested. The battle and its personified epitome become salvational representations in secular history. The statues in our parks, the names of our grand avenues, and the holidays we celebrate commemorate the salvational aspect of battle.

Neglected in Creasy's decisive battles are the thousands of indecisive ones, fought with equal heroism, yet which ended inconclusively or yielded no victory for the ultimate victor of the war; nor did these battles produce commemorative epic, statue, or celebration. Unsung heroes; died in vain; lost cause. The ferocity of battle may have little to do with its outcome, the outcome little to do with the outcome of the war. Verdun in the Great War of 1914–18 is such an example: a million casualties and nothing decisive. The significance of a battle is not given by the war, but by the battle itself.

Besides the actual battles and their monuments, the monumental epics that lie in the roots of our Western languages are, to a large proportion, "war books": the *Mahabharata* and its *Bhagavad Gita*, the *Iliad*, the *Aeneid*, the Celtic *Lebor Gabala*, and the Norse *Edda*. Our Bible is a long account of battles, of wars and captains of wars.

Jahweh presents himself in the speeches of a War God and his prophets and kings are his warriors.[1] Even the New Testament is so arranged that its final culminating chapter, Revelation, functions as its recapitulative coda in which the Great Armageddon of the Apocalypse is its crisis.

In our most elevated works of thought—Hindu and Platonic philosophy—a warrior class is imagined as necessary to the well-being of humankind. This class finds its counterpart within human nature, in the heart, as virtues of courage, nobility, honor, loyalty, steadfastness of principle, comradely love, so that war is given location not only in a class of persons but in a level of human personality organically necessary to the justice of the whole.

Have I carried my first point that battles and the martial are not merely irrational relapses into archaic pre-civilization? The martial cannot be derived merely from the territorial imperative of our animal inheritance: "this is my realm, my feeding and breeding space; get out or I'll kill you." Nor do wars arise simply from industrial capitalism and its economic distress, the mystiques of tribes and nationalism, the just preservation of a state, masculine machoism, sociological indoctrinations or psychological paranoia and aggression. (Paranoia and aggression, if explanatory principles, themselves require explanations.) No, wars are not only man-made; they bear witness also to something essentially human that transcends the human, invoking powers more than the human can fully grasp. Not only do Gods battle among themselves and against other foreign Gods, they sanctify human wars, and they participate in those wars by divine intervention, as when soldiers hear divine voices and see divine visions in the midst of battle.

Because of this transcendent infiltration, wars are so difficult to control and understand. What takes place in battle is always to some degree mysterious, and therefore unpredictable, never altogether in human hands. Wars "break out." Once commanders sought signs in the heavens, from birds. Today, we fantasize the origin of war in a computer accident. *Fortuna*—despite meticulous battle plans and rehearsals, the battle experience is a melee of surprises.

We therefore require an account of war that allows for its tran-

scendent moment, an account that roots itself in *archai*—the Greek
word for "first principle"—*arche*, not merely as archaic, a term of
historical explanation, but as archetypal, evoking the trans-
historical background, that divine epiphanic moment in war.[2]

This archetypal approach holds that ever-recurring, ubiquitous,
highly ritualized and passionate events are governed by fundamental psychic patterning factors. These factors are given with the
world as modes of its psychological nature, much as patterns of
atomic behavior are given with the physical nature of the world and
patterns of instinctual behavior are given with the world's biological nature.

I want now for us to enter more closely into the epiphany of this
archetypal principle, this God, Mars. Here is a reading from Ernst
Jünger's diary, recording the start of the last German offensive in
1918:

> The great moment had come. The curtain of fire lifted from the front
> trenches. We stood up—we moved in step, irresistibly toward the
> enemy lines. I was boiling with a mad rage, which had taken hold of
> me and all others in an incomprehensible fashion. The overwhelming
> wish to kill gave wings to my feet. The monstrous desire for annihila-
> tion, which hovered over the battlefield, thickened the brains of the
> men in a red fog. We called each other in sobs and stammered
> disconnected sentences. A neutral observer might perhaps have be-
> lieved we were seized by an excess of happiness.[3]

A scholar of Japanese culture, Donald Keene, has collected *tanka*
and hundreds of other writings expressing the feelings of major
Japanese authors (including liberals, leftists, and Christians) during
the 1941–45 war. I shall quote only passages referring to Pearl
Harbor. Nagayo Yoshio, author of *The Bronze Christ*, on hearing of
the declaration of war with the United States, wrote: "I never
thought that in this lifetime I should ever know such a happy,
thrilling, auspicious experience." The novelist and critic Ito Sei on
the same occasion said: "I felt as if in one stroke I had become a
new man, from the depths of my being." Honda Akira, scholar of

English literature, wrote: "I have felt the sense of a clearing. Now the word 'holy war' is obvious . . . a new courage has welled up and everything has become easier to do."

Glenn Gray in his book *The Warriors*—the most sensitive account of war experience that I know—writes:

> Veterans who are honest with themselves will admit the experience in battle has been a high point in their lives. Despite the horror, the weariness, the grime, and the hatred, participation with others in the chances of battle had its unforgettable side. For anyone who has not experienced it himself, the feeling is hard to comprehend and for the participant hard to explain to anyone else—that curious combination of earnestness and lightheartedness so often noted of men in battle.[4]

These positive experiences are puzzling. It is the positive experience that we must reckon with because the savagery and confusion, the exhaustion and desertion correspond with what is objectively taking place. Those responses do not need explanations. But how mystifying the lightheartedness in killing, the joy of going into battle, and that infantrymen with bayonets fixed, snipers in ambush, torpedo men in destroyers report no particular hatred, little heroic ambition, unconcern for victory, or even passion for their cause for which they stand exposed and may even volunteer to die. Instead, they sometimes report altered states of perception, intensified vitality, a new awareness of the earth's beauty and nearness of divinity—their little plot, their meager, grimy life suddenly transcendently sweet. "It is well that war is so terrible," said Robert E. Lee, "we would grow too fond of it."

And, beyond all else is the group-bonding to the platoon, the crew, a buddy.[5] Love in war. Thomas Aquinas notes that comrades in arms display a specific form of friendship. This battle-love is complex, gentle, altruistic, and fierce. It cannot be reduced merely to modern psychologisms: boosting masculinity with macho codes of honor, peer-pressure that successfully represses cowardice, the discovery and release under the duress of battle of repressed homosexual emotion. Moreover, so strong and so transcending the aims of war itself is this love that a soldier, in fidelity to his buddies, may more easily shoot down his own officer than an enemy in the opposite trench.

To illustrate this love in war, I shall condense from S. L. A. Marshall an incident from his account of the desperate American retreat from the Yalu after the failed invasion of North Korea.[6] There was a tight ravine under enemy fire through which funnel the only escape route lay. "From end to end this sanctuary was already filled with bodies, the living and the dead, wounded men who could no longer move, the exhausted ... the able-bodied driven to earth by fire. It was a sump pit of all who had become detached from their vehicles and abandoned to each other ... 200 men in the ditch so that their bodies overlapped. Americans, Turks, ROK's.... Yet there was cooperative motion and human response. Men who were still partly mobile crawled forward along the chain of bodies.... As they moved, those who were down and hurt cried: 'Water! Water!' ... Long since, nearly all canteens were dry. But the able-bodied checked long enough to do what bandaging they could ... some stripped to the waist in the bitter cold and tore up their undershirts for dressings. Others stopped their crawl long enough to give their last drop of water ... the wounded who were bound to the ditch tried to assist the able-bodied seeking to get out. Witnesses saw more of the decency of men than ever had been expected."

Love and war have traditionally been coupled in the figures of Venus and Mars, Aphrodite and Ares. This usual allegory is expressed in usual slogans—make love not war, all's fair in love and war—and in usual oscillating behaviors—rest, recreation and rehabilitation in the whorehouse behind the lines, then return to the all-male barracks. Instead of these couplings which actually separate Mars and Venus into alternatives, there is a Venusian experience within Mars itself. It occurs in the sensate love of life in the midst of battle, in the care for concrete details built into all martial regulations, in the sprucing, prancing and dandying of the cavaliers (now called "boys") on leave. Are they sons of Mars or of Venus?

In fact, we need to look again at the aesthetic aspect of Mars. Also there a love lies hidden. From the civilian sidelines, military rites and rhetoric seem kitsch and pomposity. But look instead at this language, these procedures as the sensitization by ritual of the physical imagination. Consider how many different kinds of blades, edges, points, metals and temperings are fashioned on the variety of knives, swords, spears, sabers, battle-axes, rapiers, daggers, lances, pikes, halberds that have been lovingly honed with the idea for killing. Look at the rewards for killing: Iron Cross, Victoria Cross, Medal of Honor, Croix de Guerre; the accoutrements: bamboo baton, swagger stick, epaulets, decorated sleeves, ivory-handled pistols. The music: reveille and taps, drums and pipes, fifes and drums, trumpets, bugles, the marching songs and marching bands, brass, braid, stripes. The military tailors: Wellington boots, Eisenhower jackets, Sam Brown belts, green berets, red coats, "whites."[7] Forms, ranks, promotions. Flags, banners, trooping to the colors. The military mess—its postures, toasts. The manners: salutes, drills, commands. Martial rituals of the feet—turns, steps, paces, warriors' dances. Of the eyes—eyes front! Of the hands, the neck, the voice, ramrod backbone, abdomen—"Suck in that gut, soldier." The names: Hussars, Dragoons, Rangers, Lancers, Coldstream Guards, and nicknames: bluejacket, leatherneck, doughboy. The great walls and bastions of severe beauty built by Brunelleschi, Leonardo, Michelangelo, Buontalenti. The decorated horse, notches in the rifle stock, the painted emblems on metal equipment, letters from the front, poems. Spit and polish and pent emotion. Neatsfoot oil, gunsmith, swordsmith; the Shield of Achilles on which is engraved the whole world.

Our American consciousness has extreme difficulty with Mars.[8] Our founding documents and legends portray the inherent non-martial bias of our civilian democracy. You can see this in the second, third, and fourth constitutional amendments which severely restrict military power in the civilian domain. You can see this in the stories of the Massachusetts Minutemen versus European mercenaries and redcoats, and in the Green Mountain boys and the soldiers of the Swamp Fox—civilians all. And you can see it in the casual, individualistic Texans at San Jacinto versus the Mexican officers trained in the European mold.

Compared with our background in Europe, Americans are ideal-
istic: war has no place. It should not be. War is not glorious, trium-
phal, creative as to a warrior class in Europe from Rome and the
Normans through the Crusades even to the Battle of Britain. We
may be a violent people but not a warlike people—and our hatred
of war makes us use violence against even war itself. Wanting to put
a stop to it was a major cause of the Los Alamos project and
Truman's decision to bomb Hiroshima *and* Nagasaki, a bomb to
"save lives," a bomb to end bombs, like the idea of a war to end all
wars. "The object of war," it says on General Sherman's statue in
Washington, "is a more perfect peace." Our so-called doublespeak
about armaments as "peacekeepers" reflects truly how we think.
War is bad, exterminate war and keep peace violently: punitive
expeditions, pre-emptive strikes, send in the Marines. More fire-
power means surer peace. We enact the blind God's blindness
(Mars *Caecus*, as the Romans called him, and Mars *insanus, furi-
bundus, omnipotens*), like General Grant in the Wilderness, like the
bombing of Dresden, overkill as a way to end war.

Gun control is a further case in point. It raises profound perplex-
ities in a civilian society. The right to bear arms is constitutional, and
our nation and its territorial history (for better or for worse) have
depended on a citizen-militia's familiarity with weapons. But that
was when the rifle and the Bible (together with wife and dog) went
alone into the wilderness. The gun was backed by a God; when it
stood in the corner of the household, pointing upward like the
Roman spear that *was* Mars, the remembrance of the God was there,
and the awe and even some ceremony. With the neglect of Mars, we
are left only the ego and the guns that we try to control with civilian
secular laws.

If in the arms is the God, then arms control requires at least
partly, if not ultimately, a religious approach. The statement by
the Catholic Bishops is a harbinger of that recognition. We worry
about nuclear accident, but what we call "accident" is the auton-
omy of the inhuman. Arms, as instruments of death, are sacred
objects that remind mortals that we are not *athnetos*, immortal. The
fact that arms control negotiations take on more and more ritualis-
tic postures rather than negotiating positions also indicates the
transcendent power of the arms over those who would bring them

under control. Military expenditures of course "overrun," and handguns "get out of hand." I do not believe arms control can come about until the essential nature of arms is first recognized.

Our immigrant dream of escape from conscription into the deadly games of Mars on the European battlefields cannot fit Mars into the American utopia. Hence that paradox for Americans of a peacetime draft and the violence that conscription can occasion. This clash of archetypal perspectives—civil and military—appears sharply in Sicily in 1943 when General Patton slapped two conscripted soldiers who were in the hospital for anxiety states.[9] To the appalled General (a son of Mars), they were malingerers, cowards without love for their fellows. To the appalled American nation of civilians, Patton was the coward, slapping the defenseless sick, without love of his fellows.

By the way, our customary language betrays a bias in favor of the civil—simply by calling it civil. Were we speaking from the military perspective, "civil" would be called "merchant," for these were the traditional class terms in many societies, including India and Japan, and in the Platonic division where the merchants were lower than the warriors (*Phaedrus* 248d) who were not permitted property (*Republic* IV). Traditionally, the warrior class favors the son; the merchant class, the daughter. By slapping his soldiers, Patton was treating them as sons; the civilian (i.e., merchant) reaction experiences them as mistreated daughters.

Although the office of President does combine civil and military, head-of-state and commander-in-chief, and though that office has been held by notable generals—Washington, Jackson, Grant, and Eisenhower—and men with military careers, it has been the habit in recent years for the presidency to founder upon this double role: I think of Truman and Korea, Kennedy and the Bay of Pigs, Johnson and Vietnam, Carter and Iran, and now perhaps Reagan and Central America. Unlike the Roman Republic where Jupiter and Mars could rule together, our republic pretends to have no God of War, not even a department of war. This repression of Mars rather than ritualization of Mars leaves us exposed to the return of the repressed, as rude, eruptive violence, as anxiety about armaments and military expenditures, as rigid reaction formations disguised as peace negotiations, and as paranoid defenses against delusional enemies.

So far I have been stressing the distinction between the military and civil imaginations. I have considered each to be moved by its own archetypal power, powers that do not easily accommodate in a secular, monotheistic consciousness, because that consciousness identifies with a single point of view, forcing others into opponents. Oppositional thinking and true believing are makers of this consciousness.

Now, let me make a second distinction between the military and nuclear imaginations: the martial is not necessarily nuclear nor is the nuclear necessarily martial. The civilian rejection of Mars, however, has so pushed the martial over into the nuclear that we can't think of war without thinking of nuclear war. Mr. Reagan, in fact, calls war "the unthinkable," a mystic's notion of a God beyond thought, beyond image. War is not unthinkable, and not to think it, not to imagine it, only favors the mystical appeal of apocalyptic nuclearism. Remember Hannah Arendt's call to thinking? Not to think, not to imagine is the behavior of Eichmann, said Hannah Arendt. So let us go on thinking all we can about Mars, now in distinction with the nuclear.

Mars in the Roman Republic, where he was most developed as a distinct figure, was placed in a Champs de Mars, a field, a terrain. He was so earthbound that many scholars trace the origins of the Mars cult to agriculture. This helps my point: Mars did not belong to the city. Not until Julius Caesar and caesarism were troops allowed in the city. The focus of martial activity has usually been less the conquest of cities than of terrain and the destruction of armies occupying terrain. Even the naval war in the Pacific (1941–45) followed this classical intention of gaining area.

The martial commander must sense the lay of the land. He is a geographer. The horse (an animal of Mars) was so essential for martial peoples because horses could realize the strategy of winning terrain. Martial strategy is archetypally geo-political.

The nuclear imagination, in contrast, calculates in terms of cities, and its destructive fantasies necessarily include civilians. The city (and thus the civilization, whether taken out by ICBMs or kept as intact prizes by the neutron weapon) is the main focus of the nuclear imagination. The land between Kiev and Pittsburgh (hence Europe) is relatively irrelevant.

A second contrast between the martial and the nuclear: Mars moves in close, hand-to-hand, Mars *propior* and *propinquus*. Bellona is a fury, the blood-dimmed tide, the red fog of intense immediacy. No distance. Acquired skills become instantaneous as in the martial arts. The nuclear imagination, in contrast, invents at ever greater distance—intercontinental, the bottom of the sea, outer space. Because of the time delay caused by distance, the computer becomes *the* essential nuclear weapon. The computer is the only way to regain the instantaneity given archetypally with Mars. The computer controls nuclear weapons, is their governor. Whereas the martial is contained less by fail-safe devices and rational computation than by military ritual of disciplined hierarchy, practiced skill, repetition, code, and inspection. And by the concrete obstacles of geography: commissary trains, hedgerows, bad weather, *impedimenta*.

Our civilian republic has not become fully conscious of the distinction I am laboring. The civilian soldier rebels against military rituals as senseless. He does not grasp that they serve to contain the God of War and so must be obeyed—as Patton insisted— religiously, as if the military were a religious order.

So, too, our civilian republic is not enough aware of the distinction between military and nuclear, thereby entrusting the control of nuclear explosions to the military in the person of General Grove. Considering the volatile commixture of the God of War with the spiritual, apocalyptic appeal of nuclearism, it is miraculous that we have had only test blasts.

A further difference between martial and nuclear is in their visions of transcendence. They show two elemental imaginations of fire: war and the fire of earth; apocalypse and the fire of ether or air. And two different animals: the ram of territory and head-on collision; the eagle of piercing surprise and the uplifting rapture of nuclearism.

The nuclear imagination, further, is without ancestry. Nothing to look back on and draw upon. History provides no precedents. There is a broken connection, to use Lifton's phrase, between sudden, hideous, and collective extinction and deaths modeled by the ancestors. The martial imagination is steeped in memorials. Past battles and military biographies are the ongoing texts. We tramp the battlefields, ponder the cemeteries. There are Swiss depictions of battles, for instance, showing skeletons in the ranks: here are the ancestors fighting in our midst.

The rhetoric of Mars in war-journals, poems, and recollections speaks of attachment to specific earthly places, comrades, things. The transcendent is in the concrete particular. Hemingway writes that, after World War I, "abstract words such as glory, honor, courage ... were obscene beside the concrete names of villages, the numbers of roads, the names of rivers, the regiments and dates." How rare for anyone to know the date of Alamogordo (or even where it is), the date of Hiroshima, of the first hydrogen bomb explosion, or the names of people or places or units engaged. Gone in abstraction. Glenn Gray writes: "Any fighting unit must have a limited and specific objective. A physical goal—a piece of earth to defend, a machine gun nest to destroy, a strong point to annihilate—more likely evokes a sense of comradeship."[10]

Martial psychology turns events into images: physical, bounded, named. Hürtgen Forest, Vimy Ridge, Iwo Jima. A beach, a bridge, a railroad crossing: battle places become iconic and sacred, physical images claiming the utmost human love, worth more than my life.

Quite different is the transcendent experience of the nuclear fireball. The emotion is stupefaction at destruction itself rather than a heightened regard for the destroyed. Nuclear devastation is not merely a deafening cannonade or fire-bombing carried to a further degree. It is different in kind; archetypally different. It evokes the apocalyptic transformation of the world into fire, earth ascending in a pillar of cloud, an epiphanic fire revealing the inmost spirit of all things, as in the Buddha's fire sermon:

All things, O priests, are on fire ... the mind is on fire, ideas are on fire ... mind consciousness is on fire.

Or like that passage from the *Bhagavad Gita* which came to Oppenheimer when he saw the atomic blast:

> *If the radiance of a thousand suns*
> *Were burst at once into the sky*
> *That would be like the splendour of the Mighty One.*

The nuclear imagination leaves the human behind for the worst sin of all: fascination by the spirit. *Superbia.* The soul goes up in fire. If the epiphany in battle unveils love of this place and that man and values more than my life, yet bound with this world, and its life, the nuclear epiphany unveils the apocalyptic God, a God of extinction, the God-is-dead God, an epiphany of Nihilism.

Apocalypse is not necessary to war. Let me make this very clear: apocalypse is not part of the myths of Mars. Mars asks for battle, not wipeout, not even victory. (*Nike* belongs to Athene, not Ares.) Patton supposedly said: "I like making things happen. That's my share in Deity." Apocalypse is inherent, not in the Martial deity, but in the Christian deity. Fascination with a transcendent Christ may be more the threat to the Christian civilization than the War God himself. Are not civilizations saved by their Gods also led to destruction by those same, their own, Gods?

There is one more distinction, one that may be of the most therapeutic significance. If nuclearism produces "psychic numbing," stupefaction, stupidity, Mars works precisely to the contrary. He intensifies the senses and heightens fellow-feeling in action, that energized vivification the Romans called "Mars *Nerio*" and "Mars *Moles,*" molar, massive, making things happen. Mobilization. Mars gives answer to the hopelessness and drifting powerlessness we feel in the face of nuclear weapons by awakening fear, Phobos, his Greek companion or son, and rage, *ira,* wrath. Mars is the instigator, the primordial activist. To put the contrast in eschatological terms, Mars is the God of Beginnings, the sign of the Ram. March is his month, and April, Mars *Apertus,* opening, making things happen. Apocalypse may lift veils, but it closes down into the truly final solution, after which there is no reopening, no *recorso.* Broken the wheel.

*   *   *

I seem to have been making a case for the lesser of two evils, and to have so favored Mars that you may have heard me as a warmonger. But this would be to hear me only literally. Rather than warmonger, see me as ram-monger, Mars-lover. Take my talk as a devotional ritual of imagination to constellate his awakening power. In this way we may call him up and yet deliteralize him at the same time.

It was an ancient custom and is still a modern psychological technique to turn for aid to the very same principle that causes an affliction. The cure of the Mars we fear is the God himself. One must approximate his affects in order to differentiate them. "The Homeric Hymn to Mars" (Ares), in Charles Boer's translation, makes this clear:

> Hear me
> helper of mankind,
> beam down from up there
> your gentle light
> on our lives
> and your martial power
> so that I can shake off
> cruel cowardice
> from my head
> and diminish that deceptive rush
> of my spirit, and restrain
> that shrill voice in my heart
> that provokes me
> to enter the chilling din of battle.
> You, happy God
> give me courage
> to linger in the safe laws of peace
> and thus escape
> from battles with enemies
> and the fate of violent death.[11]

It seems that the more we can love Mars, as in this hymn, the more we can discriminate (to use its words): the deceptive rush of the spirit, the shrill voice that provokes into battle, and at the same time shakes off cruel cowardice from my head.

This imaginative devotion to Mars provides a mode of deliteralizing beyond interpretation of the meaning of the God, beyond a mental act of seeing-through. Here, by deliteralizing I mean: to be fundamentally penetrated by an archetypal power, to participate in its style of love so that its compulsion gives way to its imagination, its angelic, message-giving intelligence. Then the God is experienced in the event as its image, the event no longer requiring my psychologizing for the image to be revealed.

Just this is my aim now, right now as I am speaking: not to explore war or apocalypse in the service of prevention, but to experience war and apocalypse so that their imaginations become fully realized, real. *We* cannot prevent; only images can help us; only images provide *providentia*, protection, prevention. That has always been the function of images: the magic of sacred protection.

We do not know much nowadays about imagining divinities. We have lost the angelic imagination and its angelic protection. It has fallen from all curricula—theological, philosophical, aesthetic. That loss may be more of a danger than either war or apocalypse because that loss results in literalism, the cause of both. As Lifton says, "The task now is to imagine the real." However, like so much of our imagination of the archetypal themes in human nature, the wars we now imagine are severely limited by modern positivistic consciousness. We imagine wars utterly without soul or spirit or Gods, just as we imagine biological and psychological life, social intercourse and politics, the organization of nature—all without soul, spirit or Gods. Things without images.

Wars show this decline of ritual and increase of positivism, beginning with Napoleon and the War Between the States (1861–65). The Great War of 1914–18 was stubborn, massive, unimaginative; the dark Satanic mill relocated in Flanders, sixty thousand British casualties in one single day on the Somme, and the same battle repeated and repeated like a positivist experiment or a positivist logical argument. The repetition of senselessness. Our wars become senseless when they have no myths. Guadalcanal, Inchon, My Lai: battles, casualties, graves (at best); statistics of firepower and body-count—but no myths. The reign of quantity, utterly literal.

Lacking a mythical perspective that pays homage to the God in war, we run the dangers of both war "breaking out" and "loving war too much"—and a third one: not being able to bring a war to a proper close. The Allies' demand for "unconditional surrender" only prolonged the Second World War, giving "justification" for the atomic bomb. Polybius and Talleyrand knew better: masters of war know how and where and when to ease out the God's fury. The very idea of an unconditional surrender evokes the blind rage of Mars *caecus, insanus,* the last-ditch suicidal effort. Surrender requires ritual, a *rite de sortie* that honors the God and allows his warriors to separate themselves from his dominion.

My thoughts have been intended to regain the mythical perspective. My thoughts have not been aimed at finding another literal answer to either war or nuclearism. We each know the literal answer: freeze, defuse, dismantle, disarm. Disarm the positivism but rearm the God; return arms and their control to the mythical realities that are their ultimate governances. Above all: wake up. To wake up, we need Mars, the God of Awakenings. Allow him to instigate our consciousness so that we may "escape the fate of violent death" and live the martial peace of activism.

A Frenchwoman after the Second World War tells Glenn Gray: "Anything is better than to have nothing at all happen day after day. You know I do not love war or want it to return. But at least it made me feel alive, as I have not felt before or since."[12]

Imagine! Is she not saying that war results not from the absence of the God but from his presence? For we long for purposeful action, hand-to-hand engagements, life lived in terms of death, seriousness and lightheartedness together, a clearing. The Frenchwoman's "nothing at all . . . day after day" is the nihilism of the nuclear age. Nuclear doom occurs not only in the literal future out there when the bomb goes off. Doom is already there in our numbed skulls, day-after-day, nothing-at-all. Mars can awaken us out of this nihilism, and its realization in an Apocalypse, with his *phobos,* fear. It may be our most precious emotion. We have everything to fear, except fear itself.

I have tied our numbing with a blocked imagination and the

blocked imagination with the repression of Mars and his kind of love. But fifty minutes, as we know from psychotherapy, isn't going to lift very much repression. I hope, however, that I have been able to evoke enough of Mars for you to feel him stir in your anger and your fear, and in the outward extension of imagination that will probe such questions as:

How lay out the proper field of action for Mars? In what ways can martial love of killing and dying and martial fellowship serve a civilian society? How can we break apart the fusion of the martial and the nuclear? What modes are there for moving the martial away from direct violence toward indirect ritual? Can we bring the questions themselves into the post-modern consciousness of imaginal psychology, deconstruction, and catastrophe theory? Can we deconstruct the positivism and literalism—epitomized by the ridiculous *counting* of warheads—that inform current policies before those policies literally and positively deconstruct our life, our history, and our world?

Let us invoke Mars. At least once before in our century he pointed the way. During the years he reigned—1914–1918—he destroyed the nineteenth-century mind and brought forth modern consciousness. Could a turn to him now do something similar?

Yet Mars wants more than reflection. The ram does not pull back to consider, and iron takes no polish in which it can see itself. Mars demands penetration toward essence, pushing forward ever further into the tangle of danger, and danger now lies in the unthought thicket of our numbed minds. Swords must be *beaten* into plowshares, hammered, twisted, wrought.

Strangely enough, I think this deconstruction is already going on, so banally that we miss it. Is the translation of war from physical battlefield to television screen and space fiction, this translation of literal war into media, mediated war, and the fantasy language of wargames, staging areas, theaters of war and theater commanders, worstcase scenarios, rehearsals, and the Commander-in-Chief, an actor—is all this possibly pointing to a new mode of ritualizing war by imagining it?

If so, then the television war of Vietnam was not lost. The victims died not only for their cause (if there was one) or their country (if it cared). They were rather the sacrificial actors in a ritual that may deconstruct war wholly into an imaginal operation. Carl Sandburg's phrase, "Someday they'll give a war and no one will come," may have already begun. No one need come because the services for Mars are performed nightly at home on the tube. In a media society, will not capitalist war-profiteering shift its base from a military-industrial complex to a military-communications/information complex, the full symbolization of war?

If war could be contained in imagination, why not as well the nuclear bomb? A translation of the bomb into imagination keeps it safe from both military Martialism and civilian Christianism. The first would welcome it for an arm, the second for an Apocalypse. Imagination seems anyway to be the only safe place to keep the bomb: there is no literal positive place on earth where it can be held, as we cannot locate our MX missiles anywhere except as images on a drawing board or dump the wastes from manufacturing them anywhere safe.

However—to hold the bomb as image in the mind requires an extraordinary extension, and extraordinary daring, in our imagining powers, a revolution of imagination itself, enthroning it as the main, the greatest reality, because the bomb, which imagination shall contain, is the most powerful image of our age. Brighter than a thousand suns, it is our omnipotent God-term (as Wolfgang Giegerich has expounded), our mystery that requires constant imaginative propitiation. The translation of bomb into the imagination is a transubstantiation of God to *imago dei*, deliteralizing the ultimate God-term from positivism to negative theology, a God that is all images. And, no more than any other God-term can it be controlled by reason or taken fully literally without hideous consequences. The task of nuclear psychology is a ritual-like devotion to the bomb as image, never letting it slip from its pillar of cloud in the heaven of imagination to rain ruin on the cities of the plain.

The Damocles sword of nuclear catastrophe that hangs upon our minds is already producing utterly new patterns of thought about catastrophe itself, a new theology, a new science, a new psychology, not only burdening the mind with doom but forcing it into postmodern consciousness, displacing, deconstructing, and trashing every fixed surety. Trashing is the symptom, and it indicates a psychic necessity of this age. To trash the end of the century of its coagulated notions calls for the disciplined ruthlessness and courage of Mars. Deconstructing the blocked mind, opening the way in faith with our rage and fear, stimulating the anaesthetized senses: this is psychic activism of the most intense sort.

Then—rather than obliterate the future with a bomb, we would deconstruct our notion of "future," take apart Western Futurism, that safe repository of our noble visions. Care, foresight, renewal, the Kingdom—these have been postponed forever into the future. Rather than blast the material earth with a bomb, we would deconstruct our entombment in materialism with its justification and salvation by economics. We would bomb the bottom line back to the stone age to find again values that are sensate and alive. Rather than bring time to a close with a bomb, we would deconstruct the positivistic imagination of time that has separated it from eternity.

In other words: explode the notions; let them go up in a spirited fire. Explode worldliness, not this world; explode final judgments; explode salvation and redemption and the comings and goings of Messiahs—is not the continual presence of here and now enough for you? Put hope back into the jar of evils and let go your addiction to hopeful fixes. Explode endings and fresh starts and the wish to be born again out of continuity. Release continuity from history: remember the animals and the archaic peoples who have continuity without history. (Must the animals and the archaic peoples go up in flames because of our sacred writ?) Then timelessness could go right on being revealed without Revelation, the veils of literalism pierced by intelligence, parting and falling to the mind that imagines and so welcomes the veiling. No sudden rendering, no apocalyptic ending; timelessness as the ongoing, the extraordinarily loving, lovable, and terrifying continuity of life.

13

The Warrioress Creed

by Mirtha Vega

A Warrioress . . .
is honorable;
has strength, determination, and perseverance;
is magical and optimistic;
is wise and powerful;
revels in silence;
can appreciate both inner and outer beauty;
is dedicated to the sacredness of her life;
loves to live fully;
is unwavering in her quest for the infinite;
is respectful;
can commit to those she deems worthy;
can let go of what is no longer useful, or necessary;
is compassionate;
possesses the will to walk away from illusion;
is willing to trust and surrender when appropriate;
has extraordinary vision and clarity;
faces her fears head-on;
believes.

14

The Modern Warrior: A Manifesto

by George Leonard

1. The Modern Warrior is not one who goes to war or kills people, but rather one who is dedicated to the creation of a more vivid peace.

2. The Modern Warrior honors the traditional warrior virtues: loyalty, integrity, dignity, courtesy, courage, prudence, and benevolence.

3. The Modern Warrior pursues self-mastery through will, patience, and diligent practice.

4. The Modern Warrior works to perfect himself or herself not so much as a means to achieving some external goal as for its own sake.

5. The Modern Warrior is willing to take calculated risks to realize his or her potential and further the general good.

6. The Modern Warrior is fully accountable for his or her actions.

7. The Modern Warrior seeks the inner freedom that comes from the study of esthetics, culture, and the wisdom of the ages.

8. The Modern Warrior respects and values the human individual and the entire web of life on this planet. To serve others is of the

highest good. To freely give and accept nourishment from life is the warrior's challenge.

9. The Modern Warrior reveres the spiritual realm that lies beyond appetites and appearances.

10. The Modern Warrior cherishes life and thus conducts his or her affairs in such a manner as to be prepared at every moment for death. In this light, he or she is able to view all complaints, regrets, and moods of melancholy as indulgences.

11. The Modern Warrior aims to achieve control and act with abandon.

12. The Modern Warrior realizes that being a warrior doesn't mean winning or even succeeding. It does mean putting your life on the line. It means risking and failing and risking again, as long as you live.

When the samurai Kikushi was ordained a bodhisattva (*one devoted to lifelong service*), *his master told him, "You must concentrate upon and consecrate yourself wholly to each day, as though a fire were raging in your hair."*

PART II

THE WARRIOR IN EVERYDAY LIFE

LOVING, FIGHTING, WORKING

I believe we have to be warriors. And whether it's writers or actors or rock 'n' roll players or teachers or politicians, warriors are what interest me and what I aspire to. Talent is not as important as being a warrior, working to fight your battle . . . And there are a lot of warriors whom we never hear of: the nurses and the teachers and the county commissioners and the guy who organized the neighborhood and opened up a daycare center. These are the real warriors of our time.

—KEN KESEY, FROM AN INTERVIEW IN *NEW AGE JOURNAL*

I am calm however and whenever I am attacked. I have no attachment to life or death. I leave everything as it is to the spirit of the universe. Be apart from attachment to life and death and have a mind which leaves everything to that spirit, not only when you are being attacked but also in your daily lives.

—MORIHEI UESHIBA OSENSEI

Introduction

From ancient times, the training of every Chinese warrior included the arts of peace as well as arts of war. "A single hand cannot make a clapping sound," T'ai chi master Yang said. "Whether for practical pursuits or simply the way of being a human being, how dare we neglect the two words—wen and wu, civil and martial?"

The Chinese warrior was never just a warrior. He was a warrior-scholar, a warrior-monk, a warrior-administrator, a warrior-sage. The arts of peace included everything that a cultured warrior ought to know: calligraphy, arithmetic, the Five Classics, music, and the proper performance of the rites. In *Mastering the Art of War*, Thomas Cleary has translated the sayings of Taoist warrior-sages, such as Zhuge Liang, who advised would-be generals to "enjoy social amenities and music. Familiarize yourself with poetry and prose. Put humanity and justice before wit and bravery."

Another warrior-sage, Liu Ji, taught that "the essence of the principles of warriors is responding to change." Knowing this, Taoist warriors could apply the principles of the warrior's way to all the aspects of everyday life, including the art of love. "In sexual encounter, the man's first curiosity is about the hills and valleys of the woman, and hers about the size and fire-power of his armaments," Li Yu wrote in the seventeenth-century erotic classic *The Prayer Mat of Flesh*. "Which of them has to advance and which to retreat? As in war, to know yourself is as important as to know the enemy."

The Chinese tradition of practicing both the arts of war and the arts of peace was transmitted to the Japanese samurai, where it became known as the way of the sword and the pen. During the long peace of the Tokugawa, a number of samurai "how-to" books were published. These books advised samurai to live simply; to rise early; to avoid idle chatter and other forms of self-indulgence; and to be diligent in their duty and devotion to their lord. As Yoshida Shoin, author of one of the most popular samurai guidebooks, wrote: "Take rest after death. This is a maxim, short yet charged with meaning. Perseverance, dogged determination. There is no other way."

In his study of the modernization of Japan, *Tokugawa Religion*, Robert Bellah notes that this "samurai ethic" was one of the main factors that led to the Japanese commercial success in the modern world. It is hardly surprising, then, that the American business community, looking for the "secret" of the stunning Japanese business triumphs of the sixties, should seize on a translation of a samurai swordfighting manual, *The Book of Five Rings*, and make it a surprise bestseller, which spawned other books with titles such as *Martial Arts and the Art of Management*; *Fighting to Win: Samurai Techniques for Your Work and Life*, and *Samurai Selling*. Sun Tzu's *The Art of War* has become popular for the same reason. More recently, a number of writers have begun to apply the harmonizing principles of aikido to everyday life, business, and conflict management.

Actually, when we are fully present to our everyday life, then everything we do becomes part of the warrior's training and discipline. "Every gesture is important," says Taisen Deshimaru in *Zen and the Martial Arts*. "How we eat, how we put on our clothes, how we wash ourselves, how we go to the toilet, how we put our things away, how we act with other people, family, wife, how we work—how we are: totally, in every single gesture."

We begin this section with practical instructions on "Centering as a Daily Practice" by Tom Crum, a martial artist who specializes in applying the aikido principles of nonresistance and joining to conflict management.

Next we look at relationships and family. In "The Warrior of the Heart," John Welwood introduces the "three weapons of the warrior of the heart: awareness, courage, and gentleness."

In "To Bring the Interior Warriors Back to Life," Robert Bly takes a close look at the structure of the contemporary family and considers why "the warriors inside American men have become weak in recent years."

In a personal account, "Warrior Father," Paul Shippee writes about the courage it takes not to pass on the wounds from father to son. Audre Lorde, in "Women with Breast Cancer Are Warriors Also," writes about the courage that comes from living with our wounds.

In "Accessing Power," anthropologist Angeles Arrien examines how power can manifest in a beneficial way in our daily life.

We end this section with Connie Zweig's "Becoming a Warrior Writer," in which the pen becomes a *bokken*, a sword of discrimination. "The gifts of warrior writing practice have been many," she writes. "Finally, I take my life seriously."

15

Centering as a Daily Practice

by Tom Crum

Centeredness is a true psychophysiological phenomenon that affects everything in your environment. It may appear difficult to comprehend on an intellectual level. It is only through experiencing centering that it can become comprehensible and useful.

Have you ever heard the term "mind and body integration"? Well, here it is in a simple yet extremely effective form. The mind and body are intimately connected, and it is easy to begin to experience this profoundly through these simple exercises. It is recapturing that experience throughout the day that allows you to repattern your mind and body into greater unification and stability.

This does not mean that you walk around *thinking* one point or center throughout the day. Not only would that appear foolish, it would prove ineffective as you ran into walls and people and forgot what you were supposed to be doing. Instead, periodically throughout the day, take a few seconds to recapture or reexperience the centered feeling that you acquired during the centering exercise and then go about your normal routine. Great athletes, artists, and professionals in all fields are not *trying* to be centered when they are performing at an optimum level—they are fully committed and concentrated on the job at hand. They are *operating* from centeredness, not thinking about it. Through years of practice, the "greats" have acquired, unconsciously, a certain quality of centeredness. We can optimize our own progress toward excellence by understanding and using centering *now*.

Practice and repetition bring results. There are many opportunities to practice in our daily lives. Those uncomfortable moments when conflict arises are perfect places to test the power of this centered state. You'll find that it is impossible to be angry, fearful, or at the mercy of the conflict in any emotional or physical way and still be centered.

Remember the old adage that you should "count to ten" before reacting in a conflict situation? The opportunity is yours to make this old adage really work. When that feeling of upset or irritation comes, or when fear begins to build, see and hear a big *Yes!* flash in technicolor and quadraphonic sound in your mind, then a big *Thank you for this opportunity*.

Take a moment to become centered. Take a deep breath, and on exhaling, fully release the energy you are feeling, all the while returning to center. This can be done quietly, in a nondisturbing manner. This moment of centering will give you time to really receive the communication, to silently acknowledge the situation. You can always excuse yourself and go into another room if you feel the release is more appropriately done in privacy. The main thing is to breathe deeply and return to that integrated state, to your deepest level of clarity and personal power—which also connects you sensitively and responsibly to the environment around you. You will begin to realize that it's OK to feel upset and fearful because now you don't have to operate out of those states. The energy can be released in positive and appropriate ways. Each time you recapture that centered feeling, you will find the anger or emotion naturally diminishes and your response to the conflict is appropriate and harmonious.

In the beginning stages of centering, there will be a tendency to react with the old patterns of fear or anger before remembering to respond from your center. In time, you will be able to make more subtle distinctions between the two and expand your centeredness into larger areas of your life—many of which you may have considered beyond your control. No longer can you pretend to be a victim. Your life becomes a conscious choice. It's hard not to smile when you're truly centered.

16

The Warrior of the Heart

by John Welwood

Awareness, courage, and gentleness are the basic "weapons" of the warrior of the heart. They cut through our habitual tendencies to fight or flee when we come up against painful or difficult situations. In this way, they allow us to convert whatever challenges we are facing into stepping stones in our development.

Yet most of us, if we carry these weapons at all, have let them become dull from lack of use. Fortunately, that does not disqualify us from venturing forth on love's path. For relationships provide many hard surfaces on which to sharpen these abilities. And the sharper they become, the farther we can advance along this path.

We all face certain obstacles that stand in the way of having a healthy, fulfilling relationship. We may doubt that we are lovable. We may never feel ready to make a commitment. Or perhaps we can never find the "right one" for us. Typically such impasses cause us to swing between hope—that we will somehow be rescued from our situation—and despair—that we are somehow defective or doomed. Yet telling ourselves stories like "Something is wrong with me, this shouldn't be happening," only keeps us from seeing the immediate stepping stones right in front of us.

Instead, if we can let our difficulties with intimacy touch us, they will show us what we most need to work on to come into deeper relationship with ourselves and with others. When we let ourselves feel the rawness these difficulties bring up, we start to get in touch with deeper powers—our capacities to be present with whatever is happening and to find a way to work with it. In this way, whatever seems most impossible about relationships, whatever problem, question, or confusion we have—if we see it, feel it, go toward it, *use it—is* our path.

To call upon our warrior spirit and use love's difficulties as path, we can always begin by asking of the difficulty, "What is this pointing to in me that I need to look at?" Every obstacle or challenge that we face contains an implicit question, which can help us find a new direction. *Questions are an invitation to greater awareness.* They point us toward areas of our experience that need our attention. So when we make the question that is implicit in our difficulty explicit, we are inviting our awareness to enter the situation and guide us.

When we address our impasse in this way, we can use it to generate useful "path questions" for ourselves: "What is this difficulty pointing to? What is it trying to teach me? What can I learn from this situation?" The point of asking such questions is not to come up with an immediate answer. When we try too hard to find an answer, our busy conditioned mind takes over and we only become more confused. But if we can take these questions deep inside us, using them to help us explore neglected areas of our experience, they will point us in new directions.

One woman, in considering why her prospective partners never worked out for her, discovered in herself a strong underground fear of men, as well as a distrust of her own femininity. Thus she realized that her difficulty in finding the right man pointed to some major conflicts about intimacy that she needed to resolve. In her childhood, love had become associated with guilt, debt, and pain. To be loved meant giving herself up. As long as she held that deeply ingrained belief, she was not really ready for the kind of relationship she longed for.

It took courage for this woman to bring these issues to light and deal with them. Yet painful as this was, it felt much better than remaining stuck in hope or despair. For it gave her a direction: She needed to find her own power and resolve her old fears of love before she could truly give herself to a man. Instead of complaining "Why is this happening to me?" she could start to relate to her situation more actively.

Realizing that her impasse with men was helping her take an important step forward in her development also allowed her to be more gentle with herself about her situation. Instead of blaming herself for not having a man, she began to give herself space and time to develop in new ways—to go deep within, face her tendency to give men magical power over her, and eventually find her own light which she could trust. Connecting with herself in this deeper way also helped her appreciate herself as a woman. As she expanded and filled out, she no longer expected men to fill her gaps, and she became more interested in them for who they really were. Consequently, more interesting men started appearing in her life and finding her attractive.

Thus bringing awareness, courage, and gentleness to bear on stuck and impossible areas of relationship ignites the intrinsic wisdom of the heart, which can burn through old patterns of denial and avoidance. If our heart is like a flame, our karmic obstructions are the fuel that this fire needs in order to blaze brightly. Although the burning up of old karma creates great turbulence, it also releases tremendous energy. As our habitual patterns start to break down, we gain access to a fuller spectrum of our human qualities.

So instead of trying to hide the places where we feel raw or confused, fearing that they will spoil the romance, we can, as warriors, actually invite them to come up and burn in love's fire. This allows us to discover that we have access to greater depth and power than we ever imagined. As the flame of the heart burns brighter, consuming our conditioned patterns, our confusions, and our fears, it generates warmth and lights our way.

We cannot become warriors of the heart overnight. Only through practice in working with love's challenges can our being start to unfold, step by step. This gradual unfolding is the path-quality of love. Such a path does not lead anywhere except to the heart of our humanness. Love has no other goal. The path is the goal.

17

To Bring the Interior Warriors Back to Life

by Robert Bly

The warriors inside American men have become weak in recent years, and their weakness contributes to a lack of boundaries, a condition which earlier in this book we spoke of as *naïveté*. A grown man six feet tall will allow another person to cross his boundaries, enter his psychic house, verbally abuse him, carry away his treasures, and slam the door behind; the invaded man will stand there with an ingratiating, confused smile on his face.

When a boy grows up in a "dysfunctional" family (perhaps there is no other kind of family), his interior warriors will be killed off early. Warriors, mythologically, lift their swords to defend the king. The King in a child stands for and stands up for the child's mood. But when we are children our mood gets easily overrun and swept over in the messed-up family by the more powerful, more dominant, more terrifying mood of the parent. We can say that when the warriors inside cannot protect our mood from being disintegrated, or defend our body from invasion, the warriors collapse, go into trance, or die.

The inner warriors I speak of do not cross the boundary aggressively; they exist to defend the boundary. The Fianna, that famous band of warriors who defended Ireland's borders, would be a model. The Fianna stayed out all spring and summer watching the boundaries, and during the winter came in.

But a typical child has no such protection. If a grown-up moves to hit a child, or stuff food into the child's mouth, there is no defense—it happens. If the grown-up decides to shout, and penetrate the child's auditory boundaries by sheer violence, it happens. Most parents invade the child's territory whenever they wish, and the child, trying to maintain his mood by crying, is simply carried away, mood included.

Each child lives deep inside his or her own psychic house, or soul castle, and the child deserves the right of sovereignty inside that house. Whenever a parent ignores the child's sovereignty, and invades, the child feels not only anger, but shame. The child concludes that if it has no sovereignty, it must be worthless. Shame is the name we give to the sense that we are unworthy and inadequate as human beings. Gershen Kauffman describes that feeling brilliantly in his book *Shame*, and Merle Fossum and Marilyn Mason in their book *Facing Shame* extend Kauffman's work into the area of family shame systems and how they work.

When our parents do not respect our territory at all, their disrespect seems overwhelming proof of our inadequacy. A slap across the face pierces deeply, for the face is the actual boundary of our soul, and we have been penetrated. If a grown-up decides to cross our sexual boundaries and touch us, there is nothing that we as children can do about it. Our warriors die. The child, so full of expectation of blessing whenever he or she is around an adult, stiffens with shock, and falls into the timeless, fossilized confusion of shame. What is worse, one sexual invasion, or one beating, usually leads to another, and the warriors, if revived, die again.

When a boy grows up in an alcoholic family, his warriors get swept into the river by a vast wave of water, and they struggle there, carried downriver. The child, boy or girl, unprotected, gets isolated, and has more in common with snow geese than with people.

The snow geese, treading blowing Dakotah snows,
Over the fence stairs of the small farms come,
Slipping through cries flung up into the night,
And setting, ah, between them, shifting wings,
Light down at last in bare and snowy fields.

The drunken father pulls the boy inside.
The boy breaks free, turns, leaves the house.
He spends that night out eating with the geese.
Where, alert and balancing on wide feet,
Crossing rows, they walk through the broken stalks.

—R.B.

It is no wonder that such a child, when a teenager, looks for single rooms, maternal women, gurus, systems, withdrawals, "nonattachment." When he is older, thirty or thirty-five, he will still feel unprotected, and be unable to defend himself from other people enraged at their own unprotection.

Every adult or older sibling who wants to enter the child's psychic room does so, because it is as if there is no doorknob at all on the inside of the door. The door moves freely in, opening us to improper intimacies that the mother may insist on, to improper belittling the father may insist on, to sexual fondling any older child or babysitter may insist on, to incest, physical or psychic. The door moves freely, we could say, because the doorknob is on the outside.

I think it's likely that the early death of a man's warriors keeps the boy in him from growing up. It's possible that it also prevents the female in the boy from developing. We know that Dickens, for example, endured a horrendous childhood, and we also notice that his female characters tend to be sentimental and girlish. It's possible that these girlish beings are projections of his stunted interior woman, whom his warriors could not protect from the violence all around him.

The inner boy in a messed-up family may keep on being shamed, invaded, disappointed, and paralyzed for years and years. "I am a victim," he says, over and over; and he is. But that very identification with victimhood keeps the soul house open and available for still more invasions. Most American men today do not have enough awakened or living warriors inside to defend their soul houses. And most people, men or women, do not know what genuine outward or inward warriors would look like, or feel like.

18

Warrior Father

by Paul Shippee

How many times a day do I become aware of my impulse to shame my son as my father used to shame me? My twelve-year-old son is open and vulnerable, as I was, or as any child is. Into this unguarded gap I am daily compelled to fall, like a hungry tiger. Something deep inside my body is still snarling and wants revenge for the harm done to me by my own father.

It was a hatchet job he did. It was consistent and repeated every day of my life in our family. And because this old hurt, this destruction, still lives embedded in the cells of my body, it is active now when I face my son. The impulse to shame him, to cut him down, to destroy, rises upward from my gut and takes over my thought. Quite often, it takes over my speech. But, more often than not, I can now feel the place deep in my gut from where it arises.

I am learning to change my behavior in the split second synapse where the old route of shame is traveled. The link between my wound and my shaming behavior is finally being broken by training and awareness. It may never be dissolved completely, but it is being slowed down little by little by my determination not to pass this father wound on to my son. I am going to break this link. I am going to separate the wound from the behavior.

Each time my hidden shaming impulse dies, I feel stabbed on the spot by an old pain somewhere in my heart. I feel the old pain my father inflicted on me. The temptation is obvious. I can see that I would rather avoid this little heart stab, and let the shaming missile, armed with hurt, fly out of my mouth and hit the target—my son. But I interfere, due to my determination and training. I know this is the right thing to do, even though it hurts me with the lived memory of my pain. I know this because I see that the result of these interferences is that I claim my own pain. I take responsibility for the wound I received. I feel it. I own it. I do not pass it on to my son.

19

Women with Breast Cancer Are Warriors Also

by Audre Lorde

Ten days after having my breast removed, I went to my doctor's office to have the stitches taken out. This was my first journey out since coming home from the hospital, and I was truly looking forward to it. A friend had washed my hair for me and it was black and shining, with my new gray hairs glistening in the sun. Color was starting to come back into my face and around my eyes. I wore the most opalescent of my moonstones, and a single floating bird dangling from my right ear in the name of grand asymmetry. With an African kente-cloth tunic and new leather boots, I knew I looked fine, with that brave, new-born security of a beautiful woman having come through a very hard time and being very glad to be alive.

I felt really good, within the limits of that gray mush that still persisted in my brain from the effects of the anesthesia.

When I walked into the doctor's office, I was really rather pleased with myself, all things considered, pleased with the way I felt, with my own flair, with my own style. The doctor's nurse, a charmingly bright and steady woman of about my own age who had always given me a feeling of quiet no-nonsense support on my other visits, called me into the examining room. On the way, she asked me how I was feeling.

"Pretty good," I said, half-expecting her to make some comment about how good I looked.

"You're not wearing a prosthesis," she said, a little anxiously, and not at all like a question.

"No," I said, thrown off my guard for a minute. "It really doesn't feel right," referring to the lambswool puff given to me by the Reach For Recovery volunteer in the hospital.

Usually supportive and understanding, the nurse now looked at me urgently and disapprovingly as she told me that even if it didn't look exactly right, it was "better than nothing," and that as soon as my stitches were out I could be fitted for a "real form."

"You will feel so much better with it on," she said. "And besides, we really like you to wear something, at least when you come in. Otherwise it's bad for the morale of the office."

I could hardly believe my ears! I was too outraged to speak then, but this was to be only the first such assault on my right to define and to claim my own body.

Here we were, in the offices of one of the top breast cancer surgeons in New York City. Every woman there either had a breast removed, might have to have a breast removed, or was afraid of having to have a breast removed. And every woman there could have used a reminder that having one breast did not mean her life was over, nor that she was less a woman, nor that she was condemned to the use of a placebo in order to feel good about herself and the way she looked.

Yet a woman who has one breast and refuses to hide that fact behind a pathetic puff of lambswool which has no relationship nor likeness to her own breasts, a woman who is attempting to come to terms with her changed landscape and changed timetable of life and with her own body and pain and beauty and strength, that woman is seen as a threat to the "morale" of a breast surgeon's office!

Yet when Moshe Dayan, the Prime Minister of Israel, stands up in front of parliament or on TV with an eyepatch over his empty eye socket, nobody tells him to go get a glass eye, or that he is bad for the morale of the office. The world sees him as a warrior with an honorable wound, and a loss of a piece of himself which he has marked, and mourned, and moved beyond. And if you have trouble dealing with Moshe Dayan's empty eye socket, everyone recognizes that it is your problem to solve, not his.

Well, women with breast cancer are warriors also. I have been at war, and still am. So has every woman who has had one or both breasts amputated because of the cancer that is becoming the primary physical scourge of our time. For me, my scars are an honorable reminder that I may be a casualty in the cosmic war against radiation, animal fat, air pollution, McDonald's hamburgers, and Red Dye No. 2, but the fight is still going on, and I am still a part of it. I refuse to have my scars hidden or trivialized behind lambswool or silicone gel. I refuse to be reduced in my own eyes or in the eyes of others from warrior to mere victim, simply because it might render me a fraction more acceptable or less dangerous to the still complacent, those who believe if you cover up a problem it ceases to exist. I refuse to hide my body simply because it might make a woman-phobic world more comfortable.

As I sat in my doctor's office trying to order my perceptions of what had just occurred, I realized that the attitude toward prosthesis after breast cancer is an index of this society's attitudes toward women in general as decoration and externally defined sex object.

Two days later I wrote in my journal:

> I cannot wear a prosthesis right now because it feels like a lie more than merely a costume, and I have already placed this, my body under threat, seeking new ways of strength and trying to find the courage to tell the truth.

For me, the primary challenge at the core of mastectomy was the stark look at my own mortality, hinged upon the fear of a life-threatening cancer. This event called upon me to re-examine the quality and texture of my entire life, its priorities and commitments, as well as the possible alterations that might be required in the light of that re-examination. I had already faced my own death, whether or not I acknowledged it, and I needed now to develop that strength which survival had given me.

20

Accessing Power

by Angeles Arrien

Carl Jung, the psychologist who specialized in the identification of archetypes and how they apply to personal and collective experience, stated that "myth is more individual and expresses life more precisely than does science. Science works with concepts of averages which are far too general to do justice to the subjective variety of an individual life." Through the mythic theme and archetypal expression of the warrior (an old-fashioned term for leader or leadership), indigenous societies connect to the process of empowerment and to the human resource of power. Various words have been used synonymously in both ancient and modern times to describe the warrior's way of accessing power. Those who have explored this way have been referred to variously as leader, protector, adventurer, explorer, and sorcerer.

Universally there are three kinds of power. It is believed in shamanic societies that if a person has all three powers, he or she embodies "big medicine." These three powers are the Power of Presence, the Power of Communication, and the Power of Position.

Power of Presence. Every human being carries the quality of presence. Some individuals carry such presence that we identify them as charismatic or magnetic personalities. We are drawn to them, and they captivate our interest even before they speak or we know anything about them.

Power of Communication. It is the warrior's or leader's way to communicate effectively. Effective communication is accomplished when there is an alignment of content, right timing, and right placement. Communication that empowers and inspires us is communication that is delivered at the appropriate time, and in the right place for the person involved to hear it and receive it.

Power of Position. The warrior demonstrates the willingness to take a stand. It is the capacity to let others know "where I stand and where I don't stand, what I stand for, and how I stand up for myself." Many politicians have great presence and great communication, but lose power when they allow constituencies to wonder where they stand on specific issues.

Modern-day examples of individuals who carry all three powers and who access the mythical structure and archetype of the Way of the Warrior/Leader are Mother Teresa, Gandhi, and Martin Luther King, Jr. Each has been committed to aligning the power of presence, communication, and the willingness to take a stand in arenas that have heart and meaning for them. In shamanic societies, the warrior/leader archetypes practice the Four-Fold Way™, a pervasive belief that life will be very simple if we practice these basic principles:

1. Show up (or choose to be present).
2. Pay attention (to what has heart and judgment).
3. Tell the truth (without blame or judgment).
4. Be open to outcome (not attached to outcome).

It is the warrior's task to "show up," to become "visible," and through example and intention, to empower and inspire others by what they model.

Among many native cultures these four principles are used as a guideline for leading a life of quality and integrity. A true warrior/leader is identified as someone who knows how to extend honor and respect, set limits and boundaries, and align words with actions. Shamanic cultures have different apprenticeships and trainings for developing these leadership and empowerment skills. One such method involves extensive soul retrieval work. The oldest musical instrument used for soul retrieval work among native peoples is the rattle. The rattle is humankind's imitation of rain. It is a cleansing purification instrument used to remedy "soul loss." Modern-day terms for soul loss are depression, disheartenment, and dispiritedness. Shamans use the rattle for cleansing and purifying and then, through the rattle's sound, to call parts of the soul that have been lost in the past, or in a place, or in an old relationship. The rattle is used to bring lost parts of ourselves back so that we can bring our full power into any situation. To this day, the rattle remains the one object that family and friends universally give to all newborn infants. Perhaps human beings carry a subliminal recognition of the rattle as a primal source of comfort, revitalization, and power that is still present in contemporary times and that reminds us to reclaim and remember all the parts of who we are.

Most native peoples attribute the way of the warrior to the direction of the North, the home of Father Sky and of all the winged creatures. The belief is held that during challenging times, it is essential to face our challenges with the grace, power, and dignity of "the winged ones." It is important to remember that when challenges present themselves, it is the warrior's way to embrace them with full-bodied presence rather than to constrict in fear.

Cross-culturally, the posture of standing meditation (standing in one position with arms at sides and eyes open for at least fifteen minutes) is used in the martial arts, spiritual practices, and in the military as a way of reinforcing and coalescing the three universal powers and of connecting with the greater being of who they are. When an individual has difficulty saying "no" is when he or she loses power or may have the experience of being a martyr or victim. Individuals who have developed leadership skills or the inner warrior recognize that "no" is a complete sentence. The warrior's way is to be both firm and yielding, honoring one's own individual limits and boundaries as well as the limits and boundaries of others. In the classic oriental guide to leadership, influence, and excellence,

Lao Tzu reminds us that the warrior's way of using and understanding power and the dance of life includes the following knowledge:

> To know the absolute is to be tolerant.
> What is tolerant becomes impartial;
> What is impartial becomes powerful;
> What is powerful becomes natural;
> What is natural becomes Tao.
>
> —LAO TZU

The search for full functioning of the self promises to be the most fruitful endeavor a leader can undertake. To be full of power—"powerful"—is the natural, tolerant, respectful, and impartial stance of the warrior's way.

21

Becoming a Warrior Writer

by Connie Zweig

My pen poised on the empty page, my mind resting on the empty space, I breathe down in my belly, aware of the empty moment.

Suddenly in my mind's eye a woman stands in a white *gi*, her black hair pulled back tight, her feet planted apart, her breath slow and even, her knees relaxed, her arms outstretched, right hand above left, balanced on a wodden *bokken*, which rests in midair, poised in empty space just above her *hara*. The image vanishes.

I sit upright in my fighting posture, eager to take on the enemies of the mind, as they arise on the screen of awareness. "I'm bored; I'm boring. I don't know what to say next. This isn't going anywhere."

My pen is my *bokken*, sword of discrimination, ruthless as it follows certain lines of thought onto the page and ignores others into nonexistence. My pen gives life or death to words. My pen cuts through partial truths, slashes weak verbs and, sparring and paring, uncovers a rare, gemlike image. My pen knows the ancient practice of "Neti, neti," not this, not that.

As my mind's chatter settles ever more deeply, my pen can follow a thought like a bee tracking nectar. The words appearing on the page, raw and honest, are the honey I seek. Give me the words. The words are food. We are food. We are the words.

My first writing teacher demanded twelve hours a day. I stared at the phosphorescent screen until my eyes burned and teared, until my back went knotty and my mind went numb. She hacked at my sentences like a logger clear-cutting a forest, and I watched words fly like splinters through the air.

Then I reconstructed those sentences with even greater care, certain that this time they would endure. But she took her red sword and hacked away, removing the excess I had failed to see, whittling them down until, in a flash, one phrase shone through, bright and burning—and we had a lead, or a theme, or a closing phrase.

Weeks went by ... and months ... and years. I practiced the discipline of stilling my body and emptying my mind and moving my fingers as fast as the speed of light. I learned how to contain the build-up of charge in my body, holding it inside until it ran through my legs, rolled through my belly, and rushed through my arms into my fingertips. And I discovered when to dissipate it, to shake my arms loose or get up and wash dishes, so that the container was broken and a fresh line of thought could emerge.

As I sat, I recalled a story about the Tibetan monk Milarepa, who lived for decades as a recluse eating only nettle soup. One day his teacher appeared. He asked Milarepa to build him a stone house, "over there," on a certain spot on the mountaintop. Milarepa gathered stones from miles around. He labored carefully to place each one so that it fitted neatly into the next. When the house was built, the teacher came. Pointing his finger, he said, "Oh, no. I want it over there."

Milarepa took down the house stone by stone. He carried the pieces over to the spot where the teacher indicated. And he carefully rebuilt the house so that the pieces fitted together perfectly. The teacher came, and he said, pointing, "Oh, no. I want it over there."

Again, without hesitation, Milarepa took down the house stone by stone. He carried the pieces over to the new spot. He rebuilt the house with care. Again, the teacher appeared. And again he said, "Oh, no. I want it over there." And in that moment, so the story goes, Milarepa was enlightened.

I kept this tale in mind as I built short paragraphs into longer articles, which stretched into newsletters. On rare occasions, my words burned and shined. And I imagined my writing practice to be as vital as my sitting practice, and my teacher to be a word master, who would whack me on the shoulder with her stick whenever my mind wandered or my words grew flabby.

I learned to write—I'm still learning to write—and eventually the work of building sentences changed from task to craft. I learned to muck around in the dark cellars beneath a story, and to lay the foundations piece by piece. I slowed my mind to build walls carefully, stone by stone, like Jung at Bollingen crafting a tower of solitude. And every article became a hand-made artifact.

In those years I worked the form, while the content remained newsworthy, but remote. I told tales of synaptic lightning, chaotic attractors, OBE's, and the link between chocolate and love. I had never dreamed of becoming a writer, yet I was earning my living choosing words—or learning how to let them choose me. And people noticed. Writer #1, as I came to call her, achieved an unbidden success.

But about this time, a change occurred. In the heat of deadlines, I began to hear the murmurs of another voice, the call from a parallel person living inside me, next to me, beneath me. And she wanted out—she wanted to claim territory—*she* wanted to write.

My second writing teacher helped to midwife Writer #2. This word master wields no sword; she wields few words. She sits with others in a sacred circle, and together we bear witness to one another's talent.

For the most part, this new kind of writing goes unseen. I write it from one part of myself to another. I write it like a love letter that I hope to receive. I write it because I must.

Writer #2 works by hand, no high-tech mediator between my mind and my sword. With pen on paper, I feel an immediacy, no, an intimacy with the words, which are at once removed on the green screen. Writing by hand has returned me to a sense of craft. I often feel like a painter of words, or a sculptor carefully shaping squiggly lines that somehow, magically, mean something to someone else. For Writer #2, writing is an opening.

In this new form, my psychic energy or attention has moved downward, from my mind and the realm of ideas, into my body and the realm of story. How can I say that story lives in the body? It is my experience. How can I say that imagination lives in the cells? It is my cells that sing when I write a word of power.

Sometimes the words act like reluctant lovers, withholding pleasure, refusing climax. I call out to them: "Where are you, precious words? Please point the way from formlessness to form, from possibility to actuality."

But I have to face the ruthless truth: I cannot create the words. I listen and obey. The words create me.

When they do not come, I listen to the silence—or to the noise. I listen *through* the noise to detect a signal—a word that commands me. A word that reveals me. A word that begins me again.

The gifts of warrior writing practice have been many: Finally, I take my life seriously. Rather than view it as a fleeting illusion in which I might get stuck and therefore suffer greatly, I am diving in. I am placing my feet firmly on the ground. I am planting roots. I am vowing to be here now.

I take lessons from Tom Brown, known as the Tracker, who teaches us to read the signs of the wilderness, which are everywhere once our eyes are open to them. Each animal—rodents, owls, and mountain lions—leaves a tiny track that is as unique as a fingerprint. Studying it, one can learn the age, gender, direction of travel, even speed of travel of an animal. Every plant, mound of dirt, and angle of light communicates—they cannot *not* communicate.

I want to track my life like Tom Brown tracks the wild. I want to track my observations and hold them dearly to my chest until they form a pattern, until they tell a story, which becomes part of the Larger Story, which is Life.

I don't want to worry whether my observations are new or important. I don't want to stop myself from writing down an observation because it has been made before, or said more eloquently. I want to respect my observations as a way of self-respect, and work to find the words that they deserve.

On a recent starry night I was lying out on my deck overlooking the canyon when the full moon rose. As I turned my head slightly I noticed the moon's reflection in the large window of my house, just opposite the moon itself. In my mind I heard the line, "If I lived on a world with two moons . . ." and I was jolted. I knew a poem was speaking to me and that I would lose it if I did not get up to write it down.

But I was so at home in the moment under the starry sky that I did not want to budge. In the past, I would have stayed with the moment and my writer self would have lost the battle for attention. But I had promised it respect—so I got up, found a pen and paper, returned to the deck, and gave life to a poem.

To take one's observations and images seriously is to take one's life seriously. To write them down is to offer them respect. Like dreams which respond when recognized by offering more dreams, these hunches, seed-ideas, internal pictures, and novel metaphors will respond in kind when they are given life. They will give Life in return.

In this way I have found what so many before me have found: I contain my own best *prima materia*. We are worlds within worlds. All of them deserve tracking.

One final note: When you can't write, put down your sword. And dance.

PART III

MARTIAL ARTS

FIGHTING FOR LIFE ON AND OFF THE MAT

When you get extremely soft,
then you become extremely hard and strong.

—THE TAI CHI CLASSICS

There is no enemy . . . You are mistaken if you think that **budo** *means to have opponents and enemies and to be strong and defeat them. There are neither opponents nor enemies for the true* **budo**. *True* **budo** *is to be one with the universe; that is, to be united with the center of the universe.*

—MORIHEI UESHIBA OSENSEI

Introduction

The way of the warrior is the way of action in the world. And so the point must be emphasized: the practice of the martial arts is central to the way of the warrior. It may be true that the way of the warrior can be practiced in every sphere of life; or that the proliferation of easily available automatic weapons has reduced the idea of un-armed self-defense to a quaint anachronism. Nevertheless, the prac-tice of a physical martial art, in which two (or more) people practice against each other, is the primary discipline of any warrior. Without such a practice, the way of the warrior can all too easily become heady, mere metaphor, all attitude and no substance.

Certainly, all of life is the battleground. But it is in the martial arts practice hall that the warrior trains, hones, sweats, throws, and is thrown. It is in the actual, physical contact between two partners that the warrior tests his or her ability to respond accurately. It is in the relative safety of the practice hall (*dojo*, literally "place of en-lightenment," in Japanese) that the warrior-in-training can encoun-ter danger, feel fear, lose and regain balance.

In sparring with a partner, the warrior looks directly into a very accurate mirror—a mirror that kicks and hits back. So some martial artists may discover that they are lacking in aggressive power; they may find themselves unable to deliver a true strike. Others find themselves too aggressive and unyielding; they may be unable to relax, to roll, and retreat gracefully. Either way, as aikido master George Leonard says, "The hit is a gift." But so is learning how to fall properly. One of the most important lessons of the martial arts is, according to judo black belt Trevor Leggett, "Fall seven times, get up eight."

The discipline of the warrior is practiced by way of the body. But the body, as every martial artist soon discovers, is not separate from

119

the mind. In fact, all the martial arts teach the synchronization of mind and body—"like two wheels of one cart," according to Takuan, the Zen master who taught the great swordsmen of the Yagu school. This intrinsic unity of mind and body makes it possible for the martial arts to serve as a genuine spiritual discipline, as well as a means for self-defense. In China, the martial arts were closely connected with the worldly mysticism of Taoism. The Taoist view, a kind of provisional pacifism, is given in the Tao-Te-ching:

> Weapons are instruments of fear; they are not a wise man's tools.
> He uses them only when he has no choice.
> Peace and quiet are dear to his heart;
> And victory no cause for rejoicing.
> If you rejoice in victory, then you delight in killing;
> If you delight in killing, you cannot fulfill yourself.

For the Taoist, then, the use of weapons and violence was permitted only as a last resort. Bodhidharma, the Buddhist monk who brought Zen to China from India, is credited with a similar statement: "War and killing are wrong, but it is also wrong not to be prepared to defend oneself." Because Buddhist monks did not carry weapons, Bodhidharma advocated that monks learn how "to make every finger into a dagger, every fist like a mace, every arm like a spear, and every open hand a sword."

In Japan, samurai warriors applied Taoist and Zen principles to the martial arts. No doubt this helped them to become more effective warriors. But during the long period of isolation and peace brought on by the Tokugawa shoguns, the martial arts evolved into spiritual ways. As martial arts historian Donn Draeger succinctly put it, "The desire for self-protection gave way to one of self-perfection."

The greatest martial artists, however, are able to combine both self-defense and self-protection. As Tesshu, the great nineteenth-century swordmaster and tutor of the Meiji emperor, told an aspiring student: "The secret of our Way is complete fearlessness. But it has to be complete. There are some who are not afraid to face enemies with swords, but who cringe before the assaults of passions like greed and delusions like fame. The end of our Way of fencing is to have no fear at all when confronting the inner enemies as well as the outer enemies."

The martial arts continue to evolve. Aikido is perhaps the most spiritual and influential martial art in the world today. It teaches a loving—and effective—response to conflict, in which the welfare of one's opponent is always taken into account. Kisshomaru Ueshiba, the founder's son, explains further: "Aikido teaches the way to realize absolute victory based on the philosophy of noncontention. Noncontention means to deflate the aggressive, combative, destructive instincts within a person and to channel them into the power of creative love." Or as Morihei Ueshiba himself says, "Aikido is not a technique to fight with or defeat the enemy. It is a way to reconcile the world and make human beings one family."

We open this section with "Empty Hand, Empty Self," an historical overview by John White, a well-known consciousness researcher and student of shorin-ryu karate. Reminding us "that it is a sad fact of human life that good will can be resisted and innocence slaughtered," he suggests that the way "of martial artistry offers people of peace who are still 'of the world' an avenue for understanding more deeply the nature of human conflict and how to deal with it compassionately and wisely."

This is followed by the teachings of one of the most influential contemporary martial artists, T'ai chi master Cheng Man-Ch'ing. A true example of the Chinese warrior-sage, Professor Cheng was also an adept in medicine, calligraphy, painting, and poetry. In "Eliminating the Three Faults," he focuses on lack of perseverance, greediness, and haste.

"Aikido: The Art of Loving Combat" is a first-person account by George Leonard. Unlike most martial arts masters, Leonard started late. He was forty-eight when he took his first lesson in aikido from Robert Nadeau; fifty-two when he received his black belt. Leonard, who coined the term "human potential movement," found that aikido supplied "the kind of long-term, disciplined practice that was missing in the wild and euphoric early days of Esalen and that is still largely lacking in American culture."

In "Warrior Mind," writer Sallie Tisdale reminds us that knowing how to fight for your life is still the core of martial arts. Hers is a dramatic account of a very real self-defense course, complete with a relentless Attacker wearing a huge padded helmet and heavy padding: "The rules were simple: He could attack until the woman disabled him. We couldn't fail, but we couldn't quit."

Chapter 26 is an account by the editor of this volume of a contemporary war game played with paint-ball pellets, which may possibly develop into an indigenous American martial art. This section ends with a piece by Terry Dobson, a student of the founder of aikido and a pioneer in applying the principles of aikido to everyday life. It tells how an encounter with an angry drunk on a crowded train in Japan taught him true aikido.

22

Empty Hand, Empty Self

by John White

What is the source of hostility and aggression in human affairs? Must an attack be met with violence or can it be neutralized by nonviolence? Is there a gentle way to resolve conflict between people and nations?

These questions have concerned me for decades. As part of my continuing inquiry into the human condition, I recently attended a seminar on "Zen and the Martial Arts" at the Zen Mountain Monastery in Mount Tremper, New York. The weekend, which took its name from Joe Hyams's 1979 book, was spent exploring the "warrior spirit" through talks and demonstrations by martial artists, practice sessions, and meditation.

In his discourse the first night, the monastery's abbot, Sensei John Daido Loori, pointed out that there is "common ground" between Zen and the martial arts that is profoundly spiritual. He spoke about overcoming anger, developing single-pointedness of mind, breaking through fear, and realizing the self.

Although I'd read widely in Zen literature, visited zendos, and known Zen practitioners for over twenty years, this connection with the martial arts had somehow escaped my attention. Considering myself a man of peace, I had little interest in what appeared to be the epitome of violence: Bruce Lee and Chuck Norris bashing heads or elite military forces kicking ass. I'd been involved in consciousness research and sacred traditions for decades, yet I knew Bodhidharma only as the first patriarch who brought Zen from India to China in the sixth century, not as a member of the warrior caste who trained monks at the Shaolin Temple in combat skills to strengthen themselves for meditation and defend themselves from brigands. According to Jay Gluck's book *Zen Combat*, around 528 Bodhidharma emerged from solitary meditation in a cave and announced:

"War and killing are wrong, but so also is it wrong not to be prepared to defend oneself. We may not have knives, so make every finger like unto a dagger; our maces are confiscated, so make every fist like unto a mace. Without spears every arm must be like unto a spear and every open hand a sword."

Gluck comments that Bodhidharma's system required that the fighter first divorce himself from any emotion toward his opponent and the weapon, so that "right action" is performed with "right attitude." In other words, Bodhidharma would "arm the man of peace; pacify the man of arms." Most Asian forms of weaponless combat derive from this beginning.

Thus, the common ground that Sensei Daido talked about is both historical and psychological. I was delighted to learn this several years ago when I was discussing the philosophical dimension of fighting with a friend who studies a Korean martial art. He loaned me his copy of *Zen and the Martial Arts*. It blew me away: A wholly new dimension of the martial arts emerged and converged with my long-time interest in self-transcendence and global peace. Hyams's book crystallized things for me: There is a "warrior path to enlightenment," and it is not incompatible with a desire for a peaceful world. I began to read voraciously about the martial arts and to practice an Okinawan form of karate, *shorin-ryu*, the oldest style, from which all others are derived.

To put it in simplest terms, I'll quote a friend: "The martial arts don't train you to fight: they train you *not* to fight." The traditional name for a martial arts school or practice hall, *dojo*, means "place of enlightenment," or, more precisely, "a place (*jo*) to practice the Way (*do*) to enlightenment." Enlightenment, of course, is what Zen and other sacred traditions are about, and although most practitioners of the martial arts are not enlightened or, for that matter, even aware of the possibility of enlightenment, the highest wisdom of the martial arts declares that the ultimate enemy is one's own ego. As Eugen Herrigel writes in *Zen and the Art of Archery*, quoting his master: "This is what the art of archery means: a profound and far-reaching contest of the archer with himself." Karate master Richard Kim puts it similarly in his book *The Weaponless Warriors*: "He who conquers himself is the greatest warrior."

More than technical proficiency, the ideal of the martial arts is self-mastery or ego-transcendence. The peacefulness, loving compassion, and reverence for life that flow from that state are characteristic of great martial artists. They have a sense of harmony with the universe that allows them to go through life without the chronic anxiety the ego experiences in its apparent separateness from creation. This openness to infinity, this "empty self," means freedom from the ego's habitual mental guardedness and the belligerence, defensiveness, self-aggrandizement, and power-lust that arise from the illusion of a separate self.

Yamaoka Tesshu, a nineteenth-century Zen Buddhist who engaged in thousands of contests with the best swordsmen in Japan, never took another's life. According to his biographer, John Stevens, author of *The Sword of No-Sword: Life of the Master Warrior Tesshu*, Tesshu "never resorts to the ruthless cut-the-enemy-down-by-any-means tactics of Musashi, disarming his opponents instead with the power of 'no-sword' [*muto ryo*]." The "sword of no-sword," Tesshu wrote, is a state of awareness of "the heart of things where one can directly confront life and death." Students of Tesshu's system of swordsmanship were told, "The purpose of muto ryo swordsmanship is not to fight to defeat others in contests; training in my dojo is to foster enlightenment." Despite his sometimes fierce manner, Tesshu, who attained enlightenment at age forty-five, was noted for his generosity and kindness to people and animals.

Compare his story with that of Miyamoto Musashi, far better known than Tesshu and popularly regarded in Japan as the master swordsman of all time. Cunning and seemingly invincible, he killed more than sixty people before he was thirty. Yet for all his martial prowess, he was personally unhappy and spiritually confused. Hounded by enemies created through his arrogance, he knew no peace until the last few years of life, when he retired to a cave to contemplate the mystery of existence and write *A Book of Five Rings*. "In looking back over the events of my life," he said, "I can see now that I began to understand the way of the warrior when first I began to feel compassion."

Taisen Deshimaru, a Zen master who led a session on Zen and the martial arts at Zinal, Switzerland, in 1975, pointed out that Zen became known in medieval Japan as "the religion of the samurai" because, as author and aikido master George Leonard put it in his introduction to Deshimaru's *The Zen Way to the Martial Arts*, zazen training could "still the restless mind, perceive the ultimate harmony beneath seeming discord, and achieve the oneness of intuition and action so necessary for *kenjutsu* (swordfighting)." Summarizing Deshimaru's teaching about the stages common to Zen and the martial arts, Leonard comments, "Throughout this lifelong process [of training in the martial arts], there is an inexorable shift in emphasis . . . from technique and strength of body in the beginning to exquisite intuition and a realization of spirit in the end."

Leonard adds, "Master Morihei Ueshiba, the founder of modern aikido, realized the true potential of his art only after he turned seventy, when he could no longer count on the power of his body. Most of the films which show his seemingly miraculous feats were made in the 1960s, when he was between eighty and eighty-four years old." Ueshiba, John Stevens tells us in *Abundant Peace: The Biography of Morihei Ueshiba*, was "undoubtedly the greatest martial artist who ever lived," and aikido "a path of harmony and love, unifying body and mind, self and others, man and the universe." That unity was what C. W. Nicol's karate sensei was referring to when he told Nicol, who was practicing in a Tokyo dojo, "If you practice hard you will develop a mind that is as calm as still water. Karate is moving Zen, and it is the Zen state that you must strive for."

The Zen state is characterized by tranquillity and equanimity in all circumstances, even life-threatening ones such as mortal combat. As the Tibetan Buddhist adage has it, "Insightful wisdom requires skillful means to produce effective action."

But some may wonder about the sixth commandment: "Thou salt not kill." There is a simplistic notion that it means not to take human life at all, under any circumstances. But that is a misunderstanding. Rather, it means "Do not commit murder" and is translated that way in some versions of the Bible. Specifically, it means "Do not *unlawfully* take human life or shed *innocent* blood." The Old Testament does not prohibit murder, with lesser punishments for accidentally causing death, i.e., committing homicide. Taking a life in defense of the innocent is not a crime in the Old Testament view of human affairs.

Some may also wonder about the admonition of Jesus to "resist not evil." Or Mahatma Gandhi and Martin Luther King's advocacy of nonviolence. Were they all wimps?

I don't think so; their courage is admirable and beyond question. But it is a sad fact of human life that good will can be resisted and innocence slaughtered—witness the Holocaust, the 6,000 razed temples and monasteries of Tibet, the massacre at Tiananmen Square. Sometimes turning the other cheek will only get you slapped a second time—even fatally so. How can resistance to good will be overcome effectively so antagonisms are resolved instead of perpetuated?

There is no sure and simple way. Education to enlightenment is slow, difficult, and uncertain, often requiring tremendous sacrifices in the name of love. The way of Gandhi and King is for some; I have no argument with it. However, as author and philosopher Paul Brunton notes, the person who invokes the doctrine of pacifism for universal practice misconceives a mystical doctrine meant only for inward realization and misapplies an ethical rule meant only for monks and ascetics who have renounced the world. Pacifism, Brunton says, is admirable in a mystic but out of place in a person of the world. In fact, as he points out in *Essays on the Quest*, for people who have not retired from the world "there is a bounden duty to protect human life, because of its superior value, when it is endangered by wild beasts—even if we have to kill those beasts . . . Circumstances arise when it is right and proper to arm oneself in defense of one's country and slay aggressive invaders, or when it is ethically correct to destroy a murderous assailant." He immediately adds, however, that the infliction of unnecessary pain must always be avoided.

The way of martial artistry offers people of peace who are still "of the world" an avenue for understanding more deeply the nature of human conflict and how to deal with it compassionately and wisely. In the words of Okinawan karate master Morio Higaonna, "Karate is a pacifist philosophy."

How can that be? First of all, martial arts training builds self-confidence, and with that comes a lessening of the urge to fight. Few people enter the martial arts for spiritual reasons—most simply want to learn self-defense because they're afraid of being attacked. Like any other ego-driven human, the novice martial arts practitioner has a mental attitude of fear and a constant expectation of conflict. Martial arts training can instill a degree of assuredness in dealing with an attack that, in turn, leads to calmness and the capacity to seek nonviolent means to end a confrontation. The confident person projects a certain aura or bearing that subtly signals potential aggressors that they will not find him or her an easy mark, thus further deterring the possibility of attack.

The martial arts are a reasonable, conscious alternative to the fight-or-flight reflex. Studies done at Fordham University have documented that the practice of martial arts tends to reduce and curb violent tendencies. Psychiatrist Stuart Tremlow, who has a dojo in Topeka, Kansas, told me that "at a recent gathering of experienced black belts from many traditional styles, very few indicated they had been in any sort of fight since *shodan* [first-degree black belt rank]. The answer, I think, is in the altered state of consciousness the practice produces; it is peaceful and powerful, and once this balance of opposites is achieved, there is no enemy."

Second, martial arts training clarifies the nature of violence and aggression. It provides a structured and intense but safe and supportive context for self-examination. It shows that violence and aggression are mental in nature—a mentality present in everyone until faced, inspected, understood, and transcended. With that understanding, there is no enemy. Misguided opponents, yes—enemies, no. For with understanding comes the awakening of compassion. One realizes that "there but for the grace of God go I."

When Bodhidharma found the Shaolin temple in need of security and the monks in need of personal protection from harm and greater physical endurance for spiritual practice, he took direct action that was profound in its simplicity: He gave martial arts training for nonviolent self-defense. That is still "skillful means." So as our planet heads into a new age, I look for warrior-sages, for—pardon me—Rambodhisattvas to demonstrate a new level of attainment in the human potential for self-directed growth in body, mind, and spirit aimed at the liberation of all sentient beings.

I *gassho* to the wisdom of Bodhidharma.

23

Eliminating the Three Faults

by Master Cheng Man-Ch'ing

At the outset of self-study, one must first strive to eliminate three faults. In my forty years' experience, those who are able to eliminate these three faults and study faithfully are assured of enjoying the rewards they seek. As for people who are slightly less gifted, it simply means making a bit more of an effort. Everybody is aware of these faults and the remedy is simple and readily at hand. Most often it is a case of persisting in bad habits and an unwillingness to rectify them. In my youth, I too was guilty of this, and that is why I am able to speak with such authority. Let me elaborate.

The first fault is lack of perseverance. This is what Confucius was referring to when he said, "A man who lacks perseverance cannot be a witch doctor." The medical practice of shamans is not an orthodox art, but without perseverance even this is impossible. How much more so T'ai chi ch'uan which leads us from philosophy to science. T'ai chi ch'uan's principles of "using softness to overcome hardness" and "concentrating the *ch'i* and developing softness" are based on the philosophical concepts of the *I ching*, Yellow Emperor, and Lao Tzu. When it comes to actually putting into practice "using a pull of four ounces to deflect a thousand pounds," this is what would be called a "jack" in science, or what is commonly referred to as "uncheckable pressure" in mechanics. This then is the crystallization of philosophy and science. I firmly believe that it can serve as a bridge between Chinese and Western culture. However, are principles and applications the only benefit? If one approaches the study of this art without perseverance, not only is it a waste of time, but one emerges empty-handed from a mountain of treasures. Is this not a great pity?

I often regret my lack of perseverance as a young man. Because of my poor health, I took up martial arts many times, but as soon as I made a bit of progress, I would abandon them. Finally, thirty-nine years ago, I contracted a difficult case of tuberculosis. Once again I took up T'ai chi ch'uan and fully recovered. Thereupon I determined to never give up my practice again. At that time I took all the postures in the form, and using the quickest method of practice, did a whole round in six or seven minutes. Morning and evening I did just one form, seeking only to keep up my regimen without lapsing. Actually, at the time I was very busy with teaching and other school responsibilities and had no free time even for self-study. But from this period on, before long I had made progress. In the morning immediately after rising, I would not wash or eat without first doing a form; in the evening before sleeping, I would not go to bed without also doing a form. After a long time this became habitual and I never again quit. The idea is that the greatest joy in life lies in helping others, and we should not be afraid to make sacrifices. Now if I desire health but lack perseverance in spending just a few minutes morning and evening, then how dare I set myself up as an example to others? Therefore, I was ashamed of my foolishness and determined to correct this fault.

The second fault is greediness. Hence the saying "If one is greedy nothing can be thoroughly chewed" and Lao Tzu's "Have little and receive much; have much and be confused" are true indeed. When I was young I had an older friend, Lu Chien, styled Ch'eng-pei, who was a native of Yü-yao County, Chekiang. He had travelled to Yen-tang and before returning home stopped by and said, "In former times, when gentlemen were about to take their leave, they offered some parting words. I would like to leave you with this advice. The Cheng family excels in three fields. If you take these up faithfully, there is no doubt the line will continue. But if you are greedy and attempt to learn everything, I'm afraid you will amount to little. Listen to my advice and confine yourself to poetry, calligraphy, and painting." I did follow it. This old man was a very useful friend, and if I have accomplished anything, it is all due to him. I can never forget it.

The *I ching* says, "By making it easy, it is easily understood; by making it simple, it is simply followed." Practicing T'ai chi ch'uan is no different. If one is taught a posture or two today, quietly concentrate, then polish and memorize it. Only then can something be gained. Otherwise confusion is inevitable. In the spring of 1938, while I was head of the Hunan Martial Arts Academy, the whole province was caught up in the martial arts movement. Regardless of age or sex, everyone had an opportunity to study. I wanted to popularize T'ai chi ch'uan, and therefore every two months I personally taught some forty people, the heads and teachers of martial arts schools from every county in the province who were sent for training. Because of the limited time, I decided to make certain abbreviations in the form in order to simplify it. Originally T'ai chi ch'uan had only thirteen postures, but after long transmission, the number of postures increased. It required a great deal of time to practice and could not easily be popularized. For this reason I reduced the number to thirty-seven, or twenty-four more than the original thirteen. This is adapting to the times. However, do not take my "Simplified T'ai chi ch'uan" to be simple.

After victory in the War of Resistance Against Japan, I took this manuscript to Shanghai and discussed it with senior fellow student Ch'en Wei-ming, who praised it greatly and said he agreed with me completely. He immediately wrote a preface to express his admiration. Ch'en Wei-ming is a scholar and a gentleman and would never engage in insincere flattery. Nevertheless, there are some ignorant individuals who disagree with my action and do not realize the great pains I have taken to propagate what might otherwise have become a lost art. There is nothing more I can say to them.

The third fault is haste. The saying that haste makes waste is wise advice indeed. Try to remember that as water flows it naturally cuts a channel, and that things cannot be forced. The ancients often said of the arts that we must steep ourselves in rich beauty and thoroughly savor it. They also said that difficulties will eventually disappear like melting ice, and everything will make perfect sense. I believe that we must practice T'ai chi ch'uan with this attitude. Moreover, this art includes both principles and practice, with equal attention to mind and hand, and requires that we grasp the philosophical concepts as well as master the scientific applications. Then the profit will be infinite. In summary, if we can systematically eliminate these three faults, then we can make successful progress without any obstacles whatsoever.

24

Aikido: The Art of Loving Combat

by George Leonard

The hours between 6:00 and 8:00 P.M. hold a special enchantment for me, especially during that time of year when the days are short and the nights are long and cold. I'm a homebody at heart, and there's nothing nicer, after the day's efforts and alarms are past, than to build a fire, grab a Kirin beer from the refrigerator, and listen to a record or maybe play the piano.

So most nights at about 5:30, a choice has to be made: to go to aikido class or to stay home and (I always assure myself) go *tomorrow* night. The choice couldn't be clearer. Home offers warmth, comfort, and ease. The *dojo* (training hall) offers an ambient air temperature equivalent to that of a refrigerator set on low, a training mat so hard it rattles your bones if you don't land exactly right, lung-searing physical exertion, a guaranteed minimum of manageable pain, and the distinct if distant possibility of injury.

Nevertheless, more nights than not, I find myself putting on my training outfit and heading off toward the *dojo*. When I first arrive, it's always the same: just climbing the two flights of outside stairs makes me wonder how the hell I can expect to do the warm-up exercises, much less the strenuous throws and falls that will follow. I open the door, bow respectfully to the large photograph of aikido's founder, Morihei Ueshiba, on the front wall, and enter the *dojo*.

An hour or two later I walk out of the same door a different person. My whole body is tingling, suffused with energy; I feel I could easily run ten miles. I stand on the landing and breathe deeply. The sky glistens with numberless stars, each one of them now connected with me and my life and, strangely enough, with everyone else, as well. I am completely happy and comfortable, at home in the universe. What goes on during that interlude between entering and exiting the *dojo* that can change not only the way I feel but also the way I perceive the world?

Start with the externals. Aikido is a Japanese martial art descended from *kendo* (the way of the sword) and jujutsu (a form of unarmed combat that uses the attacker's force against him). It bears a surface resemblance to the more familiar arts, such as karate or judo. There are the quilted white practice uniforms, the colored belts, the resounding slaps of open palms on the mat, the Japanese terms (*"Shomen-uchi irimi nage!"*) that roll off the Western tongue with such esoteric yet innocent charm. But the differences—the characteristics that set aikido apart from the other martial arts—are crucial.

The *dojo* is a sixty-by-forty-foot loft with exposed rafters. On one wall is the oversize photograph of the founder; on another are two racks for wooden swords and staffs, and a large wood carving of the Japanese characters for the word *aikido*. Most of the floor space is taken by a dark-green training mat. On this particular night, some thirty students are seated along one edge of the mat in *seiza*, the Japanese formal sitting position: knees wide apart, feet beneath the buttocks. The *sensei* (teacher) for this class is a woman in her late thirties, wearing a white *gi* and black *hakama*, the traditional floor-length divided skirt of the medieval samurai. At five-five and 115 pounds, with slim wrists and ankles, she might seem delicate, even fragile, except for an unmistakable presence in the way she moves.

The teacher gestures to one of the students, who rises instantly and moves swiftly toward her. He is six feet tall, slim-hipped, with a muscular chest, shoulders, and arms. Like his teacher, he is wearing the *hakama*, which marks him as of *yudansha* (black belt) rank. The teacher points casually to her forehead, and in response, the attacker rushes in and delivers a powerful, open-hand chop, as if to split her head down the center.

But the teacher is not there to receive it. At the last possible instant, she has moved *toward* the attack and slightly to one side, at the same time turning her head and body *with* the blow so that it misses her by an inch or two. This graceful, wheeling motion is accompanied by a sweeping gesture of one hand, similar to that of a bullfighter who uses his cape to invite the charging beast to go past yet stay close.

And now, as the swirling motion continues, the teacher is facing the world from her attacker's viewpoint, reaching up rather tenderly around the side of his neck to draw him even closer. By these exquisitely timed moves, she has created a human vortex in which she occupies the precise center. For a moment, the two figures seem joined, turning like inspired dancers. But the attacker's momentum is taking him even faster around the outside of the circle as the teacher gradually slows her rotation, his head down to her shoulder with one hand and sliding her other hand and arm up the front of his chest and under his chin to tilt his head backward. Her motion is something like that of a wave cresting and breaking: her arm lifts the attacker up on his toes, then slices down across his neck as she steps behind him with a thrust of her hips. The attacker is momentarily suspended, straight out, in midair. Then he crashes to the mat with a loud slap.

Seen for the first time, most of this movement, which has taken approximately two seconds, would be only a confused blur. The attack is clear enough, as is the momentary merging of the two figures and the attacker's inexplicable fall. In this culture we have become accustomed to watching the projectilelike impact of forces: a pro-football cornerback flying in to flatten a running back, two stunt men slugging it out to a fantastical symphony of knuckle music. But in this case, the aikido teacher didn't seem to *do* much at all.

But now the attacker has risen from the mat and is rushing toward the teacher again. He strikes even harder, with an audible exhalation. Again there is that inexplicable, intimate joining of the two figures. The teacher is pivoting and slipping under the attacker's arm—somehow she has him by the wrist—then throwing him in the direction he's already going, causing him to make a graceful diagonal somersault. On the next attack she unbalances her attacker by taking one of his hands in both of hers and sweeping it in a large, vertical circle while applying an outward twist of the wrist. He flips in midair and comes down with such an impact that it might seem he is badly hurt; but at the end of the demonstration he is completely unruffled, smiling appreciatively at the teacher as the two of them bow to each other.

This bow is a signal for all the students to pair off, bow to one another, take to the mat, and start practicing what the teacher has demonstrated. The scene that follows looks like a grand melee: thirty people varying widely in age, sex, shape, size, and skill taking turns attacking each other, striking, whirling, throwing, falling. With all those flying bodies, it might seem a minor miracle that there are no collisions. Even stranger is the fact that most of the people on the mat are smiling and occasionally exchanging friendly remarks.

Aikido isn't for the person who is interested in getting a quick self-defense fix or acquiring an instrument for his anger and aggression. Though the students take turns playing the attacker's role, the art itself has no aggressive moves. It *uses* the attacker's energy and intention to confound him, and its ultimate aim is peace and harmony. Aikido is a lifelong journey with many sinuous twists and turns, many opportunities for patience and humility. Even world-class athletes must be willing to endure periods of clumsiness, and the words "mastering aikido" constitute a self-canceling phrase. Analyzing the physics of aikido in the July 1980 *Scientific American*, Jearl Walker concludes that "it is the most difficult of all the martial arts to learn. Its demands for skill, grace, and timing rival those of classical ballet."

All this being so, why should anyone dedicate himself to this art? It offers, first of all, superb, all-around physical conditioning, involving the elements of strength, flexibility, coordination, balance, relaxation, and concentration. (The wind training in aikido can be anaerobic or aerobic, depending upon the intensity and duration of practice sessions.) It contributes greatly to self-confidence. Just taking the falls demanded of the attacker's role—transforming the fear of falling into the joy of flying—makes you far more sure of yourself on life's sometimes uneven path. It provides the kind of regular, never-ending practice that is rare in our culture: something reliable to fall back on during nerve-racking times. And finally, after a few years' training, it becomes a powerful and highly effective form of unarmed self-defense, perhaps the very best, since it aims ultimately at the end of all conflict. Even a student with only a few weeks' training is likely to gain some protection from attack, not through physical technique but rather through a change of attitude toward conflict and through the development of a more self-confident stance.

But these are only the externals of aikido. Beneath surface appearances lies another realm, another set of possibilities—mysterious, beautiful, endlessly fascinating. From the beginning, the founder of modern aikido, Morihei Ueshiba, conceived of the art as primarily spiritual. The word itself translates literally as "harmony-spirit-way," or, more poetically, "the way of harmonizing with the spirit of the universe." Master Ueshiba saw his art as a way of unifying the individual's mind and body through the subtle workings of the spirit-power or creative life-force the Japanese call *ki*, and also of unifying individual *ki* with the *ki* of the universe. He sincerely believed that it is possible, through the diligent practice of aikido, to become one with the universe, and, in that state, to be unconquerable.

Perhaps even more than other martial arts, aikido takes inspiration from its founder. Ueshiba was born in 1883 and died at the age of eighty-six in 1969. Early in his life he became highly skilled in classical Japanese swordsmanship and jujutsu. In the 1920s he proclaimed his own independent form of the martial arts, which he gradually developed into modern aikido.

Master Ueshiba's life was filled with the kinds of episodes from which legends are made. Once, on an expedition to Inner Mongolia with members of a religious group, he was ambushed by Chinese soldiers. Facing a hail of bullets, he discovered, according to his own account, that by remaining absolutely calm and concentrating *ki* in his mind and body, he could see "pebbles of white light flashing just before the bullets. I avoided them by twisting and turning my body." On another occasion he was surrounded by men with knives. When they rushed at him, he seemingly disappeared, only to reappear on a flight of stairs some distance away.

A founder's miraculous feats are the bread and butter of the martial arts, and are to be taken with a seasoning of salt. But those of Ueshiba occurred in recent times, and many of them are unique in having been witnessed by reliable observers or recorded on film. Most of the films were shot when he was in his late seventies or eighties, and they are truly remarkable. They show an old man less than five feet tall with a wispy white beard dressed in a *gi* and *hakama* or wearing a long robe. In one film this diminutive figure is surrounded by five powerful young martial artists holding wooden staffs. As they rush in to strike him, he "disappears" and the attackers all collapse in a heap, revealing the master smiling benignly on the other side of them. In another, Ueshiba is seated in the Japanese formal sitting position. Three young men try to unseat him by pushing on the front of his head. He remains relaxed and unmovable, then gives a sort of shrug, causing the attackers to lose *their* balance and fall.

Ueshiba took obvious delight in these set-piece demonstrations. Most of the footage, however, simply shows him performing the standard techniques of aikido with incomparable grace and ease. Attacked by three muscular young black belts, he sends them flying again and again, like chips from a woodcutter's ax. It is not physical force this octogenarian is using. It is physics, yes, but it is also *ki*. Watching the films, a trained martial artist can't miss the master's uncanny ability to anticipate the intention and then control the mind of the attacker.

Aikido is directly descended from the samurai tradition, but it is also a reform of that tradition—from dominance to reconciliation, from war to peace. In his later years Master Ueshiba stopped using the terms *enemy* and *opponent*, realizing that ultimately the only opponent is within. Students were encouraged to protect their attackers. Aikido's spirit became, in the founder's words, "that of loving attack and that of peaceful reconciliation." Aikido's techniques became more and more refined, and at the same time more and more powerful. It was a paradox: a martial art based on love, dedicated to peace, to the unification of the world family.

In practice, the paradox is resolved. The new student learns that it is possible to do something roughly approximating aikido by using muscle power alone. But it doesn't look good, doesn't feel good, and is definitely not good aikido. The subtle and exquisite moves of this art generally involve *entering* and *blending*: that is, moving toward the attacker and turning in some manner so as to face the world, if only momentarily, from the attacker's viewpoint. This requires sincerely welcoming the attacker, truly understanding the attacker's intentions, and, strange as this may seem, actually *loving* the attacker. Out of such love flows enormous power, and aikidoists use this power to send their partners flying or to control them with wrist and arm locks. The throws and locks are also expressions of love, since the partners playing the role of attacker know how to take them joyfully, without injury—as can be seen by visiting any good aikido *dojo*. In any case, the attacker's downfall expresses a universal truth: He who initiates an attack is destined, someday and in some way, to take a fall.

As on the training mat, so in the world. In the unlikely event of a street attack, the dedicated aikidoist, having an almost unlimited repertoire of responses, would ideally use the one that would provide adequate self-protection while causing the least possible harm to the attacker. The *entering* and *blending* move is, in and of itself, so surprising and, at best, so loving that it creates a stunning change of context, a shift from the probability of harm to the probability of harmony. This is also true in the case of nonphysical attacks. Psychological aikido works as well as physical aikido, and those of us who teach that skill can imagine nothing better than a world in which political leaders realize it is possible to look at a situation from an adversary's viewpoint without giving up their own.

Fourteen years ago aikido came to me as a totally unexpected gift. When a friend asked me to join him in a class, I had to confess I knew nothing about the martial arts and had never heard of aikido. But I was soon captivated by the beauty and mystery of its physical movements, and the reach and depth of its philosophy. After five years of training I passed my black belt examination. A year later I was offered a chance to start an aikido school with two fellow aikidoists: Wendy Palmer, the radiant and gifted teacher described earlier in this article, and Richard Heckler, a psychologist, author, and former world-class college sprinter. Over a period of eight years, several hundred students have passed through our school. Fourteen of those who have persevered now hold the *yudansha* rank.

As for the three of us, we keep right on training, thinking of ourselves less as teachers than as students, lifelong learners of an art that can never be mastered. Each of us teaches twice a week and trains as a student two or three times more. And if, on certain cold winter nights, we walk a little slowly and reluctantly up the *dojo* stairs, we are still rewarded: even the most ordinary night of aikido is about as good as anything ever gets.

And then, once in a very long while, there are the moments of sheer magic that occur in all intensely played physical arts, perhaps more frequently in aikido than in some others. Such moments are likely to come when you least expect them: on a night when you're not feeling well, or maybe when you're near exhaustion from par-ticularly strenuous training. Nevertheless, there you are in the calm center of the storm, with three attackers doing their very best to grab you, strike you, wrestle you down, and you have nothing at all to do except stay in the center and let yourself move with the attackers' moves, seeing without looking, hearing without listen-ing, knowing without thinking. In the magical realm you have entered, there is no concern for personal safety and dominance, not even words for such things, not even words for your own name. And if there are words and thoughts, they are the ghosts of another world, another life. You are always *here*, it is always *now*, and there is only harmony, harmony.

Then it's over, and you come back slowly, breathing very hard, the lights seeming very bright. How long was it? Maybe twenty or thirty seconds. Not long, but long enough for a glimpse into how things might be, how, in essence, things perhaps *are*: an experience you can't keep but will always have.

25

Warrior Mind

by Sallie Tisdale

Twenty years ago, I didn't worry about my physical safety. I hitch-hiked, camped out, walked alone at night, with a young person's imprudence. This unconcern gave way inexorably, first to a grow-ing caution, and then to genuine anxiety and fear. In the last few years I felt myself to be in a strange state of paralysis. My fear of physical harm, of being a victim of violence, had come to affect my behavior many times a day, limiting where I went and at what times. I felt, like most women, resigned. I was always, however unconsciously, imagining and preparing for the assault any news-paper told me to expect. I resented this feeling, which seemed to have such gravity, pulling me down, forcing me to see the world through narrowed eyes, but I also felt helpless to change it.

In my ten years as a Soto Zen Buddhist, I've considered the distinctions between activity and quiet at length. I have never been in danger of escaping to my cushion, of hiding behind a passive Buddhist face. I have a noisy mind, a restless body; my flaws have always been active ones. I envied the placid tempers of some of my fellow trainees. The last thing I thought I wanted to do was learn self-defense—learn to fight. But I believe compassion can be asser-tive, even aggressive; I believe it must take that form sometimes. While my training may be focused on the transcending of duality, I get through the day by deciding how to act. Finally, I began to see not fighting, but fighting *back*. Did I deserve to be protected? I asked myself. The answer was clear: Yes. Was I willing to face this fear? Perhaps.

I could hardly imagine hitting someone, gouging and kicking and biting the way I knew I should if attacked. But I knew that it would do neither me nor my imagined attacker good for me to be hurt. Even if my motives weren't the most generous possible, I realized that being a victim was a karmic choice as much as being an attacker. This fear confused me long enough. I signed up for the most detailed self-defense course I could find.

The class, offered by a kung fu dojo, began on a summer night in 100-degree weather. Virtually all of the eleven women involved were strangers to each other. Janesa, founder of the dojo and our teacher, was a tall, short-haired woman in long, flowing pants and a T-shirt. She began, by way of introduction, with a discussion of our histories and our fears. The youngest woman, Amy, was a shy and petite fifteen-year-old. The oldest, Karrie, was a plump, curly-haired woman of fifty, with shiny eyes, who introduced herself as an "incest survivor." There were other women, like me, who had had close calls, near-misses, enough to make us afraid all the time. Several of the students had been raped, including Lauren, a short, stocky woman. Lauren told us in a whispery voice, "I've tried for years to be invisible and inconspicuous." Rebecca was a feminine, weary-looking woman in her mid-forties. "I've worked all my life to be a good girl," she said. "I've never been raped because I always went along with sex. I wouldn't make a scene by saying no." Diane, a handsome, middle-aged woman, haltingly asked for us to protect her privacy with care. Her ex-boyfriend, she explained, was in prison for assaulting her. He was due to be released and had vowed to kill her.

Listening to these stories affected me in several ways. They reminded me that there was nothing paranoid about my fears. But I also lay awake that night thinking about how much fear I felt in my training, too. Sitting meditation has often been a battleground for me; at times, silent and upright on a cushion, I've been paralyzed by a fear as primitive and organic as my fear of being attacked in a dark street. This fear, mixed up as it is with the more quotidian emotions like depression and pride, has time after time pushed me up off the cushion and out the zendo door. I lay in bed and imagined not going back to the dojo the next day, dropping out, inventing as many excuses not to continue there as I had over the years for not going back to the zendo. Morning came, and I went.

In the first two days Janesa taught us a variety of strikes, kicks, and escape maneuvers, which we practiced until we were all sore and weary. She made us use our voices constantly, all of us reaching down for the shouts and commands women are conditioned against, and then we practiced verbal confrontations—the real goal being, we all heartily agreed, to avoid ever fighting at all.

All the while Janesa prepared us for the Padded Attacker. I had chosen this course because of the Attacker, a man in heavy protective gear against whom I could finally fight. I needed to know I could really hit, how it felt, how fighting back might work. I privately dismissed Janesa's warnings, that his presence would disturb us. He was only a volunteer, one of her black belt students, a man from whom I had nothing to fear.

I have a short temper and a sharp tongue. My own anger is one reason I had resisted the "acting out" of fighting practice. It wasn't that fighting was so foreign to me, or so far from my life, but that it was so close and familiar that worried me, that confused my fear of being hurt with my fear of inflicting harm. The line between the two is the line on which Kanzeon stands. Kanzeon, Kannon, Kwan Yin, is one side of compassion; it is she most lay trainees study. I've always been drawn to a more obscure figure, a dharma protector named Acala, or Fudo Myoo, the Immovable. Fudo holds a sword and a rope, lives in Hell, bares his teeth and glares at his enemies like a pit bull. Fudo is a symbol of clarity in action, certainty, and the power of confidence. He reminds us not to misinterpret compassion as being always soft and nice in appearance. Fudo reminds us that compassion can be cruel, and that Protectors and bodhisattvas can come in many shapes and sizes.

When the Attacker finally entered the room, already sweating in the summer heat, he was not just a man at all. He seemed the stuff of nightmares. He wore a huge helmet covered with silver duct tape, mesh screening over his eyes, hockey padding under his shirt and overalls, and gloves. The thick padding made him walk in wide, slow strides. He entered the room silently, eerie and enlarged, and all our conversation came to a halt. Janesa had been right: he was all the masked, imperturbable, attackers I have feared.

I could feel myself shrink, cower inside. "Stand up!" Janesa barked at us. "Don't let him see you're afraid!" And I thanked her, silently, and stood up straight. Cowardice is a product of the ego. It is small mind. When I sing the litany of Kanzeon, I call her "The One Who Leaps Beyond All Fear." She knows the myriad dangers of the world, of life, she knows all that can and will befall us. The Hell Realm is here; Hell is the realm full of fear. And Fudo lives here—so I told myself. This man, this volunteer, was my bodhisattva that day. But all I could feel was afraid.

For several days we were attacked. It was that simple. Each day we practiced old strikes and learned new ones, practiced combinations of escape maneuvers and added more. Then we took turns being attacked. It was up to each of us to choose our own scenario, an old or an imagined event. While Janesa whispered the scene to the Padded Attacker, whose name we never learned and whose face we never saw, the woman waiting pulled on knee pads, elbow pads, hand and wrist guards, and tied back her hair. The rules were simple: He could attack until the woman disabled him. We couldn't fail, but we couldn't quit. The fight continued until Janesa's whistle blew, signaling success. The rest of us stood around the scene, yelling, sometimes crying, giving advice, cheering on the victim as, one by one, each victim became the victor.

We were attacked from the front, from behind, on the ground; we each fought from a fully pinned-down position at least once. Jennifer, a young, long-limbed woman with a high, thin voice, reenacted two different rapes several times. Lauren reenacted a date rape and a physical assault she had suffered on the street. Karrie relived the memory of her grandfather's molestation of her when she was very young. Young Amy, pummeled by the emotional power in the room, actually stopped in the middle of an attack, giving up, submitting; we, her audience, yelled at her until she started to fight back again. Rebecca wept throughout her attacks. Diane hyperventilated once, reliving the brutal wounds she'd received in the past. Several women bore minor injuries home like trophies. At one point I felt filled with love for these women, who seemed for those several days to be my closest friends. The heat, exhaustion, and emotion charged the room, and the attacks, with rest periods between, continued. And each of us escaped every time.

When it was my turn, I could only think: I don't want to do this. I don't have to do this. My mind and body rummaged for excuses. I'm too tired, I thought. My knee hurts. I already know how to do this; I don't need to prove anything.

My fear filled me as I stood, pretending strength, and the Attacker grabbed my wrist. "I'm going to kill you," he shouted, muffled through the helmet, and it didn't matter that I had told Janesa to have him say that. He was going to kill me. To live, I had to fight back, and to fight back, I had to move—and to move was to be willing to die. Zen was the religion of the samurai, a match that, until this course, I'd never fully understood. I had not been able to understand the warrior mind. Suzuki understood it implicitly: "Zen is a religion which teaches us not to look backward once the course is decided upon," he wrote. "The fighter is to be always single-minded with one object in view: to fight, looking neither backward nor sidewise."

What I have now are memories of confusion and bewilderment, strange fragments of time speeded up and slowed down, with the voices hollering, cheering women in the background. I felt fear, fear, fear when he pulled me down and then I felt an icy rage. I don't know how many times I have sat with fear overwhelming me, fear giving way to anger, anger giving way to grief, all the while trying to remind myself that none of these states is me. Fear and hate are qualities of my ego, but it is the nature of ego states to expand and fill the spaces of our mind and heart. The "me" that is terrorized lashes out in hurt, and hurts back; that small self which is so desperately afraid to die, which sees death and injury everywhere in this uncertain world, is capable of mindless rage. And it is literally mindless; rage severs our connection to the Big Mind. Confronting fear and the anger with which we try to smother fear means to confront the mean and petty parts of ourselves. It means to see the Attacker in ourselves.

I disabled the Padded Attacker five times in seven attacks; the other two times I "killed" him. I was afraid every time, very afraid, when the attacks began. But I learned, and the fear lessened. I learned how to move, I learned that I *could do it*, which was an enormous lesson, and finally, I began to look forward, in a strange way, to the next fight. The solid blows I landed were the blows of a survivor. One of the "kills" was an accident while I was rolling away from him—a double kick which "snapped" his neck. But the second time was not. Janesa had taught us how to do a foot stomp— to the instep, the throat, the nose. I had cringed at the idea of hurting another person in this way, which seemed gratuitous even in self-defense. An hour later, we were struggling on the floor; I rolled away, stood, swung around, kicked his head, and even as Janesa's whistle blew and I was victor, I raised my foot. I didn't think at all. Wham! As hard as I could, I stomped and smashed his throat. In that moment I touched another form of compassion; in that moment, I became the Attacker.

"Compassion contains fundamental fearlessness without hesitation," wrote Trungpa. If I had been truly fearless, I wouldn't have landed that final, unneeded blow. I killed him out of a fear that I didn't even consciously feel. There is something else, too. I thought that because the Attacker was just a man, I wouldn't fear him. But it's always been men I fear, after all. My fear has made men "other" than me, it has kept me separate from men. Fear diminishes me, makes me no bigger than that part of me which fears. Fearful, I am too small to contain Thought, too small to hold real compassion. Protecting myself, I will hurt others. That is the state I was in before I took this course—always anxious, always ready, unskilled, a loose cannon in every sense of the word. Learning to fight correctly has given me not only control but the security needed to fight only as much as necessary and no more. This is true warrior mind.

The Padded Attacker is a bodhisattva to me now. Not only the real human who willingly absorbed our fear and rage, but the attackers I've yet to meet. I feel a relationship to them now that is altogether different from the way I saw them before. They attack for reasons that are disconcertingly similar to my reasons for retreat; their hostility is a mirror of my fear. Learning to fight back physically has given me another view on my training. I am afraid of violence. But I am also afraid of training, of zazen, of the depths to which meditation can take me. I have to strike back at that attacker, too. I have to fight the ego which fears not only the physical death but the death within meditation, the death of the small self within the Great Mind.

We have just had *Segaki*. Standing in the zendo, singing the *dharanis* and opening the gates, I could see myself as one ripple in an unceasing stream. All my fears, fear of rape and pain and loss, fear of assaults and injuries, of death and the future, fell away, if only for a moment. Training is nothing more than the steps between these moments, and going on as though these moments don't matter. I can't always remember fearlessness itself, but I can remember its possibility. I can remember victory over fear.

26

War Games

by Rick Fields

I am crouched at the base of a pine in a wilderness area some- where between Denver and Aspen, holding a pistol with the safety off, hardly daring to breathe, as I watch the woman I live with crawl through sagebrush and cactus, her pistol glinting in the noonday sun.

A twig cracks loudly in the trees to my right. I turn toward the sound, heart pounding, adrenaline roaring. There are other people in these woods, stalking me just as I am stalking them, and the ever- present possibility of ambush—made even more possible by the Army camouflage fatigues and green-and-black face paint we all wear—hones my attention needle sharp. The sky is a dazzling blue, the pines deep green, and the sounds of chirping birds and buzzing insects are crisp and clear.

The sudden crack of a pistol going off on the hill above us makes my friend rise just enough to see what's going on—and just enough to give me a clear shot. I have never shot anyone before, and it feels more than a little strange. But I take careful aim, and slowly and deliberately pull the trigger.

The sound is very loud and very real, and I can see immediately that I have scored a direct hit. She swings around in surprise, as if she has just been bitten by a very large mosquito, and a bright, blood-red stain of paint spreads over her khaki shirt, just below her shoulder. "You're dead," I say, and she puts on a yellow nylon vest, and leaves the field. Twenty minutes later a whistle signals the end of the round, and we all gather back at the staging area. The air is full of war stories—of sneak attacks, tactical errors, defeats and victories, close escapes and near-misses. I tell my friend about my moment of hesitation before firing, and wonder out loud if I should have pulled the trigger. "Well," she says, looking me straight in the eye, "if you hadn't gotten me first, I sure would have gotten you. Anyway"— she laughs—"you should see yourself. You look terrible."

That, no doubt, is true. My face is splattered with red paint from a shot that got me while I thought I was hidden behind a tree (I was, my arm wasn't), and I am caked with dust, sweat, and pine needles. But I feel—for reasons I cannot quite fathom—more alive than I have in a long time.

It was a puzzling, even disturbing feeling. I had come of age during the Vietnam era, and like many of my friends had gone to a good deal of trouble to stay out of the war, and then to fight against it. And yet, here I was, wearing camouflage shirt and pants, with green and black warpaint smeared over my face, and shooting a gun—for an airgun *is* a gun—at another person, and enjoying it. Of course, it was not real, but it made me look closer at some of my most cherished and basic assumptions about myself. Perhaps I was not as "peaceful" as I had thought. If I could lose myself so thoroughly in a game, then what might happen in reality? I couldn't really say, but it was enough to know that a part of me that had been barely acknowledged had come into the open, like a bullet fired from a gun.

The game that I had been playing goes by many names—the War Game, the Survival Game, the Adventure Game, the Ultimate Game, Pursuit, Skirmish, Strategy, and—most innocently— Paintball. It is played with air guns powered by carbon dioxide which shoot paint pellets that explode on impact. The paint washes off. The game itself is based on that old Boy Scout and summer camp standby, Capture the Flag. If you are hit anywhere with a paintball, you're dead, and must leave the field until the next round. (A single round takes about an hour; most people play all day, with a break for lunch.) Points are scored for every kill, so if nobody captures the flag and returns it to their own territory, the game can still be won on points.

Being hit by a paintball can sting a little, and sometimes more than a little. It hurts just enough, in any case, so that players naturally do their best not to be hit. Sometimes there are bruises. Heavy plastic goggles must be worn at all times to protect the eyes. The Game, as I'll call it, is a realistic game, which is a large part of its appeal.

I opted for defense the first round. Hidden behind the crumbling wall of an adobe shack, I peered through a crack in the wall at the heavy undergrowth in front of me. As the whistle went off, I checked to make sure my pistol was ready and that my goggles were in place. "The aim of the game is to capture the other team's flag, kill as many of the enemy as possible, and stay alive yourself," one of the yellow-vested referees had briefed us. In the silence that followed the whistle, as my adrenaline rose and my mouth dried, I realized that it was only the last of these objectives—to stay alive— that really mattered.

But we were playing against a team that called itself the Wolf Pack. They wore a snarling wolf shoulder patch to identify themselves, and they all had Darth Vader face masks, special goggles with cheek and nose guards. Many of them had rifles, more accurate than the usual pistols, if not more powerful. The Wolf Pack played at Quest nearly every weekend, and they knew the field well. Like their totemic animal, they worked together in packs of four or five. If you saw one, others were sure to be nearby, probably surrounding you. So I was understandably on edge when one of my teammates from the real-estate team hissed and pointed in the general direction of a bamboo grove off to the left. Someone was moving in there, their camos blending with the shifting shadows and leaves and branches, very close to the ground.

I had the distinct impression I was all alone. The rest of my squad seemed to have disappeared. I heard the piercing pop of an airgun going off from the far end of the town. I couldn't see a thing, but I was sure the Wolf Pack was closing in.

A helicopter from the Malibu Sheriff's Department located just next to the Quest field flew overhead. Downdraft from the swirling blades swayed the bamboo. Suddenly I heard something, someone, moving in the dense brush to the right. My goggles were foggy from the sweat I had not noticed. I turned, took aim, and held my fire. A squirrel looked me right in the eye, chirped in alarm, and darted for cover.

American kids grow up on war movies in which the hero stays alive and saves the day by shooting faster and better than all the bad guys on the other side. The message of this movie burns, I believe, in the secret hearts of men who happily have never had the opportunity to check it out against reality, and so live with the notion that if push came to shove, they too would triumph like John Wayne or John Rambo, against all odds.

Those of us who never went to war also live with the notion put forth by Hemingway and more recently William Broyles (in a cover story for *Esquire* on "Why Men Love War") that while war is hell, it is also the most intense and exciting experience a man can have. According to this view, war puts you right out there on the edge of life and death—and gives an experience civilians can never know.

I would not argue with Broyles, not about the intensification of the senses, or the camaraderie of the battlefield, or the heightening of life. Certainly I felt very alive out there in the Game, which suddenly did not seem much like a game, with adrenaline coursing through my veins and my goggles fogging up, and my fingers itchy on the trigger. But I also felt, for a long, long moment, what it really meant to be out there, alone, facing an enemy hidden in the undergrowth, an enemy that had one thought in mind—to kill you before you killed him. It was not an experience, heightened senses or not, that I would care to pursue. Whatever lingering regrets I might have had after reading the Broyles piece, whatever romanticism about war, whatever thoughts that maybe I should have gone into the jungle in that war, were shattered by the realism of the Game that morning on the playing field of Malibu. The round ended before I fired a shot.

The next round I was happy to head out on an offensive squad. Our mission was to circle behind the enemy and then rush the flag at a certain signal. At the sound of the whistle I took off at top speed through the bamboo. Fifty yards from the palms that marked the enemy perimeter we fell to our bellies and started snaking in.

Suddenly, it seemed, I was surrounded. The Wolf Pack was in front and behind. I hid behind a tree that was cover from one side, but not from both. I got off a few good shots and then I got killed.

The Quest field has a raised platform for viewing the maneuvers. Those of us who had died in action stood there, watching the rest of the battle unfold, like watching a movie. There was a Blue defender, cautiously peering around a corner, while two attackers came up behind. He never knew what hit him.

While the battle raged below us, I talked with my fallen comrades, most of whom worked together in a real-estate office. Deena, the one woman on the team, had a ponytail tucked under her floppy jungle camo hat. I asked her why she thought more women didn't play the Game. "Because it hurts so much." She laughed. "But what really hurts is your legs after running around all day." Deena said that she had played Cowboys and Indians as a kid, as well as the variation in which kids threw clods of dirt—dirt bombs, they called them—at each other. "This is like that, but more than you could ever imagine as a kid," she said. "I play for the excitement."

Craig, who was standing next to Deena, said, "It's like you're a kid again. It gives me a feeling of going back twenty years. A lot of people forget how to play as they get older. Maybe that's why I feel peaceful after I play. It's like something you lost gets put back."

"When you're playing you get to show a different kind of aggressiveness than in everyday life," said Brian. "You get to go bonzo and dive and jump and nobody thinks you're crazy."

"It allows you to build your own confidence," said Deena. "Like when your partner is taken out. You have to depend on yourself to do your best."

"But it's always scary," said Brian, "which is part of what makes it so much fun. Defending the flag is scary. Maybe there's two of you surrounded. You hear, 'I'm hit, I'm hit.' That's a real terrifying feeling."

The whistle blew, and the round was over. The Wolf Pack had won again. I asked Brian if his enthusiasm for the Game ever made him think that he might like to try the real thing. "I wouldn't want to," he said without hesitation. "It makes you think how easy it would be to get killed. Bushes stop paint, but not an M-16."

The next day, sobered but intrigued, I played against a team called the Bushmasters on a field called Skirmish.

In the last game, as the sun was disappearing behind the Santa Monicas, we decided to throw out all strategy and go for a ka-mikaze frontal assault. At the sound of the whistle, we took off through the woods until we ran into the Bushmasters' defense. I ended up playing cat-and-mouse with a Bushmaster who was perfectly hidden behind a fallen log. Our First Lieutenant signaled that he was going to circle around, up the hill, and come in behind.

It seemed to take my partner forever to make the climb, but when he was finally in position, he shot and missed. But so did the Bushmaster. Now was my chance. I leaped and charged straight on. Then I was directly above him, yelling a wild war cry of delight. He looked at me as if I were mad, aimed, and pulled the trigger.

Miraculously, he missed—and just as miraculously, I missed too. I took off toward the stream, running with all the grace of a jackrab-bit. Back at the staging area, as we discussed the day's battles, my wild charge was the object of much headshaking merriment. "You should've gotten killed," was the consensus.

And no doubt that was so. But it was also a maneuver I remem-bered from long-ago twilight games of Cowboys and Indians, a maneuver I had always loved—the feeling of throwing yourself with abandon and against all odds into the air and the battle, heedless, with no turning back. You were in the hands of the gods, then, and I for one was thankful that the Game and my fellow players, my comrades in arms, had given me the chance to be reckless and foolish once more.

A few years ago, at a symposium on the apocalypse, the neo-Jungian psychologist James Hillman said it was now crucial for us to "deconstruct war" by moving "the martial away from direct violence toward indirect ritual. Unless we enter into the martial state of soul," said Hillman, "we cannot comprehend its pull . . . it was an ancient custom and still is a modern psychological technique to turn for aid to the very same principle that causes us affliction. The cure of the Mars, the god of war we fear, is the god himself."

Imagine, for a moment, a world in which the indirect "ritual" of war games—with paint balls or laser beam guns or flour pellets or bamboo swords, for that matter—were employed in place of the unspeakable weapons we pay our best scientists to produce. Such games, if they were developed by men and women dedicated to the search for a warless world, might serve us as a kind of laboratory or testing ground for our aggressive impulses—individual or collective, innate or learned—and finally help us unravel the deadly riddle of war. I don't think this is as unlikely as it may seem. I have already come across players of the game, martial artists influenced by the samurai code of bushido, who have devised a game in which blue paint pellets are designated "tranquilizers," which merely paralyze players for fifteen minutes, while deadly red paint pellets, which "kill," are allowed, but result in penalties for the players who use them. The possibilities are as endless as the human mind.

Nearly seventy-five years ago, on the eve of the carnage of the First World War, the great American psychologist and philosopher William James proposed, in a now-famous essay on "The Moral Equivalents of War," that the martial energies that went into war be channeled into constructive social directions—social service like the Peace Corps or Vista of more recent times. If our world lasts long enough, and if we take our spirit of play and imagination seriously enough, I'd like to think that the Game, in one form or another, may blossom into something the world could use—if not a moral then at least a playful alternative to war.

27

A Kind Word
Turneth Away Wrath

by Terry Dobson

A turning point in my life came one day on a train in the suburbs of Tokyo. It was the middle of a languid spring afternoon, and the car was comparatively empty—a few housewives out shopping with their kids in tow, some old folks, a couple of bartenders on their day off poring over the racing form. The rickety old car clacked monotonously over the rails as I gazed absently out at the drab houses and dusty hedgerows. At one sleepy little station, the doors opened and the drowsy afternoon was shattered by a man yelling at the top of his lungs. A string of loud, shocking, violent oaths filled the air. Just as the doors closed, the man, still yelling, stumbled into our car. He was a big man, a drunk and exceedingly dirty Japanese laborer. His clothes were stiff with dried vomit, his hair matted and crusted with filth. His eyes were a bloodshot, neon red, and his face was apoplectic with hatred and rage. Screaming unintelligibly, he swung at the first person he saw—a woman holding a baby. The blow glanced off her shoulder, but sent her spinning across the car into the laps of an elderly couple. It was a miracle that the baby was unharmed. The couple jumped up and scampered toward the other end of the car. The laborer aimed a kick at the retreating back of the aged grandmother. "You fucking old whore," he bellowed, "I'll kick your ass!" He missed, and the old lady scuttled safely beyond his reach. Beside himself with rage, the drunk grabbed the metal pole in the center of the car and tried to wrench it out of its stanchion. I could see one of his hands was cut and bleeding. The train rattled on, the passengers frozen with fear. I stood up.

I was still young, back then, and in pretty good shape. I stood six feet, weighed 225, and had been putting in a solid eight hours of aikido training every day for the past three years. I was totally absorbed in aikido. I couldn't practice enough. I particularly enjoyed the harder workouts, the ones with the badass college jocks where teeth pattered on the floor like hailstones. I thought I was tough. Trouble was, my skill was yet untried in actual combat. We were strictly enjoined from using aikido techniques in public, unless absolute necessity demanded the protection of other people. My teacher, the founder of aikido, taught us every morning that aikido was *non*-violent. "Aikido," he would say over and over, "is the art of reconciliation. To use it to enhance one's ego, to dominate other people, is to betray totally the purpose for which it is practiced. Our mission is to *resolve* conflict, not to generate it." I listened to his words, of course, and even went so far as to cross the street a few times to avoid groups of lounging street punks who might have provided a jolly brawl in which I might test my proficiency. In my daydreams, however, I longed for a legitimate situation where I could defend the innocent by wasting the guilty. Such a scene had now arisen. I was overjoyed. "My prayers have been answered," I thought to myself as I got to my feet. "This . . . this . . . slob is drunk and mean and violent. He's a threat to the public order, and he'll hurt somebody if I don't take him out. The need is real. My ethical light is green."

Seeing me stand up, the drunk shot me a look of bleary inspection. "Aha!" he roared. "A hairy foreign twerp needs a lesson in Japanese manners!" I held on to the commuter strap overhead, feigning nonchalance, seemingly off-balance. I gave him a slow, insolent look of contemptuous dismissal. It burned into his sodden brain like an ember in wet sand. I'd take this turkey apart. He was big and mean, but he was drunk. I was big, but I was trained and cold sober. "You want a lesson, *asshole?*" he bellowed. Saying nothing, I looked coolly back at him, then slowly pursed my lips and blew him a faggotty little kiss across the car. He gathered himself for his big rush at me. He'd never know what hit him.

A split second before he moved, somebody else shouted, "Hey!" It was loud, ear-splitting almost, but I remember it had a strangely joyous, lilting quality to it—as though you and a friend had been searching diligently for something, and he had suddenly stumbled upon it. I wheeled to my left, the drunk spun to his right. We both stared down at this little old man. He must have been well into his seventies, this tiny gentleman, immaculate in his *kimono* and *hakama*. He took no notice of me but beamed delightedly at the laborer, as though he had a most important, most welcome secret to share.

"C'mere," the old man said in an easy vernacular, beckoning to the drunk. "C'mere and talk with me." He waved his hand lightly, and the big man followed as if on a string. The drunk was confused but still belligerent. He planted his feet in front of the little old man, and towered threateningly over him. "What the fuck do *you* want, you old fart-sniffer?" he roared above the clacking wheels. The drunk now had his back to me. I watched his elbows, half-cocked as though ready to punch. If they moved so much as a millimeter, I'd drop him in his tracks. The old man continued to beam at the laborer. There was not a trace of fear or resentment about him. "What you been drinkin'?" he asked lightly, his eyes sparkling with interest.

"I been drinking *sake*, god damn your scummy old eyes," the laborer declared loudly, "and what business is it of yours?" "Oh, that's wonderful," the old man said with delight, "absolutely wonderful! You see, I just love *sake*. Every night me and my wife (she's seventy-six, you know) we warm up a little bottle of *sake* and we take it out into the garden and we sit on the old bench that my grandfather's student made for him. We watch the evening fade, and we look to see how our persimmon is doing. My great-grandfather planted that tree, you know, and we worry about whether it will recover from those ice storms we had last winter. Persimmons do not do well after ice storms, although I must say ours has done rather better than I expected, especially when you consider the poor quality of the soil. But, anyway, we take our little jug of *sake* and go out and enjoy the evening by our tree. Even when it *rains!*" He beamed up at the laborer, his eyes twinkling, happy to share the wonderful information.

As he struggled to follow the intricacies of the old man's conversation, the drunk's face began to soften. His fists slowly unclenched. "Yeah," he said when the old man finished, "I love *sake* too . . ." His voice trailed off.

"Yes," said the old man, smiling, "and I'm sure you have a wonderful wife."

"No," replied the laborer, shaking his head sadly. "I don't got no wife." He hung his head, and swayed silently with the motion of the train. And then, with surprising gentleness, the big man began to sob. "I don't got no *wife*," he moaned rhythmically, "I don't got no *home*, I don't got no *clothes*, I don't got no *tools*, I don't got no *money*, and now I don't got no place to sleep. I'm so *ashamed* of myself." Tears rolled down the big man's cheeks, a spasm of pure despair rippled through his body. Up above the baggage rack, a four-color ad trumpeted the virtues of suburban luxury living. The irony was almost too much to bear. And all of a sudden *I* felt ashamed. I felt more dirty in my clean clothes and my make-this-world-safe-for-democracy righteousness than that laborer would ever be.

"My, my," the old man clucked sympathetically, although his general delight appeared undiminished, "that is a very difficult predicament, indeed. Why don't you sit down here and tell me about it."

Just then, the train arrived at my stop. The platform was packed, and the crowd surged into the car as soon as the doors opened. Maneuvering my way out, I turned my head for one last look. The laborer sprawled like a sack on the seat, his head in the old man's lap. The old gentleman was looking down at him kindly, a beatific mixture of delight and compassion beaming from his eyes, one hand softly stroking the filthy, matted head.

As the train pulled away from the station, I sat on a bench and tried to relive the experience. I saw that what I had been prepared to accomplish with bone and muscle had been accomplished with a smile and a few kind words. I recognized that I *had* seen aikido used in action, and that the essence of it *was* reconciliation, as the founder had said. I felt dumb and brutal and gross. I knew I would have to practice with an entirely different spirit. And I knew it would be a long time before I could speak with knowledge about aikido or the resolution of conflict.

PART IV

THE OUTER WARRIOR

ACTIVISM IN THE REAL WORLD

the spear shine in the sun

that warrior spirit
is too valuable to waste
on wars —
let it be placed
in a better context,
for instance,
acting to save
our Mother Earth.
then the fire-
fangled feathers
really dangle,
the bow burn gold,
the spear shine
in the sun.

—Dennis Fitzinger

Introduction

"History," William James told the assembled students and faculty of Stanford University, on the afternoon of February 14, 1908, "is a bath of blood." War had become "absurd and impossible from its own monstrosity." James looked forward "to a future when acts of war shall be formally outlawed as between civilized people."

And yet, he said, "I do not believe that peace either ought to be or will be permanent on this globe, unless the states pacifically organized preserve some of the old elements of army discipline." These elements were the martial virtues, among which he included intrepidity, contempt of softness, physical fitness, devotion to service, and universal responsibility.

This could be done, James suggested, "by finding substitutes or moral equivalents to war." To be effective, of course, such equivalents would have to be able to redirect "the innate pugnacity and love of glory," which James believed modern man had inherited from his ancestors. James's solution was to imagine a kind of domestic peace corps which would provide young men with a chance to win glory and serve the community by testing themselves against nature, rather than against other men in warfare. They would be conscripted, for a specific period, "to coal and iron mines, to freight trains, to fishing fleets in December, to dishwashing, clothes washing, and window washing, to road building and tunnel making, to foundries and stoke holes, and to the frames of skyscrapers."

Judging from the carnage of the First World War, which followed James's address six years later, it is easy to consider the "Moral Equivalents of War" as simply another utopian fantasy. And yet it remains a kind of touchstone. By calling for a "moral equivalent to war," rather than calling merely for an end to war, James opened the way for a truly radical revisioning of the warrior freed from war and domination.

James was enough of a nineteenth-century man to suggest that we substitute the productive "war against nature" for the destructive war against humanity. We know better now. Nature today needs defenders, not conquerors. It is not enough simply to make use of the warrior spirit for our own individual survival, profit, pleasure—or our own "personal power" or "personal development."

The warrior spirit is a necessary and a welcome guide in our everyday lives. But it is especially suited to do battle against injustice and oppression in the world. The awakened warrior is drawn to live what Jungian analyst James Hillman calls "the martial peace of activism."

"The war is for human survival and the survival of the biosphere," George Leonard says. "The fight is against unbridled growth, selfishness and materialism, and glorification of aggression. It's an enemy so much bigger than any we've had. But that's the battle—for the survival of life against itself, a change from aggression to gentleness. Then we can live as if each day were our last, not out of morbidity, but to come awake to its utter preciousness, like the samurai whose emblem is the brief beauty of the falling cherry blossom."

The activism of the awakened warrior may take many forms. In this section we look at a number of current battlegrounds. Chapter 28, Sam Keen's "The Virtue of Moral Outrage," focuses on the warrior as citizen. This is followed by Tibetan meditation teacher Chagdud Tulku Rinpoche's thoughts on the role of the bodhisattva in times of conflict and war.

Next we examine the awakened warrior as anti-war warrior. In "Transforming Warriors," Arthur Egendorff, a therapist and Vietnam vet, calls for the recognition that we cannot win our struggle against war "without drawing on the energy that has fueled the greatest human projects—the warrior spirit, properly healed and called to a new mission." This is followed by "They All Died in the War," by Bill Kauth, a founder of the New Warrior Training. Kauth uncovers hidden connections among the missing father, World

War II, and the confusion that results from "dishonoring the arche-typal warrior."

Glenn Gray's *The Warriors* is widely considered one of the most accurate and sensitive studies of men at war ever published. This excerpt, "The Awakened Soldier," explores what happens when soldiers wake up to the horrors of war. In "Combat and Consciousness," Richard Strozzi Heckler contemplates teaching aikido and meditation, along with other "human potential" disciplines, to a group of Green Berets. Heckler is the editor of the seminal book *Aikido and the New Warrior*, and author of *In Search of the Warrior Spirit*.

This is followed by an excerpt from peace activist and conflict specialist Danaan Parry's exploration of the truism that "power corrupts; absolute power corrupts absolutely." Not necessarily, says Parry. "Power, in itself, is neither good nor bad. Power is simply energy manifested in time." When power comes from within, as it did with figures such as Gandhi and Martin Luther King, Jr., it is one with love.

In "Freeing the Imprisoned Warrior," Harris Breiman reports on his efforts to deal with a very different sort of war—the war against poor people and minorities which has filled America's jails. Breiman is part of a movement to bring the insights of the men's movement out of the conference halls of the white middle class and into the prisons. "The Lone Buddhist Ranger" is a first-person account from the inside by Jarvis Masters, a truly gentle warrior with great courage.

Next we turn to the earth herself. Most of us feel a great deal about the war being waged against the earth. But the eco-warrior goes one step further and takes action. This section includes two pieces. Earth First! founder Dave Foreman identifies Earth First! as a true warrior society. In "Becoming an Eco-Warrior," activist Bill Devall considers the kind of training which might produce the awakened eco-warriors we need if our planet is to survive.

In "The Warrior Monk's Vision," James Channon, founder of the First Earth Battalion, imagines an army made up of awakened warriors. And in "Army Green," Stewart Brand, founder of the *Whole Earth Catalog*, puts forth a modest proposal for making good use of an army without a war.

Brand's essay is followed by a selection by the great nonviolent warrior and fighter for social change Martin Luther King, Jr.; and an updated version of a much-reprinted article, "A Better Game Than War," by peace activist Robert Fuller.

28

The Virtue of Moral Outrage

by Sam Keen

In 1974, when I first phoned Ernest Becker to see if he would be willing to do a conversation with me for *Psychology Today*, his wife, Marie, told me he had just been taken to the hospital and was in the terminal stage of cancer. The next day she called back to say that Ernest would like to do the conversation if I could get there while he still had strength and clarity. I dropped everything and went immediately to Vancouver. When I walked into the hospital room, his first words to me were, "You are catching me in extremis. This is a test of everything I've written about death. And I've got a chance to show how one dies. The attitude one takes. Whether one does it in a dignified, manly way; what kind of thoughts one surrounds it with; how one accepts his death."

In the hours we talked, I learned things I will never forget about the intellectual courage required to think clearly about the nature of evil, and the moral courage needed to confront death in a heroic manner.

During the political high jinks and revolutionary sentiment of the late 1960s, Ernest Becker was *the* professor at Berkeley to a generation of students who listened only to men whose ideas were infused with passion and animated by moral outrage. In *The Denial of Death,*

Becker took any reader who could bear the anxiety on a shamanic journey beneath the facade of personality where he revealed the defense mechanisms we "normally" use to construct our "character armor" in an effort to deny the terrifying awareness of our animality, the unpredictability of life, and the inevitability of our death. In *Escape from Evil*, published posthumously, he went further and showed that humanly caused evil results from our attempt to deny our creatureliness and overcome our insignificance. He unmasked the glorious claims of nations and the warfare state—the promise to provide us with meaning for our lives by giving us enemies whom we can destroy and thereby prove to ourselves that we are the chosen people of God—and showed them to be a demonic form of heroism. "The horror we regularly visit upon each other comes not from any innate sadism or desire to act cruelly toward others but from our desire to belong to an in-group ... And to achieve this intimate identification it was necessary to strike at strangers, pull the group together by focusing it on an outside target. ... It is not our aggressive drives that have taken the greatest toll in history, but rather unselfish devotion, hyperdependency combined with suggestibility."

By identifying the false heroism of political claims of absolute righteousness—any crime is justified so long as it is for the fatherland, the motherland, the revolution, democracy, the people of God—Becker raised the question of authentic heroism. "The most exalted type of heroism involves feelings that one has lived to some purpose that transcends one." Both his writing and his life force us to ask how we can achieve a sense that we are used for divine purposes, without falling into dangerous forms of self-righteousness.

In my pantheon of heroes the best of men are, like Ernest Becker, spiritual Warriors who are alive with moral outrage and who enter the arena to wrestle with the mystery of evil in one of its many disguises. Fierce men, rich in considered judgment, who still have thunder and lightning in them; not dispassionate spectators, or cynics. Any day of the week give me the "hot" Bill Moyers, who takes risks, calls presidents liars, and gives vent to prophetic anger at secret wars and hidden government, rather than the "cool"

McNeil/Lehrer, who nicely report the news and lead discussions on every perspective that is fashionable within the Beltway.

One of the most troubling symptoms of our time is the absence of moral outrage in the American public. The ongoing revelations that the CIA conducted covert wars, arranged assassinations, trained many of the Salvadoran military responsible for death squads, was implicated in the deaths of thousands of Indonesians, and gave the South African government information that led to the arrest of Nelson Mandela, continue to be greeted with a yawn. It is as if some invisible solvent has been leeching away our capacity for indignation. When I was first in the U.S.S.R. in the pre-*glasnost* era, I had a sense that free speech was forbidden. On returning to the U.S., I was struck with how our newspapers could print any story of corruption in high places but very little action resulted.

The hero's path in the world is bound to be filled with conflict. A man who has not been morally anesthetized cannot have his eyes opened to unnecessary suffering, disease, and injustice without feeling outrage and hearing the call to arms. From deep in the gut a sense of desecration forms itself into a judgment and grows into an impulse to act. "Goddamn it, it is wrong for governments to spend billions on weapons while children starve! Goddamn it, it is wrong for us to pursue 'progress' at the cost of destroying ten thousand species a year, the wetlands, the forests and the watersheds! Goddamn it, it is wrong for a hundred million people to be homeless, living on sidewalks, in garbage dumps and alleys!"

The sense of vocation that is central to a heroic male identity arises when we are outraged about some specific instance of evil and become warriors in defense of the sacred. If our minds are heartful, we must be outraged by the cruelty in the world, and realize that it is our vocation to become protectors of the powerless and healers of the broken.

To live in this wonderful-terrible moment of history and keep compassion and virility alive, a man must gird up his loins and decide where to enter the struggle against surplus suffering, injustice, poverty, pollution, and the rising tide of population. Suffering is a part of the human condition. In the best of all possible worlds, there would still be disease, accident, tragedy, disappointment, loneliness, death. And we require all the spiritual wisdom we can accumulate to accept injuries and losses that we are powerless to change. But above and beyond the essential suffering is the surplus suffering that results from psychological, economic, and political structures that we do have the power to change. The "just war" of the spirit is against the sources of surplus suffering, against the impulses of greed and insensitivity within the self, against those ideologies, institutions, corporations, bureaucracies, and governments that most clearly are responsible for the desecration of the earth. In this effort, the new hero must reclaim and redirect the energies and virtues of the warrior psyche—fierceness, fortitude, daring, courage, cunning, the strategic use of power—that were once used in the defense of tribe and nation.

In the struggle to preserve a sense of the sacredness of life, as in all "holy wars," identifying the enemy is a morally hazardous activity. Self-righteousness easily creeps into our judgments. It is easy to condemn the owners of coffee plantations who exploit the Indians while we are enjoying our café au lait, or rant and rail against pollution as we continue to drive to the corner store. To guard against self-righteousness, the spiritual warrior must practice the discipline of perpetual repentance. I must constantly remind myself that I am a part of the problem I am trying to solve, I am also the enemy against whom I must fight, I incarnate the evil I am called to do battle against. The demons of greed, cruelty, and fear must be fought within and without. The heart that has become hardened and careless is both individual and corporate, both mine and my enemy's. The prophetic outrage that sets the spiritual warrior in conflict with institutional incarnations of evil also sets him in conflict with his own greed and insensitivity. A man who does not know how to wage a just battle, first with himself and then with others, has no values worth defending, no ideals worth aspiring to, no awareness of the disease of which he might be healed. And no mensch worships the status quo.

When we become spiritual warriors, it must be with the knowledge that the battle is never to be won either intellectually or politically. The existentialist philosopher Karl Jaspers once said that "evil is the rock on which every system shipwrecks." There is no answer, no theodicy, no way of understanding that eliminates the insult evil poses to the human spirit. We are not in a world that satisfies our demand for moral explanations. The best approach I know is the one suggested by Albert Camus in *Resistance, Rebellion and Death:* "We are faced with evil. And, as for me, I feel rather as Augustine did before becoming a Christian when he said: 'I tried to find the source of evil and I got nowhere.' But it is also true that I, and a few others, know what must be done, if not to reduce evil, at least not to add to it. Perhaps we cannot prevent this world from being a world in which children are tortured. But we can reduce the number of tortured children."

29

Bodhisattva Warriors

by Chagdud Tulku Rinpoche

Many great Buddhist masters have prophesied that centuries from now, when the forces of aggression amass on earth and no reason can turn them back, the kingdom of Shambhala will open its gates and its enlightened warriors will come forth into battle. Whoever they encounter will be given a choice—turn away from nonvirtue to virtue or, by direct, wrathful intervention, be liberated into a pure land beyond suffering.

A Buddhist story tells of a ferry captain whose boat was carrying 500 bodhisattvas in the guise of merchants. A robber on board planned to kill everyone and pirate the ship's cargo.

The captain, a bodhisattva himself, saw the man's murderous intention and realized this crime would result in eons of torment for the murderer. In his compassion, the captain was willing to take hellish torment upon himself by killing the man to prevent karmic suffering that would be infinitely greater than the suffering of the murdered victims. The captain's compassion was impartial; his motivation was utterly selfless.

Now, as I write this, the Middle East is inflamed with war. Watching the television news, I pray that this war will prevent greater wars, greater suffering, and that those opposed to war develop the skills to bring about authentic peace.

We cannot fully discern the motivation of any participants involved in the conflict, but it is unlikely that many have the ability to bring about ultimate liberation for friends and enemies alike, or that they will be able to sustain the bodhisattva's impartial compassion as they engage in conflict.

What we can know is our own minds. We can adhere to Buddhist ideals in our activities, whether we are combatants, protesters, decision-makers or concerned witnesses. We can pray that whatever virtue there is in the situation prevails, that genuine peace be established. The Buddha has taught that throughout countless lifetimes all beings have been our parents and have shown us great kindness. Now they have fallen under the sway of the mind's poisons of desire, anger, ignorance, and they suffer terribly. Could we exclude any from our compassion any more than the sun could exclude any from the warmth and radiance of its rays?

As we aspire to peace, now and in the future cycles of our existence, we cannot deny the possibility that each of us may be confronted with the need for wrathful intervention in order to prevent greater harm. May the spiritual training we undertake now allow us to enter such situations free from the delusions of the mind's poisons. May we act with spontaneous compassion to bring ultimate liberation to all alike, both victims and aggressors.

30

Transforming Warriors

by Arthur Egendorff

Transforming warriorship becomes possible by distinguishing clearly between warriorship and warfare. In the years after Vietnam, people began to say, "We've got to separate the warriors from the war," meaning, "Don't blame Vietnam vets for what happened in Vietnam." Although the slogan was useful in campaigning for veteran benefits, it doesn't reach far enough to bring about a thorough healing. Only when we recognize that warriorship and warfare have nothing necessarily in common can we call the warrior to action without first making enemies or fueling hostility.

Reviving the warrior spirit in this higher sense is what many troubled veterans need. They will come fully to life only when properly challenged, when moved by an inspiring vision. This is also true of professional warriors in our military. Many are resigned to the prospect of future wars, but virtually all regret their predictions. "At best a necessary evil," is what the most dedicated military planners say about the human ritual that has been the most heroic calling since the dawn of history. When war is debased, the warrior spirit can be uplifted only by a new cause to serve beyond war.

The same principle applies to whole nations and to the world. Communities that suffer an absence of spirit will be roused not by condemning, repressing, or banishing the most exuberant human energies, but by directing those energies to a dignifying and ennobling purpose. Thus the treatment of veterans, the recovery of national spirit, and the historic challenge of creating a global culture demand a common vision: the possibility of transforming warriors, of turning our appetite for power to the creation of empowerment.

In the last decades of the twentieth century, people all over the world aspire to freedom and self-expression as never before. For the first time in history we have truly global markets, instant communications, and international organizations in business, science, and the arts, and even a fledgling parliament in the United Nations. However, the history now taught in our schools only rehearses various forms of provincialism. World history has yet to be written, world culture has yet to be created, and never have human beings posed such a threat to our natural environment and to one another.

The question is, What can we envisage to make healing from war a plausible prospect? What can convert the task from a do-gooder's hope to an objective for which most dedicated, undaunted people on earth would give their lives?

What we need is an alternative service, one that frees warriorship from its enslavement to the cult of domination. We must give the warrior spirit within and among us a new cause, to achieve victory for life on earth by cultivating the power of empowerment.

One of the visionaries who has issued this call is Robert de Ropp, a biologist and author of several books on the development of consciousness. De Ropp makes the connection between spiritual power and warrior virtues with this prescription:

> We develop [this alternative] power through . . . the sacrifice of our favorite daydreams, our pet negative emotions, our habit of doing the easy rather than the difficult, our vanity and self-importance. This struggle is "the moral equivalent of war"—the Warrior's Way. We become, through this struggle, the creators of ourselves. We become food for a higher level of the cosmic process, "food for archangels." We enter the way of return, which is an uphill path and leads to that level that is rightly ours, [when we do not] waste our energies on inessentials. The kingdom of heaven is indeed within us, but we cannot reach that kingdom if we insist on living in squalid little hells of our own creating.

De Ropp states openly what William James only hinted—that warriors have a crucial role to play in the struggle to outgrow war. We cannot hope to accomplish this without drawing on the energy that has fueled the greatest human projects—the warrior spirit, properly healed and called to a new mission.

31

They All Died in the War

by Bill Kauth

The mystery: As a man devoted to doing men's work, I'm constantly invited to explore the question, "Where did our fathers go?" I know well that current wisdom says our dads lost their sense of manhood in meaningless work that resulted from the industrial revolution. But I sensed there was more. Within one generation something dramatic happened. They were gone! Where did they go? The more I learn about the archetypal warrior, the more I think our fathers all died in World War II.

Personal history of the mystery: On the Fourth of July 1988, I was alone watching a TV movie on the building of the Vietnam war memorial. The show, called *To Heal a Nation*, was a re-creation of Vietnam veteran Jan Scruggs's personal and political struggle to get the memorial built. A way into the story I began feeling, in my breathing, an impending sadness, which soon became tears and sobbing. I was confused by my unexpected deep emotional response.

The next day I told my friend, Doug, about my emotional experience, and he told me that both he and his wife had also cried as they watched the same program. He speculated that it was a natural grief reaction, as he had known men who had been killed in Vietnam. It almost made sense, except that I had only one distant acquaintance in college who had died in Vietnam. My response had been way too strong.

It plugged me into remembering a similar response three years before, while reading *National Geographic*'s account of the building of the Vietnam memorial wall. It was a very technical account of the political and aesthetic conflicts surrounding the building of the memorial, yet I cried through damn near the whole dry article.

As a psychotherapist, I've trained myself in emotional awareness. These emotional responses perplexed me. My reactions were not logical. Yet they were very viscerally real. My body knew something I didn't. It was a mystery and I wanted an answer.

Nearly everyone I talked to within my age range (thirty-five to fifty) who had read the same article or had been to the wall felt the same emotional response whether they were veterans, draft dodgers, men, or women. There was some *emotional commonality* here. And while many people had some specific rationale for their responses, none fit generally. I tucked it away as one of those mysteries that would come to light someday.

The theory: A year later this mystery, which I had carried for over three years, popped open. I knew from reading, and from seventeen years of men's work, that manhood as it once had been known had been fading since the industrial age replaced the agrarian age. As our great-great-grandfathers moved from the farms to the cities into essentially meaningless work, they lost that strong male identity a man finds in his work. A man often identifies with what he does or builds out in the world, external to himself. It was this focus he passed on to his sons. Men's ability to pass on a meaningful sense of manhood has been waning for over 200 years.

Then something big and fast happened with World War II. It seemed to strip away what was left of our fathers' ability to pass on to us whatever sense of manhood remained. I knew this from years of observing and talking to many men as well as from reading accounts of men's pain, anger, and confusion around their sense of manhood.

One sunny morning while discussing shame with my friend

Tony, the pieces of the puzzle jumped into place. I imagined the correlation between my own inexplicable grief feelings about Vietnam, the mystery of our lost WWII dads, the women's movement, and the insane fact that we humans have at least enough bombs to destroy all life on the planet twenty times over and that we keep building more of them every damn day.

The answer seems to be *shame from dishonoring the archetype*. I think it is important at this point to define "shame" and consider male "archetypes" with a focus on the warrior.

Shame: I've seen shame defined as the painful belief in one's basic defectiveness as a human being. I learned about shame and how it is different from guilt from a 1986 article by Francis Baumli in *Transitions* (a men's rights newsletter). He said, "Shame is often referred to as a void. A person who is ashamed feels empty inside, without ballast, lacking a sense of self-centeredness or emotional certainty. Shame is something quite indeterminate and unspecifiable. Shame is felt in terms of what one is as opposed to what one does, which is guilt."

Shame is difficult to grapple with because it has no specific form. Attempts at dealing with it tend to leave one feeling helpless. So shame is much more likely than guilt to persist as a toxic, crippling feeling compensated for by an anger which, if turned inward, becomes self-destructive. And shame is *always secret*. Nobody talks about it.

The "warrior" archetype: I believe the male archetypes exist as part of the male psyche. According to C. G. Jung, archetypes are "the hidden foundations of the conscious mind . . . the two-million-year-old man that is in all of us . . . an inherited mode of functioning." The archetype has existed 100 or 1,000 times before, so the imprint is left in our minds.

Thanks to Robert Moore and Robert Bly, we've come to know some of these archetypal "patterns of behavior" as the King, Warrior, Magus, Lover, Blacksmith, and Clown. Another one is the Natural Man, whom some of us have come to value deeply as the "Wildman." It is when we are in touch with this one that we know instinctively we are men.

The archetypal warrior is the keeper of order and safety. He serves the sacred king. He is loyal, faithful, and disciplined. He is dedicated to his cause and unswerving in his mission, be he an author, musician, businessman, or doctor.

When we open ourselves to look deeply into our inner warrior who has existed for thousands of years, it feels right. Every man is intuitively in touch with that raw masculine energy that protected and preserved our distant ancestors. His warriorship was meaningful work. It was the essence of who he was, and it felt right. However, there is a shadow side.

World War II: Our dads took on the awesome mission of WWII with great courage, and they were wounded, deep inside. They were in the first fully automated war. The sense of genuine "warriorship" was grotesquely distorted or absent. These were men (like their fathers, doing meaningless work) who were operating cold machines that delivered death miles away or miles below. And the final blow, the climactic culmination of WWII, was the atomic vaporization of thousands of men, women, and children.

Our fathers fought WWII against the covertly rageful, grandiose, narcissistic insanity of Hitler's Germany. This enemy was made up of men so severely damaged emotionally as to be possessed by the shadow warrior. Cynical and without compassion, they released the Mars energy of war in ways that violated every code of honor a warrior has. I suspect that, in the way members of a dysfunctional family get drawn into its craziness and secrets, our fathers too got close to that shadow warrior.

Here is the subtle part: Beneath the rationale, beneath the good, solid, logical reasons (Pearl Harbor, stopping Hitler), is the reality that they killed millions of people. Beyond the rationales that "the enemy did it too, we had to protect ourselves, we saved one million American lives," lies the fact that they did it. Beyond whatever reasons they used to justify it, they did it. And they stuffed it down inside themselves. Well below conscious awareness lay their horrible secret, and there they kept it.

True warriorship is a way of being that includes integrity and honor. It is a highly intimate experience. I've read of samurai warriors who could face off in mortal combat for many hours and be so utterly present and in contact with one another that neither would swing their swords. The warriors of millennia *faced* their opponent, respected him. War became a ritual process of respectful men. The warrior knew who he was, why he was doing what he was doing, and he felt good about himself.

Our fathers did not feel good about themselves as warriors because they were mechanics operating machines of death. They were part of the slaughter of millions (all rationale aside) and so were the folks back home who made the bullets and saved the tin foil. Their spirits died in the unconscious shame associated with dishonoring the archetypal warrior. The shame of WWII was secret. They rarely, if ever, talked about their experience of the war. Later they threw themselves into work, bottled spirits, or other addictions to salve the shame.

Warriorship and manhood died an inglorious death. Civilization had evolved into an inhuman killing machine, and manhood died in the gears.

The women's movement: With the demise of manhood there was a void of male energy in the Western world. Authentic male energy was in very short supply. Because nature abhors a vacuum, the deficit of male spiritual and emotional energy led to several social responses.

Wives went crazy with frustration, living with men who came home to them spiritually dead. They felt powerless to do anything about it. In their desperation, too often, they tried making their sons into the man they were missing.

Sons took to the skies, emulating Peter Pan, the *puer aeternus* or eternal boy living out various playboy and spiritual lifestyles to compensate for what their environment lacked. Growing up without an emotionally alive father and experiencing the emotional incest with Mom made intimate relationships with both men and women difficult.

Daughters' attempt to fill the void by becoming as like men as possible was the most dramatic manifestation. The women's movement was, beyond all the rationale (unequal pay, men had all the power, housework is slavery), a deeply felt need to balance out what was missing. In some ways young women tried to be men. So desperate was their need for male energy that they attempted to create it themselves. Most found it very unrewarding and have created ways to embrace their feminine selves again.

Overall, I think the most socially destructive result of the male energy void was Mom's anger toward Dad, which our generation unconsciously took in. It became the social prejudice against men. Man bashing is still acceptable. Women often admit that among themselves they rarely have much good to say about men. The saddest part is that too many men hold the same prejudice. They do not like men.

The bomb: The bomb? What bomb? After WWII the number of bombs kept growing, despite public knowledge that we were long past the amount it would take to eliminate human life on the planet. Shame is always a secret, so the absurdity and nihilism of the bomb had to be kept secret or justified in some way.

As world alliances rearranged themselves into two superpower camps, each side could logically point to the other as the enemy from which they needed to be protected. That protected the secret. It was the same secret for both sides, rooted in the same shame.

The "Atoms for Peace" program built nuclear power plants, and men felt they could logically say, "See, this atomic stuff isn't so bad; it produces electric power." They, too, protected the secret. Our legacy is cost-ineffective, billion-dollar water boilers with toxic waste products that we can't get rid of.

The healing: As long as our fathers stayed in power, the secret remained. Their shadow of shame was so great that they were willing to face death rather than look at it. Now something has changed. Perhaps the shame of their sons in Vietnam opened the door. Since the war ended, 50,000 Vietnam veterans have committed suicide. Perhaps this agonizing fact engendered a deep, quiet feeling of empathy. Perhaps they could see for the first time their own pain in the mirror of their sons: men coming home broken from a similar war. This time there was no rationale, no reason to be there. The shame could not be denied with good reasons.

On a spring day in 1989, Robert Bly said, "Warriors do not make war. It is the lack of connectedness to the warrior archetype that causes war."

Men are taking back their archetypal warrior spirit. I believe that the ending of the "cold war" in Europe was the shadow coming into the light. Some men are looking inside and consciously living out the warrior archetype. Devoted to a mission greater than themselves, they engage in conflict, and they trust their use of power. They are no longer afraid of their inner warrior.

Tears of joy come to my eyes as I think, for the first time in my life, that we may survive. Yet I know too well that those bombs are still out there, and that Mother Earth is badly wounded. She will need several million men with true warrior spirit rooted in a mission of service to heal her. So, warrior brothers, let us complete our battles within and together take joy in the battles without!

32

The Awakened Soldier

by Glenn Gray

There are degrees and kinds of guilt, and not merely a formal declaration of simple guilt or innocence by the inner tribunal. Those soldiers who do respond to the call of conscience find themselves involved in the most baffling situations, in which any action they could take is inappropriate. They learn soon that nearly any of the individual's relations to the world about him can involve him in guilt of some kind, particularly in warfare. It is as pervasive in life and reflection as is human freedom itself. Awakened to his personal responsibility in one aspect of combat action, the soldier is not necessarily awakened to finer nuances of guilt. Yet it sometimes happens that the awakening is thorough and absolute in character, demanding of the subject an entirely different set of relations to friend and enemy.

It is a crucial moment in a soldier's life when he is ordered to perform a deed that he finds completely at variance with his own notions of right and good. Probably for the first time, he discovers that an act someone else thinks to be necessary is for him criminal. His whole being rouses itself in protest, and he may well be forced to choose in this moment of awareness of his freedom an act involving his own life or death. He feels himself caught in a situation that he is powerless to change yet cannot himself be part of. The past cannot be undone and the present is inescapable. His only choice is to alter himself, since all external features are unchangeable.

What this means in the midst of battle can only inadequately be imagined by those who have not experienced it themselves. It means to set oneself against others and with one stroke lose their comforting presence. It means to cut oneself free of doing what one's superiors approve, free of being an integral part of the military organism with the expansion of the ego that such belonging brings. Suddenly the soldier feels himself abandoned and cast off from all security. Conscience has isolated him, and its voice is a warning. If you do this, you will not be at peace with me in the future. You can do it, but you ought not. You must act as a man and not as an instrument of another's will.

I shall always remember the face of a German soldier when he described such a drastic awakening as this. At the time we picked him up for investigation in the Vosges in 1944, he was fighting with the French Maquis against his own people. To my question concerning his motives for deserting to the French Resistance, he responded by describing his earlier involvement in German reprisal raids against the French. On one such raid, his unit was ordered to burn a village and to allow none of the villagers to escape. (Possibly the village was Oradour and the soldier was one of the participants in that grisly atrocity; at that time we knew little of what was happening elsewhere and I did not ask him for names.) As he told how women and children were shot as they fled screaming from the flames of their burning homes, the soldier's face was contorted in painful fashion and he was nearly unable to breathe. It was quite clear that this extreme experience had shocked him into full awareness of his own guilt, a guilt he feared he would never atone. At the moment of that awakening, he did not have the courage or resolution to hinder the massacre, but his desertion to the Resistance soon after was evidence of a radically new course. Terrible as was his self-reproach at what now could be undone, he had won himself through this experience and would never again be available as a functionary.

In the Netherlands, the Dutch tell of a German soldier who was a member of an execution squad ordered to shoot innocent hostages. Suddenly he stepped out of rank and refused to participate in the execution. On the spot he was charged with treason by the officer in charge and was placed with the hostages, where he was promptly executed by his comrades. In such an act the soldier has abandoned once and for all the security of the group and exposed himself to the ultimate demands of freedom. He responded in the crucial moment to the voice of conscience and was no longer driven by external commands. In this case we can only guess what must have been the influence of his deed on slayers and slain. At all events, it was surely not slight, and his example on those who hear of the episode cannot fail to be inspiriting. Were it not for the revelation of nobility in mankind, which again and again appears in time of war, we could scarcely endure reading the literature of combat.

33

Combat and Consciousness

by Richard Strozzi Heckler

It was about the fifth day of a one-month retreat, and everybody was just starting to get into the groove of what we were trying to do there. So after sitting for about fifteen minutes, everything started to quiet down, and a certain kind of focus began to happen. I opened my eyes and I slowly looked around the room.

The person to my right, I could tell, was pretty concentrated and pretty still. Just naturally my eyes gravitated toward him, and the first thing I saw was this T-shirt that he was wearing. He was a very big man, big barrel chest, big biceps, a really physical person. He had this black T-shirt on, and in the middle of it it had a skull and crossbones. Written across the top it said "82nd Airborne Division," and underneath, in big white glaring letters that kind of screamed out at me, it said "DEATH FROM ABOVE." So this isn't your normal meditation T-shirt that you see at retreats. And this guy was sitting like someone does at a meditation retreat. He was very straight, he was very still, his breathing was very deep in his belly, and he happened to be a member of the Special Forces, which all of you probably know as the Green Berets. He was one of twenty-five men that I taught from the end of last July to the end of February of this year. I worked with two other team members, one man who did most of the administration and psychological values and another who was the head of the biofeedback lab.

It started three years previously, through a group based in Seattle that I work with called Sportsmind. We had worked with a lot of Olympic athletes and professional athletes and had redesigned the Third Army Division's physical training program. And while that was going on, a major from the Special Forces said, "Do you think it's possible that you could do a special program for Special Forces?" And we said, "Well, let's try to do it." We took three years designing it, taking it through the Army bureaucracy, and getting it signed before that program actually started. It was a six-month program, and one of the Army's goals in the program was physical enhancement: they wanted the men to have more physical endurance, more physical strength, more physical flexibility. They also wanted what they call "mental enhancements": they wanted to improve concentration and attention span, and they wanted the men to have more control over their autonomic nervous system— simple things like controlling blood pressure and heart rate, and being able to have more intense concentration after longer periods of extended sleeplessness. And the third thing they wanted is what they called team cohesion. Basically that was interpersonal work. They wanted to improve the communication between their teams, between the officers and enlisted men, and also between the team members and their families.

Usually when I tell this to people I see a kind of balloon over their heads like in the cartoons, and it reads something like a *National Enquirer* headline. "I meditated with twenty-five Green Berets and lived to tell about it." Or "He's teaching them to kill with awareness." And the basic questions people ask are: Why did the Army want to do this? What are they really up to? and Why would I do something like this? These are really good questions. When I was asked to do this, the deepest place in me said, "Yes. I want to do this. This is important for me to do." I felt really prepared to do it. I felt like a good person to do it. The person that asked me was a guy named Jack Cirie, a friend of mine who did two tours in Vietnam and retired as a colonel from the Marine Corps. He was mostly our liaison between the Army and our Sportsmind group. Jack had studied aikido with me, and that's how we knew each other. I was hired on board to teach aikido and to teach psychological values and what we call psychology of the body. A lot of my colleagues in the psychological community were very much opposed to me doing this. They had a lot of very strong considerations about it, basically coming from a point of view like, "How could you give the secrets to the Army?"—that whatever the Army was doing, this would add to the sinister or nefarious ways that Special Forces might use this stuff. And that's not without historical precedent, actually. I think everybody knows that Hitler had a whole background in the occult and the psychic, and knows about his ability to use hypnotic suggestion.

Anyway, one reason I did the program was because I just wanted to do it. Another reason is that the things I do that have really influenced me—aikido, meditation, and a body-mind psychology—I have really seen transform a number of other groups who hold the same kind of ideas about living in the world. I've worked with prisoners. I've worked with police departments. I've worked extensively with a lot of the gang kids from East Oakland and East Los Angeles. And I wanted the opportunity to express what I felt is the real ideal of being a warrior, what a warrior could be.

The ideal of a military for me would be one that could make America secure without making somebody else insecure. That's a basic stance of aikido, too. You can make your own self secure without making somebody else insecure. Those two questions— why I did it and why they did it—bring up a basic question: "How do these things fit?" Well, I'll tell you right away. It was the most challenging professional experience I've ever had, because it had daily, hourly obstacles in it, and some of the obstacles were just as simple as personality clashes between the instructors and the soldiers. Another obstacle was the fact that civilian instructors were teaching these Special Forces, and these men, who are the military elite and who hold themselves at the top of the heap, were saying, "What can you possibly teach me?"

One of the main things that we did for them is show them their weaknesses. Because our point of view was that basically everybody's strength is also their weakness. And that really brings up this whole central dilemma around the idea of teaching these kinds of things to Special Forces soldiers or the Army as an institution. And I also hold that the dilemma which I'll talk about is the same dilemma you find in teaching in any institution, not just the Army. The dilemma was this: The Army wanted these soldiers to have certain skills, certain physical, mental, mind-body skills. Interpersonal skills. In order to get those kinds of skills you have to feel yourself more deeply than you ever have. You really have to take your attention inside yourself and to tap the kind of potential that's there, and in doing that, what happens is that all of your humanity comes up. You see yourself more deeply, more widely than you ever have. Your level of self-knowledge grows. Along with your ability to become self-educating, self-knowing, and self-healing, you will also naturally become more compassionate and more sensitive. It's simply part of the package. It doesn't work any other way.

What the Army wanted to do is to be able to say, "Okay, you be able to ruck with a hundred-pound pack on your back for a hundred miles in two and a half days and be able to stay wide awake for the next two hours." Well, you can learn how to do those kinds of things, but in learning to do those things, this other level comes up. In other words, you start to feel yourself as a person, you start to feel your fellow soldier as a person, and you start to feel the enemy as a person. The Army doesn't want that. Consciously and unconsciously, the Army does not want that.

I want to quote from something that a guy named J. Glenn Gray wrote. His book *The Warriors* is really the most sensitive and intelligent book on men and war. He says:

> The military man finds it almost a condition of his vocation that he regard men in terms of force. That is, as objects, and disregard all those subjective factors that distinguish every man from every other. The personality of each man becomes of interest to him, not for itself alone, but for its military effectiveness. Hence, the professional is caught in a world of means and instruments, himself one among others. The total human being has no chance to break through to consciousness because there's no official interest in the whole human being.

This was the central dilemma which all the obstacles came out of, and I think that if you wanted to, you could replace the military with IBM or AT&T. This in some way could even be the institution of the family:

> *The total human being has no chance to break through to consciousness because there's no official interest in the whole human being,* so the professional image of the enemy is a consequence of the pattern of life imposed on those who serve as instruments and not ends. The abstraction of the image is more or less inevitable.

So there we were with these men. And in our own naïveté, we didn't discover this dilemma until about two months into the program. And in order to get to this stuff, we asked these people to go in more deeply; in other words, we did a one-month meditation retreat, where at times they meditated for up to sixteen hours a day. We did bodywork on them. They did a lot of interpersonal skills with each other and with their families in order to get these physical, mental, and interpersonal enhancements. But as these things started to come up, so did their humanity.

Here's one story. We were doing a ruck, a big, long ruck. One guy, a really bright guy who I got close to particularly fast because he liked aikido, sprained his ankle. He couldn't go on, so we decided the rest of the team would go ahead, get a Medivac, and I'd stay back there with him. So he was there; he was really grumpy about it, really pissed off about hurting his ankle. And as we started to talk about it, he started to get a level of self-responsibility about actually how that happened. In other words, as we were talking about it, he backtracked to the moment when he hurt his ankle and realized that he wasn't aware at that time. He saw that. And as we went further into it, he realized that he was critical of one of my team members for something that had happened before on this ruck, something insignificant, but he was thinking about him and pissed off at him about being irresponsible for what he was doing. And then he hurt his own ankle.

So while he was telling me this and gaining this kind of self-knowing and putting these pieces together—in other words, as he quit projecting out from the outside that somebody had done something to him, that there was somebody to be mad at—he started to cry. It was a very tender moment. I mean here we were way out in the boondocks. We were both pretty exhausted. We were carrying these hundred-pound packs. And this guy started to cry. And he was fighting his crying. I didn't say anything, which he couldn't have taken: I was just trying to encourage the expression of his anger and his grief about that whole incident as a natural thing that just needed to come out. He was fighting, and then in the middle of it, he said, "My wife is going to be so pissed off at me." I said, "What do you mean, your wife is going to be pissed off?" He said, "This is what she's always wanted from me. She has wanted me to cry with her and show my emotions, and I'm doing it with you." He really didn't have any kind of a relief from it, but it was the same kind of thing: what came forth from him was that Green Berets, Special Forces soldiers, don't cry. Now I'm not saying these men aren't sensitive. They're quite sensitive. But again, it was that going back to that central dilemma of the official interest versus what came up with the tools and skills we were trying to bring up. Well, he told me he hadn't cried since he was thirteen, when his dog died, and he had cried deeply about that. He was about twenty-eight the time that he had cried after that. And it just didn't fit into the official interest.

These kinds of things happen daily. And as small or insignificant as the story sounds, it was like all those things built, and it became very educational to me. I personally feel that it's the very reason that people who are guerrillas fighting for their land are going to win, and are proving that they're going to win over and over again, because they can feel that kind of passion and feeling and love from their depths. They're allowed to do that, because they're fighting for something that's very close to them. They're fighting for their own land, for farms to till: and they're fighting for people they love—their children and their wives, their families. They can pull up that kind of passion, that kind of feeling, along with the skills. When we get into our huge technological army, fighting someplace a long ways away, it's very difficult to do that. And there are endless accounts of Vietnam veterans who are talking about that, that what they really wanted to do was to survive. "How can I get out of this place alive?" It wasn't like, "How can I win this or fight this?" or "What's my support system?" It was more like, "Can I just survive this?" And I think it puts the huge technological army at a huge disadvantage. Not only that, it points to something very important about people who are struggling in the world for different liberties and freedoms that are theirs.

Throughout the program we brought in fourteen experts in their fields. One of them was a guy named Brother David Steindl-Rast. He's a Benedictine monk, an extraordinary, exemplary person. Very unsoldiery type of guy, although he was in the Austrian army at one time, and he gave a beautiful talk to these guys about the similarity between a monk and a soldier. At the very end of the program, I set up a hypothetical situation. I said, "Let's take all the visiting instructors and I want you to choose. If you had to be with one of them for six months, like they might live with you, they might be in garrison, go on operations, or maybe even be called to do something in the field, be in combat, who would you choose to be with?" We had a number of speakers, but a lot of them were martial artists and more, you would think, in their image. Well, three-quarters of them chose Steindl-Rast. They said, "This is the guy I'd rather be with." And the first hit was that it was basically because he drew this similarity between being a monk and being a soldier. But the other thing they said is they felt that whenever he was with them he would really be able to take care of himself, that he wouldn't lean on them. Now, Brother Steindl-Rast is small in stature, and he probably weighs about 130 pounds. He's a very unassuming type of a person. But I think really what they felt from him was an inner power. And I saw that that had some kind of meaning to them. Especially since I asked this at the end of the program, when they were starting to be able to see beyond just physical force and physical strength.

Anyway, the real question is: Can a Special Forces soldier be a Special Forces soldier and still have these new experiences and these new attitudes and these new feelings? It's a good question, and I don't think that it really is answerable or even possible until the official interest changes. Going back to J. Glenn Gray's statement, for example, these guys were mission-specific. If certain political events constellated in a certain way, they would go out on an intelligence-gathering mission, and then they would exfiltrate after a certain time. One guy told me that never before has he thought of the question of exfiltrating from a mission and running into some civilian fifteen-year-old farm boy. What he knows he's trained to do at that time is to shoot him. So that everybody gets out free and they bring back the information. So at the end of meditation retreat, he says, "What do I do? What do I do with that?"

This was enlightening to me in a sense because I saw on some level we're creating a certain kind of double bind. The worst kind of double bind will create a schizophrenic. The most creative kind of double bind will create a new, creative possibility. In other words, I'm giving him one piece of information that's saying one thing. He's getting another piece of information this way, so he's bound up on both sides. One thing that he respects is saying this; another thing he respects is saying that. And he is put in this quandary. I didn't know how to really answer that. After the first week of aikido, one guy says to me, "How are we going to do this for six months and then drop any bombs on anybody?" I really didn't know how to answer him. But it's a really good question. And all I can say is that I think it really keeps coming back to the official interest. A few of the men wrote in their after-action report, "Oh, I get it. It's not any one of these things: our diet is different; our training is different; we concentrate differently; we feel better with our kids or with our work; it's none of that. You're really asking for a change in lifestyle." And that's really what it comes down to: a change in lifestyle, a whole different attitude. And an attitude isn't a mental phenomenon. An attitude is a bodily phenomenon. So we're really talking attitude in terms of how they're going to behave in the world.

Ways that I felt successful in it were like this. I asked one soldier what he had gotten out of aikido. He was a guy who liked aikido, and I know he'll follow up and do it later. He said, "I don't hit my kids anymore." He said, "It's this idea of being centered: when I'm centered I realize I shouldn't do that." For me that was like a personal win. If that happens with his kids and their kids, I think that is important. Other members of these two Green Beret teams would have tremendous changes in the objective tests—their physical fitness tests, their mental tests, and our subjective evaluation. And right to the end they denied anything had happened. Even though you could see that they were stronger, they were more flexible, they were more relaxed, they had lost weight, and their blood pressure had gone down, right to the end they denied that anything had happened at all and said that basically it was kind of a waste of time for them, and they wanted to get on with being soldiers. There were levels of resistance like that. Some of my detractors would always say to me, "Gee, maybe some of them would leave the Army," which a lot of them felt like maybe after this program they should. My whole hope is that they would stay in the Army, that they would actually be able to teach this, and it would move on.

The program was taken and debriefed down at Special Operations Command. They thought it was worthwhile enough to do an iteration of it. The group commander—there are four Special Forces groups—had been rotated out, the guy who had supported us, and a new group commander came in. And his reaction was like, "What are you? Meditation? Biofeedback? I don't want to hear about that." And so basically the program has been put in the dead-letter file, in the back.

34

Taking Power

by Danaan Parry

POWER

What a powerful word! The mere mention of the word usually scares the pants off of people. The concept of Power is so intimately related to the warrior path that we must go beyond its boogey-man facade and seek to understand power for what it truly is.

> When the power of love overcomes the love of power, then there will be true peace.
>
> —SRI CHIN MOI GOSH

I'm sure that you are familiar with the phrase "Power corrupts; absolute power corrupts absolutely." If this is true, how can you as a Warrior of the Heart aspire to the conscious ownership of your full range of power? Yet this is exactly what must occur for you to know yourself and to be effective in the world.

The answer is that "Power," in itself, is neither good nor bad. Power does not corrupt. "Power" in its essential state has no value judgment associated with it, just as "behavior" has no positive or negative connotation until someone *does* something with it. *Power is simply energy manifested in time.* What the individual chooses to do with that manifestation of energy is what determines its positive or negative inclination. Throughout history the primary inclination has been to use Power in a negative fashion, rather than positive, because it is a matter of where the power comes from, the "locus of power."

It would be a worthwhile venture for one embarking on today's warrior path to study the figures in history that utilized large amounts of Power. A study not of "what they did" but of "who they were" will clarify the concept of Power and its positive and negative use. There are only two types of world leaders that have successfully wielded Power. One type is personified by arch-villains such as Hitler, Mussolini, Nero, and Herod. The other type, at an extreme in behavior style, is personified by passionately loved heroes such as Jesus, Gandhi, Buddha, Mother Teresa, Dag Hammarskjöld, and Martin Luther King, Jr. It's fascinating to uncover the very simple common denominator present in each type and also the simple difference between the types. It's not complicated at all. It's just a matter of *where* their power comes from.

In the case of the arch-villains, a look at their early childhood clearly shows that they came from a position of utter powerlessness. For them, their center of Power was somewhere *external* to their being. Power was something out there that had to be seized and manipulated. Lacking a sense of internal Power, they grabbed on to external power and misused it to its extreme.

A look at the lives of the folk heroes shows men and women who felt their Power from *within*. The source of their tremendous Power lay inside their being, not outside where it must be achieved. When they used their Power in the world, there was never any fear that it could be stolen from them or used up or worn out. Their source of Power was as a wellspring deep within their Self, never faltering, never decreasing in its flow. Power and love were one for them, and the more they gave of these, the more there was to give.

It is so with the Heart Warrior. Power does not corrupt. Those who cannot sense their internal wellspring of Power and love are the ones who *choose* to corrupt with the Power that they have stolen from outside themselves.

The warrior knows that his or her internal wellspring of Power and love is constantly renourished by self-power and self-love. The warrior's sense of Self can never be taken away.

The warrior walks the path of Power as did the high beings of pure love and pure Power who are known to us now as Jesus,

Gandhi, Buddha, Krishna, and White Eagle. If you wish to deepen your knowledge not only of Power, but of total love and yielding (the art of giving up "position" to make a space for everyone to win), then there can be no finer place to begin than with the lives of these beings.

On your own personal journey, you will encounter moments wherein you will know your source of Power. It may occur in the midst of deep meditation. It may overtake you as you immerse yourself in a moment of intensity. It may fill you as you consciously yield in the face of aggressive challenge. Or, it may simply come unannounced and uninvited in the mundane "getting on with life." But you will know briefly that you are different, unique. You are. In a flash, you will understand that you have everything you could ever need to be whatever you wish to be. You will know that a Source flows within you that will never cease.

This awareness occurs to *all* conscious beings, everywhere. *But* almost everyone chooses instantaneously to disregard this moment, to discount it. When we have been trained from childhood to fear and mistrust our own Power, it's understandable that we would try to deny it when it bubbles up. But if you choose the path of the warrior, you must learn to cherish this gift and to utilize your Power in the service of love. Your Will—your conscious Will—will make the difference between the correct and incorrect use of your Power.

35

Freeing the Imprisoned Warrior

by Harris Breiman

As a boy I was terrified of the schoolyard bullies. I would hide my chubby body from their cruel teasing and brutal violence and was bewildered by the hateful, hurtful energies they radiated. My strategy for remaining safe was to become invisible or to cleverly befriend and seduce them with offers of academic assistance or free milk during lunch breaks. These early encounters were initiations into the shadow side of masculine power which triggered psychic scars.

No one ever mentored me in the martial arts or the skills of self-defense. My world was neatly divided into the good boys who were kind, gentle, and meek and the bullies who were destructively aggressive. My father and I prided ourselves on our capacity to endure and to transcend the negativity of others through a shared search for the miraculous experience of a "higher consciousness." Little did we know that we were embracing a masochistic style of suffering which masqueraded as forgiveness. Jesus, Gandhi, and Martin Luther King, Jr., who each espoused the path of non-violence and love, were later to become my saints. Though I aspired to their noble ideals in college anti-war activities and embraced the philosophy of peacemaking, inwardly my soul remained passive and fearful of conflict. I learned to demonize all aggression and froze my body into rigidity in the process. My sword became stuck in the stone.

Little in the ensuing years offered an opportunity to enthusiastically embrace the full range of masculine selfhood. The Women's Movement rightly critiqued our culture's oppression of women and the devaluation of the feminine. Unfortunately this truth turned into a dogma wherein feminist fundamentalists equated masculinity with testosterone poisoning and shamed men in a reverse version of the doctrine of original sin. Now men carried the face (or was it the phallus?) of the enemy. It became politically correct to presume that masculinity and patriarchy were identical. The option of our becoming androgynous or unisex eunuchs was encouraged as a way of liberation from the gender genocide being perpetrated upon women by the male mutants of the human species. Was there to be no choice between toxic macho stereotypes, on the one hand, and psychic castration on the other?

Years of immersion in the Men's Movement has decisively answered this question for me by initiating an ongoing journey into "mature masculinity," a phrase suggested by Robert Moore and Douglas Gillette to describe their decoding or discovery of the deep structures of the male psyche. Throughout the poetry, mythology, and folktales which appear across all cultures there are universal depictions of key figures such as the King, the Warrior, the Magician, and the Lover. Envisioning an integration of such forces within myself has provided a compass by which to navigate the stormy seas of my soul's transformations. Being able to distinguish between the empowering energies of these inner allies and their distorted or abusive forms has released me from the trance of my childhood traumas . . . especially my passivity. I have gained an appreciation for what I would now call the angelic aspects of aggression as personified in the figures of the Rainbow Warrior from the Native American tradition and the Knights of the Round Table from the Arthurian legends. The necessity to defend that which is sacred from attack and to fight for that which is holy, just, and true now makes sense to me in a much more visceral way.

Along this pathway I am also learning a capacity for discipline and focus which cuts through obstacles, the cultivation of courage in the face of fear, the capacity to endure pain or suffering for a profound purpose or goal, and the ability to engage in creative conflict or confrontation without willfully wounding my adversary in the struggle. All of this energy emerging from imprisonment within my soul has also inspired me to move beyond my personal healing by offering service to my community. This has taken the form of doing volunteer work with men at the Shawangunk Correctional Facility, a New York State maximum security prison.

I have brought into the prison environment perspectives and models which have guided Men's Work across the country. Our Men's Prison Council has become a forum where we explore what it means to move beyond the psychology of criminality. The men I have worked with to develop the council are all convicted of violent acts and many are serving life sentences. Half of the inmates at Shawangunk Correctional Facility have murder convictions.

When I first arrived at the prison I had to make my way through a labyrinth of security checkpoints and locked iron doors to enter an island of isolation. It was easy to fantasize that here—in the belly of the beast—I would meet the citizens of Hell and look into the eyes of the enemy. It was my presumption that here I would find only those worthy of punishment and incarceration for their crimes against civilized codes of conduct. I was sure that these men would make the schoolyard bullies of my childhood seem like wimps, and so I wasn't surprised when the memories of a terrified boy echoed in my underground and activated my anxiety.

What I have slowly discovered to the contrary is a shocking truth. Without being naive or sentimental and with utmost concern for the victims of crime and their survivors, my conviction is that these particular prisoners have used the punishment of incarceration as an opportunity for education, initiation, and rehabilitation. They are striving to return to society as redeemed men who will make a valuable contribution to our collective life. These men are moving away from the violent, abusive, death-dealing energies which are acted out by the shadow side of the warrior and moving toward the virtues and noble characteristics of the Rainbow Warrior or Knight of the Round Table. My own journey has been from the passive side of the victim who was bullied toward this very same sacred common ground. The prisoners and I have, then, offered to each other mirror reflections of a distorted masculinity. Our shared quest for healing is quickened by the community-building process and dialogue within the Men's Council.

Within prison, just as within the culture beyond prison, the warrior energies of the male soul can be expressed in creative or destructive ways. The men in the Council express sorrow and frustration that other prisoners still remain caught up in adult versions of the schoolyard violence and macho, bully behavior which horrified me as a child. It is as though the energies of the rainbow and of the storm clouds exist side by side and are always in need of our conscious stewardship and containment. I have only to look to the experience of my ancestors in the Nazi Holocaust of the Jews to be reminded of this polarity of possibilities in the manifestation of warrior energy. For there I am struck by the images of the Warsaw ghetto fighters resisting the genocidal brutality of the storm troopers.

What then becomes the evidence of a successful warrior initiation? The capacity to make choices is not enough in and of itself. We must allow ourselves to wonder: to whom am I dedicated? To what vision am I devoted? For what purpose am I seeking empowerment? My imprisoned brothers ask these questions, which are helping to shape my still-evolving understanding of Men's Work. These men bring a prophetic passion for economic and social concerns to my still-developing sense of conscience and communal responsibility for the life of the world. They ask me to engage the realities of racism and poverty and to move from the comfort of my middle-class lifestyle into the streets and the trenches of transformation. The words of one of the imprisoned men echo powerfully in my mind:

> Let arise among you the Warrior-King of Brotherhood, ready and prepared to ascend the noble throne of humanity, wielding his spiritual sword of social justice with the wisdom and compassion of Solomon.

What does it mean to listen to and honor his voice? Will I recognize it as my own? Will I free the imprisoned warrior? Will we?

36

The Lone Buddhist Ranger

by Jarvis Masters

We had only been out on the San Quentin maximum security exercise yard for an hour when I noticed a new prisoner entering the yard gate, looking as though he were a woman. I couldn't believe it. No San Quentin exercise yard hated homosexuals more than this yard. Gays came in second only to informants to be stabbed and killed. My mind instantly said this was some kind of mistake, or a dirty ploy by the prison administration to get someone killed. Wondering which of these two evils it could be, I peeked up at the tower gunmen. I asked myself what a Buddhist teacher would do at this point.

My blood pressure boiled with anger and frustration at the prison administration's negligence for letting something like this happen. It made absolutely no sense to put a "he-she," who looked more like a woman than a man, out here on this high security exercise yard. "This is totally insane," I thought, trying to not show any facial anger.

According to the laws of prison life, none of this was supposed to be any business of mine. But secretly, it was. This time it had to be. For all the life in me, I wasn't able to look at this gay person, who was now sitting alone, against the back wall of the exercise yard, and not see an innocent human being there. Yet I did not want to have to summon up the courage to become a snitch and risk my own life for his to warn him off this yard. Why me, anyway? I felt crossed up.

I looked up again at the gunmen, hovering over the exercise yard, and saw they had already gotten in position. They both had their semi-automatic rifles hanging over the gun rail, readying themselves to fire down on the north wall of the exercise yard. Obviously, they already knew what everybody else knew.

I had to do something. Not later, but now. I began walking alongside the wall of the exercise yard. What could I possibly do? Violence was just waiting to happen. Dammit, I asked myself, why are things like this happening even more since I took my vows? What would all the thousands of people outside these walls who call themselves Buddhists tell me to do? Would they say, "Let's all be Buddhists and everybody just put their knives up and smile"?

I made my way around to where the homosexual was sitting against the wall. Not stopping, I passed him several times, wanting to give myself a really good look at him. I wanted to find out if he was aware of what was going on, that someone was about to stab and kill him. The fool was not! He sat there like a tiny fish in a shark tank. Now I needed to get away from this guy, quick. I needed to think, because I felt time was running out—even for me.

I spotted Crazy Dan on the opposite side of the exercise yard. He was squatting down, and secretly cuffing a long prison-made shank in the sleeve of his coat. "Damn!" I mumbled, "No! Not Crazy Dan." My heart began to pound as I watched Dan, a really good friend of mine, preparing himself to kill this innocent person, whose only offense was that he was gay.

Dan and I had known each other for more than eight years in San Quentin, and it just figured that this good friend of mine wasn't feeling as I was about all this. I didn't want Dan to risk his own life, trying to take the life of another with these two ready gunmen watching.

Then my mind went blank. Without thinking, I began walking down the wall, on the opposite side of the yard from Dan. It wasn't until we both suddenly turned the corners, coming toward each other, with the lone gay man, squatting quietly against the back wall, that I saw the long shank slowly sliding down from Dan's coat sleeve, into his right hand. I quickened my pace to get there before Crazy Dan. I didn't have time to be scared, or even to think. I knew I had to get there first.

Quickly, I knelt down in front of the gay man and asked if he had a spare cigarette. Dan was only six feet away. I glanced up and saw Dan stopped dead, standing there with his right hand hiding behind his leg, gripping the long shank. Dan was stunned. I could see all the adrenaline in his body freeze, as his eyes like those of a ferocious beast stared into mine. I'd never seen those eyes before. They were not those of the Dan I knew. For that split second I thought my friend was going to kill me instead.

Then something happened. Dan's eyes blinked hard several times, as he suddenly began to realize my silent plea. I could see that he was remembering the time when I had once stood by him when he, too, had been marked for death. Dan turned and calmly walked away.

I'd personally never held anything against homosexuals, but I knew that the prisoners on this particular yard hated them. Some hated them just for hate's sake. Others hated them out of fear: especially those who had arrived at San Quentin in the early '80s with life sentences or those who were waiting on Death Row to die, and had long ago been taken in by the very first media reports of how AIDS was just a homosexual disease. Later, prison officials told us that other diseases like tuberculosis were something else that homosexuals were spreading throughout the prisons. The men on this yard had come to believe all this. They were scared of homosexuals and hated them all.

I stared with disbelief at this gay person waiting at the entrance of the yard gate. I thought, "This guy isn't going to last one full hour out here!" I didn't have to turn around to know that there were other prisoners behind me, looking on coldly. Everyone was watching. I could just feel it. There was silence all over the yard. I didn't have to see all the prison-made shanks being pulled out of waistbands to know what some of the men had begun doing. I wanted so badly to holler out, and warn this stupid person who was still standing at the yard gate, "Man, this isn't your damn yard. Don't bring your ass out here." But I couldn't say this. I could not say anything. It would've been considered snitching. And I am not a snitch. So I swallowed and kept my mouth shut, and prayed.

Then came the loud clinking and whining sound of the motorized gate letting this person onto the yard. When the gate slammed shut, my heart dropped. He had just become another walking dead man. I had seen a few others like this in my eleven years of incarceration.

The entire yard, from everyone on the basketball and handball courts to the scattered groups of others over by the pull-up bar, all watched in total silence as this fragile-looking man with tiny breasts, his hair in a ponytail, Vaseline on his lips, dressed in really tight state jeans, began swishing along the yard fence.

"Hey, Daddy, did you want this cigarette, or what?" the homosexual asked in a female voice, holding one out between his fingers.

"No, I don't smoke." He looked around confused.

When I realized what I had just done, I almost choked on my fear. Why had I put my life on the line for somebody that I didn't know, or hadn't even seen before? "Am I crazy or just plain stupid?" I wondered, looking in the face of this gay man who was still totally unaware of what I had just done.

I stood up and walked away, knowing that I was going to take a lot of heat later that day from everyone on the exercise yard. But I realized that I could make the case to the whole yard that all this had been one big setup. I would say that the prison authorities had been intent on shooting and killing some of us and that I wasn't about to let anybody that I knew, especially Crazy Dan, get killed by tiptoeing into their trap. The truth that I would purposely leave out, in justifying what I did that day, was that I honestly cared about the homosexual person too. He meant absolutely nothing to me—except that he was just as human as all of us. He never came back to our yard after that day, but he left me with a lot of questions.

Is what I did a Buddhist deed? Can't it just be a human deed? Can't everybody or anybody do this? Am I alone? Am I the only Buddhist out here? Does this mean I have to do this all the time? Am I the Lone Buddhist Ranger, expected to be here to stop all this stuff? I imagine myself raising my hand and yelling "Stop! A Buddhist is here!"

I'm not going to stop it all. It hasn't stopped at all. There are stabbings every day in this place. All I have is my practice. Every morning and night I fold my two bunk blankets and sit on them on the floor of my cell.

37

Earth First! Is a Warrior Society

by Dave Foreman

Human beings are primates, mammals, vertebrates. EF!ers recognize their animalness; we reject the New Age eco-la-la that says we must transcend our base animal nature and take charge of our evolution in order to become higher, moral beings. We believe we must return to being animal, to glorying in our sweat, hormones, tears, and blood. We struggle against the modern compulsion to become dull, passionless androids. We do not live sanitary, logical lives; we smell, taste, see, hear, and feel Earth; we live with gusto. We *are* Animal.

Not all Earth First!ers monkeywrench, perhaps not even the majority, but we generally accept the idea and practice of monkeywrenching. Look at an EF! T-shirt. The monkeywrench on it is a symbol of resistance, an heir of the sabot—the wooden shoe dropped in the gears to stop the machine, whence comes the word *sabotage*. The mystique and lore of "night work" pervades our tribe, and with it a general acceptance that strategic monkeywrenching is a legitimate tool for defense of the wild.

And finally: Earth First! is a warrior society. In addition to our absolute commitment to and love for this living planet, we are characterized by our willingness to defend Earth's abundance and diversity of life, even if that defense requires sacrifices of comfort, freedom, safety, or, ultimately, our lives. A warrior recognizes that her life is not the most important thing in her life. A warrior recognizes that there is a greater reality outside her life that must be defended. For us in Earth First!, that reality is Earth, the evolutionary process, the millions of other species with which we share this bright sphere in the void of space.

Not everyone can afford to make the commitment of being a warrior. There are many other roles that can—and must—be played in defense of Earth. One may not constantly be able to carry the burden of being a warrior; it may be only a brief period in one's life. There are risks and pitfalls in being a warrior. There may not be applause, there may not be honors and awards from human society. But there is no finer applause for the warrior of the Earth than the call of the loon at dusk or the sigh of wind in the pines.

38

Becoming an Eco-Warrior

by Bill Devall

The prospect of nuclear holocaust frightens most people. The prospect of loved ones and beloved places being completely destroyed in an instant brings up death images and grave anxiety. But nuclear holocaust is only one logical outcome of the social dynamics of our civilization. A state of war already exists and nuclear holocaust, as terrible as it would be, is only a continuation of that war. Mother Earth has been raped. The rain forests have been raped. Rape, an ugly, violent, abusive crime, is a shocking metaphor to use to describe the situation but a most appropriate one.

Warriors have been raped. All are victims but not humiliated and shamed. Warriors don't have to be filled with self-hatred or pity. Fully accepting their situation, new warriors remain sensuous, erotic, touching their place, active, fully committed, alive to possibilities. Bells and drums announce the warriors' presence. They are not passive, sullen, or cynical.

Greenpeace tells the prophecy of an old Cree grandmother more than two hundred years ago—a mother with the name Eyes of Fire. She prophesied a time when fish would be poisoned in their streams and birds would fall from the sky and the seas would be "blackened"—all due to white man's technology and greed. Native American peoples would almost completely lose their spirit, but some would find it and teach some white people to have reverence for the body of the earth. Using the symbol of the rainbow, the races of the world would band together to bring an end to desecration and destruction of earth—Warriors of the Rainbow.

Warriors are not necessarily pure, in this society. Gary Snyder says they "must realize that these are abnormal times and there's no way that any of us can keep ourselves pure." All people carry a portion of the world's poisons.

Warriors are aware of the dangers. One great danger is the tendency to be too abstract, too intellectual. Some warriors want to build elaborate arguments for deep ecology, but in the context of the dominant mind-set of Western society, the intuition of deep ecology cannot be completely justified. It is also dangerous to hold too much attachment. Many feel attached—ego involved—in winning and losing. Non-attachment is practiced by Buddhists through several methods. Warriors can learn this practice.

New warriors also face the temptation of desiring to be heroes. Today's heroes are usually media figures or extraordinary individuals. In contrast, heroes in deep ecology are all those involved in the real work. Warriors may become heroes, but not of their own choosing, not from their own desire. New warriors seek transformation of self but *not* egotistical growth, not what some critics call "spiritual materialism." Social and political transformation are part of Self-realization.

New warriors train themselves with two weapons, one being the insight that they are connected with the net of life, that everything is connected and intermingled with everything else. The other weapon is compassion. Warriors take on the suffering of the world, feeling immense compassion. They also act effectively in politics. Persons who intellectually understand environmental problems and develop complex mathematical models of ecosystems or rivers yet never *know* the forest or the river as part of their "body," have not fully experienced the joy of the warrior.

Warriors do not deny their situation or its painfulness. While denial is a useful psychological mechanism in certain circumstances, denying the human impact on the Earth or evolution might tempt warriors to yield to an arcadian fantasy. Deep ecology warriors create ecotopian visions against which they compare the present situation; ecotopia is not a fantasy but rather a statement of an ecological and ethical ideal toward which all can strive.

Neither do warriors retreat into a private cave, attempting through spiritual practice to avoid the pollution and dangers of this world. They are engaged in live blade practice in everyday affairs.

Warriors with deep self-identification with a territory, a place or another species of animals, defend it. There is nothing passive or boring or nihilistic about deep ecology warriors. They have affective, erotic relationships with bioregion, river, mountain, and they are passionate, aroused—sometimes even angry.

Most of all the deep ecology warriors live fully, rightly, and deeply with the dilemmas and paradoxes of post-modern civilization. They live in the midst of a war zone, recognizing peril. Even when filled with suffering, they are calm. If even one person is calm in the midst of the terror, others are also. If warriors panic in the war, if they feel there is too much challenge and are overwhelmed with fear, then they become incompetent and their energies are scattered.

If warriors are uncommitted or too arrogant, if they feel they have control over the situation or are overconfident or lethargic, they will become boring to themselves and will never be able to act effectively.

Clear thinking, commitment, confidence, calmness. These are attributes which engage minds and bodies in the real work with centered charity.

New warriors are morally bound not to shrink from responsibility. "For if we shrink, we close our eyes to reality, and therefore become as guilty of causing the earth's demise as those who produce the weapons and push the buttons," says the Beyond War Woman's Convocation.

Some people see the new warriors as dangerous, because they are serious about their real work. But they continue to practice, are practicing, diligently, and that is affirmation. Ordinary people in extraordinary times expand their capacity for suffering and become warriors.

For the warrior, every campaign may be his or her last; therefore it is the one most real. Warriors feel alive in the midst of the campaign—alive to possibilities in what Buddhists call the great emptiness.

Warriors recognize and accept the suffering, the wounds of the world. They take on the suffering of the rapist and the humiliation of the rape. Even under the best circumstances it is highly likely that they will witness massive human-induced destruction. They do not despair. They simply live.

The simple life is not easy. But warriors are not seduced by the comfortable life, the easy compromises with the dominant worldview. Nor are they seduced by romanticism, idealism, or sentimentalism. Ecological realism is a profoundly objective spiritual *way*.

They are exploring many possibilities for a graceful civilization. What a challenge. What a rich opportunity.

They are settling into *practicing*. In the midst of this war they are searching for ways of dwelling richly and complexly.

There is no opponent, no enemy, in this war. All action comes from the center of a great empty circle full of possibilities. Do nothing. Accept everything. Warriors have no great part to play in the mountain's destiny. Absorb the mountain. Listen to the mountain. Settle onto the mountain.

Perhaps a more mature person, one dwelling in a mixed community, is settling into a space not yet discovered. Some will say our destiny is in the stars. They plan great voyages to other planets. But many supporters of deep ecology say, "Well and good. Plan your trips to other planets. That may be a great adventure. But we hardly know this earth. We are just learning ways of dwelling here. In this lifetime it is better to know this earth as a friend, not to dream of escaping to a distant planet."

So warriors stay in their homelands, thrilling to the adventures here. This work requires strength, but not the strength of a weight lifter. No search for perfection, no great achievements. Practice speaking for the rat, the wolf, the kangaroo. Practice mindfulness. Practice nothing. Nothing forced. No heroic gestures. Practice diving deeper into the river, dwelling now here, now there, now here again.

All data is in a sense ambiguous and most statements made (if they are interesting) are paradoxical.

What then are warriors to do? If they agree that most human-induced changes during the past three hundred years have been destructive, that the dominant worldview is anthropocentric, what must they do?

Paradoxically they must attempt to change everything in the culture that is anthropocentric and human-centered, and do nothing.

Warriors withdraw from the most violent and destructive elements in society. They withdraw support from political regimes which encourage warfare, development of nuclear weapons, and massive, destructive projects in the name of economic development. They actively avoid taking sides between capitalism and Marxism, between the U.S.A. and the U.S.S.R., between science and religion. They are neither left nor right. They are affirming the inherent worth of rain forests and grizzly bears. They are encouraging broader identification and solidarity.

Warriors work in political campaigns which are congenial with principles of deep ecology—restoring the Damaged Lands, protecting habitat, protecting biological diversity, helping people to richly experience their place. But they make no great plans, build no great monuments, do not encourage more mega-technology.

They are most active when affirming with their bodies what is not fully expressed in words.

Aikido's method of defense is seeing the openings in the attacker and filling them. It is a method for protecting both the attacked and the attacker. It is also an art. Each person practicing aikido develops his or her own style within the general principles. Each person who is a supporter of deep ecology develops his or her own style within those deep ecology principles.

Warriors are constantly advised, "Work only on yourself, not on your opponent. . . . When you try to force, throw, take down or defeat your opponent, you are using your willpower and not your power. Keep to your own center. Let the action occur."

When they feel tired, depressed, defeated, discouraged, without hope of ever really learning aikido, "Keep practicing."

Of course warriors will at times feel frustrated, irritated, despairing. To say that they must feel good all times is to deny the full range of emotional response. In the context of the "great emptiness," emotions are part of the greatness.

Practicing diligently and precisely is challenging, engrossing, vital, and energizing.

Practicing, warriors can take on great suffering with dignity.

Practicing means sharing insights with others, but it also means realizing that those others must discover the insights of deep ecology for themselves, in their own place.

Practicing simply.

Practicing deep ecology means cultivating a sense of the wild center in a civilization out of balance. Action comes from the center of the circle where all is condemned, potential energy.

Practicing deep ecology is a win-win game. Engage the process and the process will continue to engage us. The more cooperation, the more living beings gain realization.

Practicing is subtle.

Practicing is simple.

Practicing is just practicing.

Nothing forced, nothing violent, just settling into our place.

39

The Warrior Monk's Vision

by James Channon

I envision an international ideal of service awakening in an emerging class of people who are best called *evolutionaries*. I see them as soldiers, as youth, and as those who have soldier spirit within them. I see them come together in the name of *people* and *planet* to create a new environment of support for the positive growth of human-kind and the living earth mother. Their mission is to protect the possible and nurture the potential. They are the evolutionary guardians who focus their loving protection and affirm their allegiance to people and planet for their own good and for the good of those they serve. I call them *evolutionaries*, not *revolutionaries*, for they are potentialists, not pragmatists. They are pioneers, not palace guards.

As their contribution to a hopeful future, the warrior monks bring evolutionary tactics. They recognize that the world community of peoples demands hope from those who would operate as servants of the people. Services rendered by the warriors of the First Earth Battalion are specifically designed to generate workable solutions to defuse the nuclear time bomb, promote international relations, spread wise energy use, enforce the ecological balance, assist wise technological expansion, and above all, stress human development. Armies are both the potential instruments of our destruction and the organized service that can drive humanity's potential development. They are the "turn key" organizations that could either shift the energy of our world into a positive synergistic convergence, or bring us to the brink of the void. We have no choice but to encourage world armies to accept and express the nobility they already strive to attain. I can see their action expanding to include evolutionary work like planting vast new forests, completing large canal projects, helping in the design and construction of new energy-solvent towns, helping to clean up the inner cities and working with the troubled inner-city youth in young commando groups, and working harmoniously with other nations to see that the plentiful resources of our mother earth are equally shared by all peoples.

This will not be the first time that warrior monks have been active. In Vedic traditions, the warrior monk was a philosopher and teacher, and therefore a powerful transformational player. In the Chinese culture, the warrior was both a healer and teacher of martial arts. History affirms our own belief that there is no contradiction in having the warrior and the service-oriented monk prototypes live a completely harmonious, blended, and parallel path when the basic ethic and service is "loving protection" of evolution and humankind. There is no contradiction in having armies of the world experience the same ethic as they evolve in peaceful cooperation toward the greater good of all.

It is sometimes difficult to determine how we have set ourselves against each other as nations, and even the more frustrating when we realize that the people of these nations are not really very different inside, and in fact have the same desires for growth and environmental balance and for prosperity that we have. But this is reality. And soldiers who have grown up in an "arms race" world are obviously doing their job of protection when they come up with a new and more effective weapons package. But it is time for another approach, to use all of this military power for another end. It is time to give as much reward for the evolutionary contribution made by a soldier or an army as we have given in the past for the destructive contributions made on behalf of national defense.

I know that this process will begin with the transformation of soldiers and evolutionaries everywhere on the face of our planet home. There are young men and women who already aspire to this level of service and who are ready to make a permanent commitment. They will begin to meet in small groups to provide a support system for the personal transformation of group members. And on a small scale these groups will begin selected evolutionary programs in their units and their communities.

All national-level armies will begin to cooperate on ventures that stabilize the nuclear balance of terror. Joint teams could then patrol space and counter local terrorist activities that threaten stability in any given areas. Evolved cooperation will stifle the arms race. Cooperation between the Soviets and American military could insure that neither side "flies off the handle" in direct collision in some local arena of tension, which would precipitate both sides into a major nuclear war. And there are precedents for this type of cooperation unknown to the public. The U.S. and Soviet military have partied together in Potsdam. They have exchanged academics at the Staff College level, and they have viewed each other's military exercises in recent years.

The great flow of historical events, habits, and international relations is not easy to change. It will take the patient, focused, loving, and dedicated effort of warriors all over the world, people of different languages and cultures and all examples of humanity's infinite variety of expression.

40

Army Green

by Stewart Brand

The arms race is running backwards. NATO is without a mission. The few Communist governments that haven't crumbled have turned inward. In the absence of a Soviet-scale threat, present or foreseeable, what is the U.S. Defense Department supposed to defend in the coming decades? What are we supposed to do with the prodigious instrument that won the Cold War and encored with a dazzling victory in the Gulf? That is the deeper debate these days around the Pentagon, accompanying the immediate issue of how to scale down severely and gracefully.

Meanwhile a famous global problem, the deteriorating natural environment, is gradually being reunderstood in economic terms. America is finally becoming alarmed about the decay of its engineered infrastructure—highways, water systems, communications systems, and even the education system. In the same way, the whole world is worried about the *natural* infrastructure—soils, aquifers, fishable waters, forests, biodiversity, and even the atmosphere. The natural systems are priceless in value and nearly impossible to replace, but they're cheap to maintain. All you have to do is defend them.

The natural and engineered infrastructures together constitute the world's economic infrastructure—the ecostructure.

Suppose our military took on the long-term role of protecting the global ecostructure. From one point of view it did so in the Persian Gulf, defending the world's access to the major source of inexpensive energy when U.S. direct interests in the region were relatively limited. Could we build on that success? When the global economic infrastructure is understood as including natural infrastructure, we might defend rain forests and diverse ecosystems for the same reasons we defend freedom of the seas and global communications.

An example which has scarcely been reported: tropical hardwood such as teak is a global, renewable resource being criminally squandered. Environmental groups are acutely aware of the issue and acutely powerless to do anything about it in some places, such as Burma ("Myanmar," but who expects the name to last?). Would a threat of UN-sanctioned military intervention keep the vandal government of Burma from selling off its hardwood forests and its people's future livelihood? The idea seems unthinkable now. A few years from now it may seem unthinkable *not* to take action.

But seldom does environmental protection need to be that militaristic. Is there any reason to believe the military would be good at the mostly gentle role of environmental steward?

A rare federal hero of environmentalists these days is, of all things, the Army Corps of Engineers. In the last fifteen years the Army Corps has reversed its behavior, from destroying wetlands, channelizing rivers, and marching roughshod over local conservation interests, toward increasingly creating wetlands, restoring rivers, and responding to local conservation calls for help. All this from an agency that started with no environmental mandate at all.

By contrast, the recent record of federal agencies directly charged with solving serious environmental problems is more mixed. The Environmental Protection Agency's toxic-cleanup Superfund is bogged down in escalating legal costs of a scale to threaten the national economy. The National Park Service is facing its own infrastructure breakdown, having deferred maintenance on basic facilities so long that repair work often consists of "painting the rot." In the Forest Service, programs for actively preserving public lands are constantly being proposed by staffers and just as constantly shot down in Washington for interfering with commercial interests (cattle, timber, mining) in the National Forest system.

How can that happen? It has to do with expectations. People

expect *positive and immediate* results from agencies like the National Parks, Forest Service, and EPA—happy vacationers, income, cleaned-up toxic sites. No one has positive or immediate expectations of the military, only negative, long-term ones—keep war from our land at home and our interests abroad. Environmental problems are best addressed in similarly negative, long-range terms—keep the natural systems from crashing. Such slow, preventative programs are evidently better run by career officers, as in the Army Corps, than by political appointees, as in the EPA, National Parks, and Forest Service.

An element in the military's favor for an active environmental role is its experience in making radical programs work by sheer decree. Way back in 1948 President Harry Truman declared that the U.S. military shall integrate the races in its ranks, starting now. The Pentagon took a deep breath, saluted, and complied, the first and most powerful of American institutions to integrate. A man of Colin Powell's abilities as head of the Joint Chiefs of Staff was a natural result. The same occurred with giving the sexes equal opportunity in the military, a fact overlooked by the public until the Gulf War but long lauded by studious feminists such as Betty Friedan.

If there is an example of socialism that works in the world, it is the U.S. military, capable of carrying out large, slow missions, funded by the seething market economy it protects. I saw it work during two years of active duty as an Army officer in the early '60s. You have job security, lifetime benefits, and a relatively money-free personal economy. You go where you're told and do what you're told, and you feel surprising personal freedom from the gibbering options and threats of American civilian life. You can relax and do your job, and often the job you do makes you proud.

Following the Gulf War, the U.S. military is bursting with pride and a sense of competence to undertake any task. It prefers humanitarian tasks, such as defending Kurds or aiding Bangladesh typhoon victims. But America has a habit of forgetting its military between wars and giving it no assignments besides laying low and being ready. So the talent and the money get spent on training (with a side-benefit of public education) and on weapons systems (with a fractional side-benefit of technology transfer).

Occasionally a rogue program such as the old ARPA—Advanced

Research Projects Agency—puts a few million dollars into a long-term-benefit program such as basic research in computer science in the early '60s. That single project gave America a ten-to-twenty-year lead on the world in computer technology and led directly to the personal computer revolution and its associated economic boom (and also a lower-casualty victory with smart weapons in the Gulf). The perhaps lamentable fact is that the best funder of basic science in Washington is the Pentagon. Environmental science needs money—long-term, reliable, large-scale money. Where could it be better spent to protect the world from war over the long run?

Military people are public servants, dedicated to the point of risking and sometimes losing their lives—it is called "the service." A frustration I remember of military life is not being called upon to actually serve the public very often; you feel a keen regret for all that ability going to waste in variations on the exercise of digging holes and filling them in. My platoon could have made short work of restoring a salmon stream, assisting a controlled forest burn, helping protect African wildlife from poachers, or planting native shrubs at the edge of a growing desert. I wonder if they might get the opportunity.

41

Pilgrimage to Nonviolence

by Martin Luther King, Jr.

When I went to Montgomery as a pastor, I had not the slightest idea that I would later become involved in a crisis in which nonviolent resistance would be applicable. I neither started the protest nor suggested it. I simply responded to the call of the people for a

spokesman. When the protest began, my mind, consciously or unconsciously, was driven back to the Sermon on the Mount, with its
sublime teachings on love, and the Gandhian method of nonviolent
resistance. As the days unfolded, I came to see the power of nonviolence more and more. Living through the actual experience of
the protest, nonviolence became more than a method to which I
gave intellectual assent: it became a commitment to a way of life.
Many of the things that I had not cleared up intellectually concerning nonviolence were now solved in the sphere of practical action.

Since the philosophy of nonviolence played such a positive role
in the Montgomery Movement, it may be wise to turn to a brief
discussion of some basic aspects of this philosophy.

First, it must be emphasized that nonviolent resistance is not a
method for cowards; it does resist. If one uses this method because
he is afraid or merely because he lacks the instruments of violence,
he is not truly nonviolent. This is why Gandhi often said that if
cowardice is the only alternative to violence, it is better to fight. He
made this statement conscious of the fact that there is always another alternative: no individual or group need submit to any wrong,
nor need they use violence to right the wrong; there is the way of
nonviolent resistance. This is ultimately the way of the strong man.
It is not a method of stagnant passivity. The phrase "passive resistance" often gives the false impression that this is a sort of "do-
nothing method" in which the resister quietly and passively accepts
evil. But nothing is further from the truth. For while the nonviolent
resister is passive in the sense that he is not physically aggressive
toward his opponent, his mind and emotions are always active,
constantly seeking to persuade his opponent that he is wrong. The
method is passive physically, but strongly active spiritually. It is not
passive nonresistance to evil, it is active nonviolent resistance to
evil.

A second basic fact that characterizes nonviolence is that it does
not seek to defeat or humiliate the opponent, but to win his
friendship and understanding. The nonviolent resister must often
express his protest through noncooperation or boycotts, but he
realizes that these are not ends themselves; they are merely means
to awaken a sense of moral shame in the opponent. The end is
redemption and reconciliation. The aftermath of nonviolence is the

creation of the beloved community, while the aftermath of violence is tragic bitterness.

A third characteristic of this method is that the attack is directed against forces of evil rather than against persons who happen to be doing the evil. It is evil that the nonviolent resister seeks to defeat, not the persons victimized by evil. If he is opposing racial injustice, the nonviolent resister has the vision to see that the basic tension is not between races. As I like to say to the people in Montgomery: "The tension in this city is not between white people and Negro people. The tension is, at bottom, between justice and injustice, between the forces of light and the forces of darkness. And if there is a victory, it will be a victory not merely for fifty thousand Negroes, but a victory for justice and the forces of light. We are out to defeat injustice and not white persons who may be unjust."

A fourth point that characterizes nonviolent resistance is a willingness to accept suffering without retaliation, to accept blows from the opponent without striking back. "Rivers of blood may have to flow before we gain our freedom; but it must be our blood," Gandhi said to his countrymen. The nonviolent resister is willing to accept violence if necessary, but never to inflict it. He does not seek to dodge jail. If going to jail is necessary he enters it "as a bridegroom enters the bride's chamber."

One may well ask: "What is the nonviolent resister's justification for this ordeal to which he invites men, for this mass political application of the ancient doctrine of turning the other cheek?" The answer is found in the realization that unearned suffering is redemptive. Suffering, the nonviolent resister realizes, has tremendous educational and transforming possibilities. "Things of fundamental importance to people are not secured by reason alone, but have to be purchased with their suffering," said Gandhi. He continues: "Suffering is infinitely more powerful than the law of the jungle for converting the opponent and opening his ears which are otherwise shut to the voice of reason."

A fifth point concerning nonviolent resistance is that it avoids not only external physical violence but also internal violence of spirit. The nonviolent resister not only refuses to shoot his opponent but he also refuses to hate him. At the center of nonviolence stands the principle of love. The nonviolent resister would contend that in the struggle for human dignity, the oppressed people of the world must not succumb to the temptation of becoming bitter or indulging in hate campaigns. To retaliate in kind would do nothing but intensify the existence of hate in the universe. Along the way of life, someone must have sense enough and morality enough to cut off the chain of hate. This can only be done by projecting the ethic of love to the center of our lives.

In speaking of love at this point, we are not referring to some sentimental or affectionate emotion. It would be nonsense to urge men to love their oppressors in an affectionate sense. Love in this connection means understanding, redemptive good will. Here the Greek language comes to our aid. There are three words for love in the Greek New Testament. First, there is *eros*. In Platonic philosophy *eros* meant the yearning of the soul for the realm of the divine. It has come now to mean a sort of aesthetic or romantic love. Second, there is *philia*, which means intimate affection between personal friends. *Philia* denotes a sort of reciprocal love; the person loves because he is loved. When we speak of loving those who oppose us, we refer to neither *eros* nor *philia*; we speak of a love which is expressed in the Greek word *agape*. *Agape* means understanding, redeeming good will for all men. It is an overflowing love which is purely spontaneous, unmotivated, groundless, and creative. It is not set in motion by any quality or function of its object. It is the love of God operating in the human heart.

Agape is disinterested love. It is a love in which the individual seeks not his own good, but the good of his neighbor (I Cor. 10:24). *Agape* does not begin by discriminating between worthy and unworthy people, or any qualities people possess. It begins by loving others *for their sakes*. It is an entirely "neighbor-regarding concern for others," which discovers the neighbor in every man it meets. Therefore, *agape* makes no distinction between friend and enemy; it is directed toward both. If one loves an individual merely on account of his friendliness, he loves him for the sake of the benefits to be gained from the friendship, rather than for the friend's own sake. Consequently, the best way to assure oneself that Love is disinterested is to have love for the enemy-neighbor from whom you can expect no good in return, but only hostility and persecution.

Another basic point about *agape* is that it springs from the *need* of the other person—his need for belonging to the best in the human family. The Samaritan who helped the Jew on the Jericho Road was "good" because he responded to the human need that he was presented with. God's love is eternal and fails not because man needs his love. St. Paul assures us that the loving act of redemption was done "while we were yet sinners"—that is, at the point of our greatest need for love. Since the white man's personality is greatly distorted by segregation, and his soul is greatly scarred, he needs the love of the Negro. The Negro must love the white man, because the white man needs his love to remove his tensions, insecurities, and fears.

Agape is not a weak, passive love. It is love in action. *Agape* is love seeking to preserve and create community. It is insistence on community even when one seeks to break it. *Agape* is a willingness to sacrifice in the interest of mutuality. *Agape* is a willingness to go to any length to restore community. It doesn't stop at the first mile, but it goes the second mile to restore community. It is a willingness to forgive, not seven times, but seventy times seven to restore community. The cross is the eternal expression of the length to which God will go in order to restore broken community. The resurrection is a symbol of God's triumph over all the forces that seek to block community. The Holy Spirit is the continuing community creating reality that moves through history. He who works against community is working against the whole of creation. Therefore, if I respond to hate with a reciprocal hate, I do nothing but intensify the cleavage in broken community. I can only close the gap in broken community by meeting hate with love. If I meet hate with hate, I become depersonalized, because creation is so designed that my personality can only be fulfilled in the context of community. Booker T. Washington was right: "Let no man pull you so low as to make you hate him." When he pulls you that low he brings you to the point of working against community; he drags you to the point of defying creation, and thereby becoming depersonalized.

In the final analysis, *agape* means a recognition of the fact that all life is interrelated. All humanity is involved in a single process, and all men are brothers. To the degree that I harm my brother, no matter what he is doing to me, to that extent I am harming myself. For example, white men often refuse federal aid to education in order to avoid giving the Negro his rights; but because all men are brothers they cannot deny Negro children without harming their own. They end, all efforts to the contrary, by hurting themselves. Why is this? Because men are brothers. If you harm me, you harm yourself.

Love, *agape*, is the only cement that can hold this broken community together. When I am commanded to love. I am commanded to restore community, to resist injustice, and to meet the needs of my brothers.

A sixth basic fact about nonviolent resistance is that it is based on the conviction that the universe is on the side of justice. Consequently, the believer in nonviolence has deep faith in the future. This faith is another reason why the nonviolent resister can accept suffering without retaliation. For he knows that in his struggle for justice he has cosmic companionship. It is true that there are devout believers in nonviolence who find it difficult to believe in a personal God. But even these persons believe in the existence of some creative force that works for universal wholeness. Whether we call it an unconscious process, an impersonal Brahman, or a Personal Being of matchless power and infinite love, there is a creative force in this universe that works to bring the disconnected aspects of reality into a harmonious whole.

42

A Better Game Than War

by Robert W. Fuller

So long as anti-militarists propose no *moral equivalent of war*, they fail to realize the full inwardness of the situation.

—WILLIAM JAMES (1910)

WHAT *DOES* WAR DO FOR US?

The reason there has never been a satisfying response to William James's call for a "moral equivalent of war" is that no *moral* equivalent exists. Spellbound by its glories and barbarities, we hardly notice its amoral role in delivering people to that open, empty place of surrender where they become capable of changing their fundamental shared beliefs—their collective identity—and embarking on a new course. The unconscious belief that we cannot do without war has surely been a barrier to finding a substitute for it. Any substitute for war has to do for us what war, despite its horrible costs, has done, and that's a tall order.

Not long after James called for a moral equivalent to war, H. G. Wells answered his call with a phrase destined to become equally famous: "Human history becomes more and more a race between education and catastrophe." To see war as a problem and education as the solution was prescient in the early years of this century, but today it isn't enough. We have to figure out what we've been going to war to learn, and just what sort of education might become a substitute teacher.

We speak openly of our hatred of war, but we hide our love for it. We deny our dependence but demonstrate it by returning to war again and again. When we are not actually at war, it lives in our imaginations, taking on the attributes of a great game. The reason we remain susceptible to war is that it has served as a forge for identity, summoning us over and over again with the promise of uniting our divided souls in high purpose.

But we've reached an evolutionary impasse: War doesn't work anymore. It's obsolete. Not only do modern weapons threaten the very things we would fight for, but the questions we now face are simply not resolvable through war. Such crucial issues as human rights, the shape of political and economic systems, and environmental and educational policies are already being argued *within* each society more intensely than they are *between* different societies. Even if one nation managed to win a clear-cut victory in war, these issues would inevitably arise within it and with equal urgency. War has become self-defeating before we have ended our dependence on it.

War has served many purposes but none is more fundamental than its role in identity formation. Laurens van der Post pierces to this root cause when he characterizes war as "the terrible healer of one-sidedness and loss of soul in man." In the game of war the stakes are even higher than life and death—they are the identities of the players. Win or lose, all parties to war are changed in the process. We have overridden our fear and chosen war again and again, because it provides an experience of exhausted openness that enables us to embrace fundamental changes in our societies and ourselves—to give birth to new identities and to bury dead ones.

We have honored warriors because they've served as forerunners in the formation of group identity. Furthermore, the warrior's is the only identity that, by placing *itself* at risk, shows people that they are not limited to their current identities. Our explanations for war are incomplete unless we take into account the recurring need for transformation, both individual and collective. People follow their leaders to war to discover who they are—to put a new tribal or national identity to the test or to discard one they've outlived. Van der Post, who spent World War II in a Japanese prison, wrote of his captors, "The war was ... an instinctive search for renewal by destroying a past they could not escape except through the disaster of utter collective defeat."

Grand projects like building the Pyramids, going to Mars, or ending world hunger are sometimes suggested as substitutes for war. But there isn't enough risk in them, not enough opportunity to transcend ourselves. In pursuing them, aspects of our image are at stake, but we do not feel that our fate is on the line. War and tribalism (or its modern-day counterpart, nationalism) have gone hand in hand precisely because the tribe is the locus of our collective identity and the battlefield is where that identity either has been affirmed or lost.

The alternative to war is so simple that at first it looks inadequate. The truth that can save us is that *we don't have to risk our lives to risk our identities*. This innocent-looking proposition is not easily lived, but the results of doing so are revolutionary. If we give up the unconscious belief that we *are* our personas—the constellation of beliefs and images in which we currently take pride—we can send *them* into battle in our stead. Our beliefs and self-images must be defended, yes, but to *their* death, not ours—and defended only until we are able to replace them with transcending identities, which themselves are likewise provisional, just like scientific models.

If there are no ultimate, absolute beliefs, it doesn't make sense to kill others in the name of them. On the other hand, if others try to impose their beliefs by force of arms, it does make sense to resist, by force if necessary. Absolutism must be resisted absolutely. Tolerance and relativism are stances that work only so long as conflict is avoidable. Once it isn't, then a new synthesis must be sought "to the death" of old relative, partisan beliefs.

Conflict exists. Always has, always will. We'd be bored without it. Conflict is the lifeblood of change. It signals the existence of a hidden message, one it's hard work to decipher. If we identify with our position—take it to be "right" and the messenger's position "wrong"—then we may see the message as borne by an "enemy." Alternatively, we can view the disagreement as meaning "we" and "they" have different answers to the same question, and likely different questions as well. A proper response to the conflict—one that ends it—consists of finding a synthesis of one's own and the other's questions and answers. Responding to an unwelcome message by going to war is simply killing the messenger.

In the past we have relied on violence and war to open ourselves to change; but at this juncture in history we have the opportunity to choose a way that is at once gentler and more precise. Changing one's mind while holding to the facts amounts to the creation of a new, higher truth embracing several perspectives at once. Creating new, mind-changing truth is an open-ended task that summons intelligence, will, integrity, and grace—in a word, enlightenment. Such truth allows for a change not only of one's own mind and of the other's mind but also of the world—without making war. More and more, individuals now possess the flexibility of mind to apprehend new truths and create new synthesizing understandings—whether of self or non-self.

Establishing ourselves irrevocably in a postwar world means making enlightenment the norm. This may sound utopian, but Jefferson's call for "the enlightenment of the people," interpreted in its day as establishing universal literacy, once appeared equally unlikely. Although literacy has largely been stripped of its mystery and reading and writing are now taught routinely in schools worldwide, enlightenment—in the sense of creative use of mind—remains the province of elites.

Illiterate peoples are vulnerable to enslavement. Likewise, a world short on enlightenment is vulnerable to war or stagnation—T. S. Eliot's "bang" or "whimper." Literacy is to the formation of national identities what enlightenment is to the formation of global identity, and we shall have to get as good at teaching the latter as we have the former. Enlightenment demystified—as the capability to change our minds, and thus our very identities—is an educational goal long realized by the elites and well within reach of everyone else. The establishment of a global identity, far from precluding national and cultural sub-identities, will support their individuation by providing a context wherein their uniqueness is prized and their continuity assured.

PART V

SPIRITUAL COMBAT

THE BATTLE WITHIN

The Bodhisattva is like
   the mightiest of warriors;
But his enemies are not
   common foes of flesh and bone.
His fight is with the inner delusions,
   the afflictions of self-cherishing
      and ego-grasping,
Those most terrible of demons
That catch living beings in the
   snare of confusion
And cause them forever to wander
   in pain, frustration and sorrow.
His mission is to harm ignorance and delusion,
   never living beings.
These he looks upon with kindness,
   patience and empathy,
Cherishing them like a mother cherishes
   her only child.
He is the real hero,
   calmly facing any hardship
In order to bring peace, happiness
   and liberation to the world.

—THE THIRTEENTH DALAI LAMA
(TRANSLATED BY GLENN MULLEN)

Introduction

In the end, every warrior comes to recognize that the battle is within. This does not mean that the "spiritual warrior" turns from the world. But it does mean that he and she knows that in order to be truly effective in the war that truly matters—whatever you think that is—it is best to wield the diamondlike sword of Manjusri, the bodhisattva of wisdom, which cuts through ignorance and self-deception.

In the end, the greatest act of bravery may well be to simply face ourselves as we are rather than as we fear or hope to be. For it is the denial of our own death which gives rise to the illusion of invulnerability that is the most hidden and powerful of all our self-deceptions. When we face death, we open ourselves to both our own vulnerability and the world with one stroke, and the warrior's compassion is born.

This spiritual combat is especially dangerous, however. For the battle with our inner enemies can lead to a devastating inner war. In such a battle, gentleness may well be the most skillful tactic of all. The idea of conquest itself must be conquered. This battle can be fought best with the weapon of a spiritual discipline such as meditation or prayer, a practice in which, as Trungpa Rinpoche says, "you are completely open, with nothing to defend and nothing to fear."

In this way, we defeat our inner enemies by recognizing them as ourselves. Only then can the warrior draw strength from and protect our wildest, most vulnerable nature.

In "Milarepa and the Demons," the Tibetan hermit-poet defeats five demons who have taken possession of his cave, by recognizing them as phenomena of his own mind. This excerpt, from *The*

Hundred Thousand Songs of Milarepa, begins when he returns to his cave with an armful of wood, to find the demons waiting for him.

Sufi master M. R. Bawa Muhaiyaddeen outlines an Islamic view of "The Holy War Within." The true *jihad*, or holy war, has nothing to do with fighting or killing others, he says, for "Allah has no enemies." The true holy war was in the inner *jihad*.

In "The Fight with the Shadow," Carl Jung relates the inner to the outer war: "Anything that disappears from your psychological inventory is apt to turn up in the guise of a hostile neighbor . . . It is surely better to know that your worst enemy is right there in your heart."

Jung's essay is followed by an excerpt from Ralph Metzner's essay "From Inner Warfare to Inner Peace." Metzner writes: "I used to believe one had to make friends with the inner enemy, the shadow self. I now feel that making friends is perhaps not necessary, that this 'other side' of our nature may always stay in opposition to our true nature."

Finally, in "Personal Disarmament," poet and novelist Deena Metzger discovers a divided country within herself. She finds, "I couldn't hope to accomplish change in the outside world until I changed the inner one."

We conclude with "The Battle," a tale about Coyote, the great trickster warrior, by poet Peter Blue Cloud.

43

Milarepa and the Demons

Translated by Garma C. C. Chang

Exalted, Milarepa adjusted his robe and carried a handful of wood back to his cave. Inside, he was startled to find five Indian demons with eyes as large as saucers. One was sitting on his bed and preaching, two were listening to the sermon, another was preparing and offering food, and the last was studying Milarepa's books.

Following his initial shock, Milarepa thought, "These must be magical apparitions of the local deities who dislike me. Although I have been living here a long time, I have never given them any offering or compliment." He then began to sing a "Complimentary Song to the Deities of Red Rock Jewel Valley":

> This lonely spot where stands my hut
> Is a place pleasing to the Buddhas,
> A place where accomplished beings dwell,
> A refuge where I dwell alone.
>
> Above Red Rock Jewel Valley
> White clouds are gliding;
> Below, the Tsang River gently flows;
> Wild vultures wheel between.
>
> Bees are humming among the flowers,
> Intoxicated by their fragrance;
> In the trees birds swoop and dart,
> Filling the air with their song.

In Red Rock Jewel Valley
Young sparrows learn to fly,
Monkeys love to leap and swing,
And beasts to run and race,
While I practice the Two Bodhi-Minds
    and love to meditate.

Ye local demons, ghosts, and gods,
All friends of Milarepa,
Drink the nectar of kindness and compassion,
Then return to your abodes.

But the Indian demons did not vanish, and stared balefully at Milarepa. Two of them advanced, one grimacing and biting his lower lip, and the other grinding his teeth horribly. A third, coming up behind, gave a violent, malicious laugh and shouted loudly, as they all tried to frighten Milarepa with fearful grimaces and gestures.

Milarepa, knowing their evil motives, began the Wrathful Buddha Meditation and recited forcefully a powerful incantation. Still the demons would not leave. Then, with great compassion, he preached the Dharma to them; yet they still remained.

Milarepa finally declared, "Through the mercy of Marpa, *I have already fully realized that all beings and all phenomena are of one's own mind. The mind itself is a transparency of Voidness. What, therefore, is the use of all this, and how foolish I am to try to dispel these manifestations physically!"*

Then Milarepa, in a dauntless mood, sang "The Song of Realization":

Father Guru, who conquered the Four Demons,
I bow to you, Marpa the Translator.

I, whom you see, the man with a name,
Son of Darsen Gharmo,
Was nurtured in my mother's womb,
Completing the Three Veins.
A baby, I slept in my cradle;
A youth, I watched the door;
A man, I lived on the high mountain.

Though the storm on the snow peak is awesome,
I have no fear.
Though the precipice is steep and perilous,
I am not afraid!

I, whom you see, the man with a name,
Am a son of the Golden Eagle;
I grew wings and feathers in the egg.
A child, I slept in my cradle;
A youth, I watched the door;
A man, I flew in the sky.
Though the sky is high and wide, I do not fear;
Though the way is steep and narrow, I am not afraid.

I, whom you see, the man with a name,
Am a son of Nya Chen Yor Mo, the King of fishes.
In my mother's womb, I rolled my golden eyes;
A child, I slept in my cradle;
A youth, I learned to swim;
A man, I swam in the great ocean.
Though thundering waves are frightening,
  I do not fear;
Though fishing hooks abound, I am not afraid.

I, whom you see, the man with a name,
Am a son of Ghagyu Lamas.
Faith grew in my mother's womb.
A baby, I entered the door of Dharma;
A youth, I studied Buddha's teaching;
A man, I lived alone in caves.
Though demons, ghosts, and devils multiply,
  I am not afraid.

The snow-lion's paws are never frozen,
Or of what use would it be
To call the lion "King" —
He who has the Three Perfect Powers.

The eagle never falls down from the sky;
If so, would that not be absurd?

An iron block cannot be cracked by a stone;
If so, why refine the iron ore?
I, Milarepa, fear neither demons nor evils;
If they frightened Milarepa, to what avail
Would be his Realization and Enlightenment?

Ye ghosts and demons, enemies of the Dharma,
*   I welcome you today!*
It is my pleasure to receive you!
I pray you, stay; do not hasten to leave;
We will discourse and play together.
Although you would be gone, stay the night;
We will pit the Black against the White Dharma,
And see who plays the best.

Before you came, you vowed to afflict me.
Shame and disgrace would follow
If you returned with this vow unfulfilled.

Milarepa arose with confidence and rushed straight at the demons in his cave. Frightened, they shrank back, rolling their eyes in despair and trembling violently. Then, swirling together like a whirlpool, they all merged into one and vanished.

"This was the Demon King, Vināyaka the Obstacle-Maker, who came searching for evil opportunities," thought Milarepa. "The storm, too, was undoubtedly his creation. By the mercy of my Guru he had no chance to harm me."

After this, Milarepa gained immeasurable spiritual progress.

44

The Holy War Within

by M. R. Bawa Muhaiyaddeen

My brothers, the holy wars that the children of Adam are waging today are not true holy wars. Taking other lives is not true *jihad*. We will have to answer for that kind of war when we are questioned in the grave. That *jihad* is fought for the sake of men, for the sake of earth and wealth, for the sake of one's children, one's wife, and one's possessions. Selfish intentions are intermingled within it.

True *jihad* is to praise God and cut away the inner satanic enemies. When wisdom and clarity come to us, we will understand that the enemies of truth are within our own hearts. There are four hundred trillion, ten thousand spiritual opponents within the body: satan and his qualities of backbiting, deceit, jealousy, envy, treachery, the separations of I and you, mine and yours, intoxicants, theft, lust, murder, falsehood, arrogance, karma, illusion, mantras and magics, and the desire for earth, sensual pleasures, and gold. These are the enemies which separate us from Allah, from truth, from worship, from good actions and good thoughts, and from faith, certitude, and determination. These are the enemies which create divisions among the children of Adam and prevent us from attaining a state of peace.

Among the seventy-three groups of man, there are only a few who understand and fight the war against the enemy within themselves, the enemy who stands between them and Allah, the enemy who does not accept Allah and will not bow down and prostrate before Him. To cut our connection to this enemy who is leading us to hell is the true holy war.

Brothers, once we realize who is the foremost enemy of this treasure of truth which we have accepted, then we can begin our battle against that enemy. That is the holy war of faith, of the *kalimah*, and of Islam. That is the one holy war which Allah accepts.

We must not kill each other. Instead, we must wage war against the evil qualities within ourselves. When a child has bad qualities, what does the mother do? She tries to teach him and help him to develop good qualities. Does she call him an evil child? No. If he steals the belongings of another because he wants to play with them, that is a bad quality no doubt, but the child is not evil. Does the mother strike down the child just because he has some bad qualities? No, the mother explains things to him and tries to expel the bad qualities and teach him good qualities. That is her duty, is it not?

Likewise, Allah, who created us, does not strike down His creations for the evil they have committed. It would not make sense if He did that. They are all His children, the children of the Lord of all creation. As their Father and Mother, He helps them to dispel their evil ways and tries to bring them to the straight path. He seeks to make His children happy and good. That is the way God is. And just as God does not kill His children because they have evil qualities, we must not murder others or cut them down. Instead, we must try to improve them by showing wisdom, love, compassion, and God's qualities, just as a mother teaches her mischievous child to change. That is our duty.

No good can come from cutting a person down. If a mother constantly shows unity and love to her child, that will get rid of the child's bad tendencies. In the same way, we must help others to remove the evil qualities, teach them good qualities, and lead them to the state where they can become the princes of God.

My brothers, if we act with love and unity, we can dispel all our evil qualities and live as one family, as one race, as children bowing to one Lord. Once we understand this truth, we will become good children. But as long as we do not understand and do not cast off the evil, then we are bad children.

Of course, when you cut these qualities, it might hurt. It might cause difficulty and suffering. When a child is cut, the pain makes him cry. He may scream and fight or maybe even bite you. He may shout, "I will kill you!" But you must embrace him with love and patiently explain things to him, always remembering that the qualities within the child are the enemy, not the child himself.

My brothers, man has two forms, each with its own set of qualities. The war is between these two forms. One is composed of the five elements and is ruled by the mind; it lives in the kingdom of illusion, creation, and hell. The other is a pure form made of Allah's light, of His resplendence and purity. That form lives in the kingdom of heaven, in the world of pure souls. When man dwells within this good form, he speaks and acts in good ways. When he moves into the form of the elements, he speaks and acts in evil ways. One body exists within him in a formless state; the other exists outside as his form and shadow. These two bodies have opposite qualities and duties.

The heart also has two sections: one is the innermost heart and the other is the mind. The mind is connected to the fifteen worlds, which are ruled by the energies of earth, fire, water, air, and ether. Just as these five elements are mixed together in the earth and in the sky, they are also mingled within the body.

The fifteen worlds are connected to all of creation, to all forms. Seven of the worlds are above, seven are below, and the fifteenth world, which is the center, is the mind. It is there, in the world ruled by the mind, that the holy war must be waged. The mind and the energies of the elements roam up and down throughout the fifteen worlds, manifesting as the four hundred trillion, ten thousand miracles that create differences and divisions among men. We have to fight against all these energies in all fifteen worlds. This is the major battle. Once we complete this war, then we are ready to begin our work within the innermost heart.

The innermost heart is the kingdom of Allah. That is where His essence can be found. The secret of the eighteen thousand universes and the secret of this world are contained within that heart. Allah's messengers, His representatives, the angels, prophets, saints, the resplendently pure souls, and His light within the soul are all to be found in a tiny point within the heart. Within the atom is contained His entire kingdom, the kingdom of truth and justice and purity, the kingdom of heaven, the kingdom of enlightened wisdom. The eighteen thousand universes are within that kingdom of light and divine knowledge, and Allah is the ruler of all those universes. His infinite power, His three thousand gracious qualities, His ninety-nine attributes, His compassion, peace, unity, and equality are all found within those universes. That is the innermost heart, His kingdom of true faith and justice, where one can find peace.

Until we reach that kingdom, we have to wage a holy war within ourselves. To show us how to cut away this enemy within and to teach us how to establish the connection with Him, Allah sent down 124,000 prophets, twenty-five of whom are described thoroughly in the Qur'an. These prophets came to teach us how to wage holy war against the inner enemy. This battle within should be fought with faith, certitude, and determination, with the *kalimah*, and with the Qur'an. No blood is shed in this war. Holding the sword of wisdom, faith, certitude, and justice, we must cut away the evil forces that keep charging at us in different forms. This is the inner *jihad*.

My brothers in *Iman Islam*, we must cut away the qualities which oppose Allah. There are no other enemies. Allah has no enemies. If anyone were to oppose Allah, the All-Powerful, Unique One, that person could never be victorious. You cannot raise or lower Allah. He does not accept praise or blame.

Praising Allah and then destroying others is not *jihad*. Some groups wage war against the children of Adam and call it holy war. But for man to raise his sword against man, for man to kill man, is not holy war. There is no point in that. There can be no benefit from killing a man in the name of God. Allah has no thought of killing or going to war. Why would Allah have sent His prophets if He had such thoughts? It was not to destroy men that Muhammad came; he was sent down as the wisdom that could show man how to destroy his own evil.

Once we have completely severed those qualities of satan within us, there will be no more enmity among human beings. All will live as brothers and sisters. That is true Islam, the affirmation of the unity of Allah, the oneness of Allah. Once we accept this, Allah accepts us. Once we fight and conquer these enemies of our faith, these enemies of our prayers, we will find peace within ourselves. And once we have found peace within, we will find peace every-

where. This world will be heaven, and we will have a direct connection to Allah, just as Adam had that original connection. Then we
will understand the connection between ourselves and all the children of Adam.

Every child must know this and fight the enemy within. We must
fight the battle between that which is permissible under God's law
and that which is forbidden. If we do not do this, then the qualities
of evil will kill that which is good, and the truth will be destroyed.
But if we can win this huge battle, we will receive Allah's grace, and
that will enable us to know His eighteen thousand universes. If we
can conquer the world of the mind, we will see the kingdom of the
soul, His kingdom.

May every one of us think about this and wage our own holy war.
Only when we finish the battle and progress beyond will we realize
that we are all children of Adam, that we are all one race, that there
is only one prayer, and that there is only One who is worthy of
worship, one God, one Lord. He is the Compassionate One, He is
the Merciful One. He creates and sustains all lives, He does not cut
them down. Once we realize this, we will stop the fighting, the
spilling of blood, the murder.

We will never attain peace and equality within our hearts until we
finish this war, until we conquer the armies that arise from the
thoughts and differences within ourselves, until we attack these
enemies with faith, certitude, and determination and with patience,
contentment, trust in God, and praise of God. With divine knowledge, with justice and conscience, we must fight and win this inner
jihad.

May the peace of God be with you. Allah is sufficient for all.
Amen.

45

The Fight with the Shadow

by C. G. Jung

In Hitler, every German should have seen his own shadow, his own worst danger. It is everybody's allotted fate to become conscious of and learn to deal with this shadow. But how could the Germans be expected to understand this, when nobody in the world can understand such a simple truth? The world will never reach a state of order until this truth is generally recognized. In the meantime, we amuse ourselves by advancing all sorts of external and secondary reasons why it cannot be reached, though we know well enough that conditions depend very largely on the way we take them. If, for instance, the French Swiss should assume that the German Swiss were all devils, we in Switzerland could have the grandest civil war in no time, and we could also discover the most convincing economic reasons why such a war was inevitable. Well—we just don't, for we learned our lesson more than four hundred years ago. We came to the conclusion that it is better to avoid external wars, so we went home and took the strife with us. In Switzerland we have built up the "perfect democracy," where our warlike instincts expend themselves in the form of domestic quarrels called "political life." We fight each other within the limits of the law and the constitution, and we are inclined to think of democracy as a chronic state of mitigated civil war. We are far from being at peace with ourselves: on the contrary, we hate and fight each other because we have succeeded in introverting war. Our peaceful, outward demeanor merely serves to safeguard our domestic quarrels from foreign intruders who might disturb us. Thus far we have succeeded, but we are still a long way from the ultimate goal. We still have enemies in the flesh, and we have not yet managed to introvert our political disharmonies. We still labor under the unwholesome delusion that we should be at peace within ourselves. Yet even our national, mitigated state of war would soon come to an end if everybody could see his own shadow and begin the only struggle that is really worthwhile: the fight against the overwhelming power-drive of the shadow. We have a tolerable social order in Switzerland because we fight among ourselves. Our order would be perfect if only everybody could direct his aggressiveness inwards, into his own psyche. Unfortunately, our religious education prevents us from doing this, with its false promises of an immediate peace within. Peace may come in the end, but only when victory and defeat have lost their meaning. What did our Lord mean when he said: "I came not to send peace, but a sword"?

To the extent that we are able to found a true democracy—a conditional fight among ourselves, either collective or individual—we realize, we make real, the factors of order, because then it becomes absolutely necessary to live in orderly circumstances. In a democracy you simply cannot afford the disturbing complications of outside interference. How can you run a civil war properly when you are attacked from without? When, on the other hand, you are seriously at variance with yourself, you welcome your fellow human beings as possible sympathizers with your cause, and on this account you are disposed to be friendly and hospitable. But you politely avoid people who want to be helpful and relieve you of your troubles. We psychologists have learned, through long and painful experience, that you deprive a man of his best resource when you help him to get rid of his complexes. You can only help him to become sufficiently aware of them and to start a conscious conflict within himself. In this way the complex becomes a focus of life. Anything that disappears from your psychological inventory is apt to turn up in the guise of a hostile neighbor, who will inevitably arouse your anger and make you aggressive. It is surely better to know that your worst enemy is right there in your own heart. Man's warlike instincts are ineradicable—therefore a state of perfect peace is unthinkable.

Moreover, peace is uncanny because it breeds war. True democracy is a highly psychological institution which takes account of human nature as it is and makes allowances for the necessity of conflict within its own national boundaries.

If you now compare the present state of mind of the Germans with my argument you will appreciate the enormous task with which the world is confronted. We can hardly expect the demoralized German masses to realize the import of such psychological truths, no matter how simple. But the great Western democracies have a better chance, so long as they can keep out of those wars that always tempt them to believe in external enemies and in the desirability of internal peace. The marked tendency of the Western democracies to internal dissension is the very thing that could lead them into a more hopeful path. But I am afraid that this hope will be deferred by powers which still believe in the contrary process, in the destruction of the individual and the increase of the fiction we call the State. The psychologist believes firmly in the individual as the sole carrier of mind and life. Society and the State derive their quality from the individual's mental condition, for they are made up of individuals and the way they are organized. Obvious as this fact is, it has still not permeated collective opinion sufficiently for people to refrain from using the word "State" as if it referred to a sort of super-individual endowed with inexhaustible power and resourcefulness. The State is expected nowadays to accomplish what nobody would expect from an individual. The dangerous slope leading down to mass psychology begins with this plausible thinking in large numbers, in terms of powerful organizations where the individual dwindles to a mere cipher. Everything that exceeds a certain human size evokes equally inhuman powers in man's unconscious. Totalitarian demons are called forth, instead of the realization that all that can really be accomplished is an infinitesimal step forward in the moral nature of the individual. The destructive power of our weapons has increased beyond all measure, and this forces a psychological question on mankind: Is the mental and moral condition of the men who decide on the use of these weapons equal to the enormity of the possible consequences?

46

Getting to Know One's Inner Enemy

by Ralph Metzner

In some of our experience, the duality of good and evil is felt as a defensive stand-off, a separation, a gulf, a rejection. We are unconscious of the shadow aspects, blind to our faults, we want to separate from that in us which we feel is rotten. In other phases of our experience, there is a more active struggle or conflict going on. We may love and hate simultaneously, or feel both attraction and aversion toward the same object or person. We may be in turmoil as our fears and inhibitions struggle with impulses of lust or aggression. In meditative states, or dreams, or psychedelic visions, we may witness what seems like a clash of opposing tendencies in our psyche, like armies battling in the night.

The task of personal transformation is to turn this inner warfare to inner peace. We need to come to terms with "enemies," both inner and outer. The clashing opposites must be reconciled. Forces, tendencies, and impulses that are locked in seemingly endless conflict must learn to co-exist. I used to believe one had to make friends with the inner enemy, the shadow self. I now feel that making friends is perhaps not necessary, that this "other side" of our nature may always stay in opposition to our true nature. We may want to keep this figure, to function as what Castaneda's Don Juan calls a "worthy opponent," for warrior training. But we need to understand this enemy. Making friends with the inner enemy may be possible. Getting to know him or her is essential.

All spiritual traditions agree that the seeds of warfare, the violent, destructive forces are within us, as are the peaceful, harmonizing forces. A Hindu teacher, Swami Sivananda, writes, "the inward battle against the mind, the senses, the subconscious tendencies (*vasanas*), and the residues of prior experiences (*samskaras*), is more terrible than any outward battle." A text by one of the fathers of the Eastern Church, from the Philokalia, states, "there is a warfare where evil spirits secretly battle with the soul by means of thoughts. Since the soul is invisible, these malicious powers attack and fight it invisibly." The good Christian, in order to be saved, is exhorted to battle temptations, to ward off demonic invaders and harmful external influences. A poem by the Persian Sufi Rumi states: "We have slain the outward enemy, but there remains within us a worse enemy than he. This *nafs* (animal self, or lower self) is hell, and hell is a dragon . . ." I cite this imagery because it illustrates how widespread, across many religious traditions, is this symbolism of inner warfare.

As a psychologist, I have been investigating the many metaphors used to describe the transformation process in order to determine their origins. I pose the question: How does the feeling of being in a state of inner conflict arise in us in the first place? And I suggest partial answers to this question from three different perspectives: the personal/developmental, the evolutionary/historical, and the theological/mythical.

The *personal/developmental basis* for the experience of conflict may very well be (in part) the phenomenon of sibling rivalry in early childhood. Competition between brothers and sisters for the attention and approval of the parents and other adults is extremely common. This competitive attitude may be maintained into adulthood and carried over into personal and work relationships with peers. Alternatively, it may be internalized, so that one feels that there is an inferior and a superior self-image competing and struggling with each other. The founder of gestalt therapy, Fritz Perls, called this the conflict between top dog and underdog.

There are numerous myths about bitter and protracted competition between rival brothers, such as Cain and Abel, or Osiris and

Seth, and stories about hostile sisters, such as Cinderella, or the daughters of King Lear, that illustrate this theme of sibling competition. From the perspective of the psychology of transformation, we interpret such stories as referring to an internal process. Both the good sibling and the wicked sibling are aspects of our own nature. In the words of the English Boehme disciple, William Law: "You are under the power of no other enemy, are held in no other captivity, and want no other deliverance but from the power of your own earthly self. This is the murderer of the divine life within you. It is your own Cain that murders your own Abel."

In addition to its childhood origin in sibling rivalry, this theme of inner conflict also has probable *evolutionary* and *historical* antecedents—the age-old, long-continuing struggles between tribes and societies for territory and economic survival. The cutthroat competition of the haves and the have-nots is a deeply ingrained factor in the consciousness of the human race. Whether humanity, as a species, can transform this territorial and economic competition into peaceful and cooperative co-existence is perhaps our most difficult challenge.

Going even further back into mammalian evolution, one could speculate about the possible residue in human genetic memory of the millions of years of competitive interaction between predators and prey. The ecologist Paul Shepard has argued that the predator carnivores developed a different sort of consciousness, a different kind of attention from the prey herbivores, related to their different lives of hunting or escaping. Predator intelligence is searching, aggressive, tuned to stalking and hunting. Prey intelligence is cautious, expectant, tranquil, but ready for instant flight. I suggest that these different styles of awareness, these opposing modes of relating, form a kind of substrate to the human experience of aggressors (predators) and victims (prey). Don't we still hunt, prey on, and victimize our fellow humans for survival? Don't we still, in the paranoid mode, vigilantly watch for threats, prepared to flee or defend?

In the human imagination, the encounter with the shadow is often experienced as a confrontation with a dangerous beast. When the ideal-ego feels attacked by a monster who emerges out of the unconscious, it feels like a victim. Transformation involves realizing that this ideal-ego is also the beast, the aggressor, the predator. We are both the hunter and the hunted. When we realize this, then the two can make peace—first within, and then in external relationships. In the final days, when planetary transformation is completed, according to ancient prophecies, "the lion and the lamb shall lie down together"; erstwhile victims and aggressors will co-exist peacefully.

The third perspective on the origin of the inner conflict is theological/mythical. Many ancient mythologies offer a cosmic story of the world inherently split by discord and strife. Heraclitus said, "War [of opposites] is the father and king of all." In the Zoroastrian religion of ancient Persia, competition between the forces of light and darkness was given a most dramatic expression: Here we find the myth of the long-drawn struggle, and alternating rulership of the world between Ahura-Mazda, the Light Creator, and Ahriman, the Prince of Darkness. This Zoroastrian conception of a fundamental cosmic dualism undoubtedly had a profound influence on both the Jewish and the Christian religions. The Manichaeans and Gnostics were particularly affected by this myth, with their strong emphasis on the fundamental duality of the Creator, and the parallel duality of the created cosmos.

In this complex of conflict and warfare, made up of personal, evolutionary, and mythological elements, we find the story of man's inhumanity to man—destructiveness, violence, cruelty, sadism, intentional injury, and violation of another's physical or psychological integrity. Recalling the earlier discussion of judgment, I offer the following perspective on these manifestations of human evil: They represent a combination of judgmentalism with violent rage. The judgment is expressed and acted upon in a destructive and aggressive way. Those who are judged *bad*, or *evil*, or *opposite*, are attacked and destroyed.

To put it another way, the judgment that is rendered serves as a rationalization for the naked expression of rage. The rationalization may be literary or aesthetic, as with the Marquis de Sade; or it may be spuriously racial or genetic, as with Hitler's genocidal holocaust; or it may be religious, as with the torturers of the Inquisition—the pattern is everywhere the same. The conflict of the judge-persecutor with the judged victim is perhaps the most vicious of all the warring opposites we know. This variant is also played out within the psyche: We are ourselves the punitive judge (in Freudian terms, the super-ego) *and* the punished victim of persecution (psychologically, the guilt-ridden ego).

For transformation to take place, we need to learn to become wise, impartial judges of ourselves, not punitive, vindictive judges. And again, we must start by realizing that the opposing enemies, the clashing and competing forces, are all within—both the judge and the accused, the jailor and the prisoner, the executioner and the condemned.

ON FACING ONE'S DEMONS

In traditional and contemporary folk religions, demons are the relatives of the devil—they are personifications of evil forces, of alien and destructive influences and impulses. They are definitely regarded as something outside of us, something not-self. In primitive or native cultures, living in a state of "participation mystique" with Nature, demons, like giants, often represent the destructive, violent energies of hurricanes, storms, lightning, wildfires, avalanches, floods, earthquakes, or volcanic eruptions. By inventing or imagining living beings, whether spirits or demons, who guide these forces, their terrifying character is somehow made more tolerable.

Conversely, our own inner states may at times feel to us to be out of control, like the forces of Nature. We then find it natural to describe these inner states as analogous to these forceful aspects of Nature. We speak of someone as a "tempestuous character," or of being in a "stormy mood," or "flooded with grief," or having a "volcanic explosion" of temper. Our inner life, like Nature around us, seems at times to be dominated by violent, clashing energies that seem alien and overwhelmingly powerful to us. This is one aspect of the experience of the demonic.

In the East, both Hindu and Buddhist mythology offer a somewhat different perspective on demons, or *asuras*, also known as "angry gods," or "titans." In many myths, the *asuras* are seen as playing a kind of counterpart role to the good gods, or *devas*. They are the opponents of the gods, analogous to a kind of cosmic Mafia, with values opposite to those of normal humans and gods. In the Buddhist Wheel of Life, which symbolically portrays six different types of lives one can be born into, the world of *asuras* is one of the six worlds, one possibility for existence. Buddhists say these demons are dominated by feelings of pride, jealousy, and anger, and are engaged in perpetual competitive struggle and conflict.

From a psychological point of view, we are in this world of demons when we are dominated by feelings of pride, jealousy, anger, and competitive struggle. The mythic picture of the *asuras* is shown to us as a kind of reminder of how our feelings, our thoughts, and our intentions create the kind of reality in which we live. The chaotic, murderous existence of the demons and of humans dominated by demons, is an external consequence of an inner state.

In Western culture the concept of demon has an interesting history. For the Greeks and Romans, the "daimon" (Latin *genius*) was not evil at all, but was a protective spirit, a divine guardian, something like what later European folklore called the "guardian angel." Socrates was wont to say that he would converse with his daimon in order to obtain guidance. It is only under the later influence of Christianity that the word demon came to connote something malevolent or destructive. As is well known, Christianity tended to turn old pagan gods such as Pan and Dionysus into devils or demons.

Generally speaking, there appears to be a much greater tendency in the Western, Judaic-Christian tradition to polarize good and evil as absolute opposites. Only the three monotheistic religions have a concept of an evil deity—the devil or Satan, who opposes God and the spiritual aspirations of human beings. In the Asian traditions and in the Egyptian and Greek polytheistic religions, we more often find a pluralistic view that accepts a multitude of different perspectives and states of being of various origins and values. And although there may be numerous harmful spirits, demons, and enemies, there is not one personification of all evil. There are gods of death—Hades, Pluto, Yama, Mara—but these are not like the devil or Satan.

The figure of Satan, at least in Western culture, has all the traits and qualities that are part of our shadow or unacceptable side. He is the liar, the slanderer, the destroyer, the deceiver, the tempter, the one who brings guilt and shame, the adversary, the unclean and dark one, who denies and negates everything that enlarges and enhances life, who opposes everything that we value and hold most sacred.

In Jungian terms, the devil represents or embodies the collective shadow of the entire Western Judaic-Christian civilization. He is an amalgamated projection of the shadow image of all the thousands and millions of individuals who have believed in him through the centuries. As with other projections, by attributing dark impulses and feelings to the devil, someone not-self, one is relieved of any responsibility for them—as expressed in that most classic of all excuses, "The devil made me do it." Satan exists in the same sense that the ancient gods and goddesses exist and live in the psyches of individuals who express their qualities and characteristics, whether consciously or unconsciously. The legion of forms and names that the devil can take, the many variations on this theme of clashing opposites, are a tribute to the creative imagination of human beings.

This is the multifarious figure whose features can be detected somewhere behind the persona-mask of every man and woman. It is the beast that haunts every beauty, the monster that awaits every hero on his quest. But if we recognize, acknowledge, and come to terms with it, a great deal of knowledge formerly hidden, unconscious, in the shadows, becomes conscious. When we recognize this devil as an aspect of ourselves, then the shadow functions as a teacher and initiator, showing us our unknown face, providing us with the greatest gift of all—self-understanding. The conflict of opposites is resolved into a creative play of energies and limitations.

47

Personal Disarmament: Negotiating with the Inner Government

by Deena Metzger

In a small, segregated country, called Zebra, the Sun minority has relegated the Shade majority to reservations far from the cities and the centers of power. Some Shades work for the Suns or are exhibited in the lavish national parks developed for the enjoyment of foreigners. The government is a theocracy, with a dictator who has allegiance to the oligarchy and priests.

The dictator, as well as the majority, knows nothing of the culture, mores, values, or spiritual inclinations of the Shades; nevertheless, fear and control of the Shades is behind every governmental decision. It is fully believed that if the Shades came near prominence or power, the entire way of being of the country would be altered. The Suns do not fear for their lives; they fear for their way of life. To change this would be worse than death.

One day there is a serious power outage. The power lines have been cut. Up to this point, energy has been the major export of this country. The country is paralyzed. The Shades do not deny they cut the lines, but assert that the power has always belonged to them. . . .

This scenario could describe conditions in any one of numerous countries. In fact, it is a description of my own inner state of being, a political description of the nation-state of my own psyche. I have come to understand that an individual is also a country, that one contains multiple selves who are governed as nations are governed, and that the problems and issues that afflict nations also afflict individuals. For most of my life, I have been completely unconscious of the real mode of government and the status of the beings within my territory.

A few years ago, confronted by an inner coup in the making, I realized that, despite my politics and activities, I was not identifying with the Shades, the oppressed and disenfranchised majority within, notwithstanding the rumors of their vitality, spiritual development, and artistic skills. To my horror, I was identifying completely with the dictator, the official church, and the empowered. Unthinkingly, I was supporting the status quo, order for its own sake, separatist minority tradition, efficiency, production, export, and growth, and I was acting in loyalty to priests who had long forgotten the true meaning of a spiritual life. Forced to consider negotiating with the Shades (not to mention having to contemplate a coalition government or the demand that the Sun minority abdicate power absolutely), I was overcome with terror and despair. I knew nothing of the Shades, whom I distrusted and denigrated. I co-opted their cultural resources while forcing them to work as slaves at cultural tasks or menial labors. I believed that the Shades were irrational, incompetent, irrelevant people, who were emotionally manacled, distracted by sentimentality, and bewitched by occult practices and so-called literary distractions, and who now wanted to impose their silliness upon Zebra. I ridiculed the preposterous assertion that they could govern themselves, let alone the entire country, and take their chances in the modern world.

Until then, Zebra had been developing into one of the largest, most valuable and respected energy exporters in the region. Now the lines were cut, the energy sources occupied, and the army and police without energy were totally immobilized. Against my will, I had to learn to negotiate with these "barbarian" and threatening forces.

Feeling the demand to arbitrate from this position of extreme fear and distrust, I learned invaluable political lessons as real politics—personal politics—became real life. There was no choice; my country—that is, my life—was at stake. Having once had a life-threatening disease whose underlying causes in the psyche I'd come to understand, I knew the gravity of the situation.

When I began to think about myself as a country, as well as an individual, I was struck by what seemed an overwhelming truth. While nations suffer the delusions that they can destroy one segment of their populations and remain intact or thrive, a nation-state such as I was, like a physical body, cannot hack off one limb or cut out one vital organ, and remain intact. I had managed to suppress some selves up to this time, but I suspected, and even the Suns and later the Shades came to know, that extermination of the opposition meant death. Therefore, albeit unwillingly, slowly, and painstakingly, I began to dismantle the minority supremacist government. I did this although the Suns insisted this meant the end of progress and growth, that it meant disaster.

Attentive to the alien feelings and ideas of the Suns inside myself, it occurred to me that this new empathy could serve me later in political activities in the world at large.

I found it most difficult to give priority to the needs and demands of the Shade people when these challenged the "national" goals of production, export, and defense. But the Shade council government was adamant and threatening. Inevitably, I couldn't please everyone. Elements of both the Suns and Shades were dissatisfied, wanting to take things into their own hands. The internal Sun police continued working out of habit and desperation, and, although they no longer had authority, they remained eerily competent. The deposed minister of culture continued to control the thoughts and habits of the dominant Sun population he was serving so that the theocracy and oligarchy maintained, for a while, its unofficial but tenacious way of being. The Shades, still being repressed, remained mysterious and frightening.

Terrorism existed on both sides. Time and again, I was deprived of sufficient energy to do work while, in response, books and other creative projects were burned; there were many other atrocities. Censorship and spying still flourished, if ex officio. I fell into the pattern of punitive, relentless, even mindless work, followed by periods of utter collapse. The work was insisted upon by the deposed Suns while the collapse was the retaliation of the not-yet-enfranchised Shades.

But while this desperate cycle continued, something new was

occurring. There was someone in me watching it, some interim government or peacekeeping force that managed to hold another vision and to continue the careful process of change. Somehow, against inner public opinion, I made a decision to forgo violent revolution or a new military coup and was not drawn into either alternative, despite provocations against each other and against the interim regime itself. It was difficult not to panic during the cycles of terrorism and hostilities.

I don't know what finally changed the balance of power and led to the development of a new government and a new country. Perhaps it came from empowering a group of international advisors and observers, or from instituting an interim regime. Certainly it derived from the inner realization that all-out war was untenable. Perhaps it was the occasion of declaring a national holiday period and allowing the Shades a limited opportunity to rule. Slowly, very slowly things began to shift.

The real crises of conscience occurred after I regained a more natural affiliation with the Shades. Within the reality of my own psyche, I learned that the former brutality and ethnocentricity of the Suns came from enormous trauma, grief, and pain in their ancient and forgotten history. Sometime in the past, Zebra had suffered a series of crises that threatened the existence of the nation. At that point, the Suns came to power through certain naive but necessary decisions. These became entrenched—both the cause and the motives vanishing. Later these emergency procedures were codified as holy law. The culture of the Suns followed from this, developing out of the real need to protect the country. This ancient grief did not mitigate the contemporary suffering of the Shades but it had to be acknowledged. Just as I was finally reunited with the Shades, I had to recognize the value of the Suns. It became clear that if the Suns were massacred, imprisoned, or brainwashed, the entire country would become demoralized and disoriented. Energies would be diverted endlessly and unproductively toward defense and armaments, and the cycle would begin again in the other direction. I had to find a way to allow the Shades to govern with the Suns, despite the Shades' history of persecution and the Suns' connection with power.

This was not metaphor. Each time something interfered with the process of change in government, I could feel it in my body. The reality of the necessary integrity of a self or a country became physically and emotionally manifest. I experienced on the inner plane the risks, dangers, violence, and terrorism that characterize contemporary political life.

Soon it became clear that a lost function of government was being restored: to nurture, sustain, and protect the entire population, to support distinction, and to provide dynamic communication between the disparate elements.

Protection took on an entirely different tone. It did not have to do with police, prisons, armies, walls, or armaments. It meant providing for diverse needs, even without petition. Sleuthing the inner needs, motivations, and practices that had long been disguised and hidden became an honorable and essential activity. This time, however, the intent was not to eradicate them but to support them adequately. Rather than being militaristic or aggressive, protection began to feel maternal or paternal in the sweetest way. It was characterized by tenderness.

There were many limitations and deprivations in the recovery period: foreign travel, for example, was curtailed. Emphasis was put upon domestic travel (inner exploration). All public transportation was free and encouraged. Bus lines, trains, and domestic airlines were highly subsidized, and free phones, computers, and modems were widely distributed. Publishing increased. But this emphasis upon communication was also potentially dangerous. How could this level of contact, these modern systems, be introduced without destroying the Shades? After all, their culture was based upon the occult; to expose this might have dire consequences. Also, the Shades needed time to solidify their own culture, find the means to protect their ways and oral traditions against corruption and co-option, for their own sake as well as the nation's. So, while access to the lands of the Shades was encouraged, there were to be no new hotels, highways, or tours. When Suns came to the Shades territory, they had to live exactly like Shades. The Shades did not support themselves through tourism, nor could they be subsumed into the entertainment industry. The government had to provide without interfering in their way of life, so the Shade culture once more became the living vibrant source of meaning in Zebra.

Also, technology could not determine development as it had in the past. It was only one of many tools. It had no meaning in itself.

Of course, while this transition was in progress, there were grave economic difficulties, and, accordingly, the country, by one of the first national agreements, isolated itself from the outside world. Ironically, it did not matter so much now when people strayed across the borders in one direction or another. When immigration and emigration restrictions were eased, when no one needed a visa or passport one way or another, it happened that interest in international affairs (in the outer, public world) momentarily diminished. The decrease in publications for export similarly diminished international interest in the country's domestic affairs. Zebra was aided by the fact that its energy resources were depleted, so there was little reason for a foreign takeover. There was nothing to gain. After a while, it became possible to make new and surprising alliances on different bases altogether.

Power was no longer the primary motivation even when a modified energy system was restored. There were no longer plans to build nuclear power plants. Those that existed—even those which had supplied the outer world with energy—were slowly being dismantled, although the problem of atomic wastes was serious and had to be solved. I was not a dreamer; I knew that traces, even huge pools of toxicity, might remain in my psyche for my lifetime. If they could not be neutralized, they needed to be contained. This was also a national priority. I hoped that I would no longer pass their effects on, that they would diminish in time.

Now I was ready to attempt the most difficult work of all. Having achieved some harmony within my own nation, having begun to dismantle the inner police force and the system and values upon which it depended, I turned to the outer world and foreign relations (friends, family, community, and career). I had come to the realization that the inner enemy had been the heroic substance of my domestic life for eons, and that I had been dependent upon it as a source of identity and control. The concept of enemy had been a false and dangerous premise, wasting my resources and diverting my nature, especially because I'd been unconscious of the extremity and implications of the inner conflict. I hadn't known how severely I'd been deprived by being alienated from half myself. Now I was ready to examine my system of defenses and armaments vis-à-vis the public world. Because I had some experience in reviewing the enemy, if only within my own borders, I turned to the enemy without.

In this period, I'd learned that the enemy is the "beloved." The enemy can almost single-handedly bolster and maintain a sense of who we are. It was in contrast to the enemy that the Suns, for example, falsely considered themselves good, strong, spiritually disciplined, intellectual, hardworking, God-fearing, moral, and courageous. It was in opposition to the Shades that they became holy warriors. I had to see how that operated between Zebra, between myself, and others in the world.

I began to identify my external so-called enemies and drop the distinction of self and other in this sphere. I had to learn how I could maintain my own diversity and sense of self while yielding to the value of others, even those who seemed so contrary to myself. I had to see how we could coexist. Perhaps instead of declaring war, we could write treaties asking for help in protecting our differences. I had to examine the weapon arsenals I had created. Secret information, hidden even from myself, had to be exposed, so that I knew the number and nature of every weapon I had.

Finally, I wanted to bring myself at least to a single, sincere act of unilateral, personal disarmament as a sign, primarily to myself, of sincere desire to trust, sincere abdication of the notion of enemy, sincere interest in peace.

I did begin this process of disarmament. It is slow, difficult work.

Long before I could begin to enact these changes, I came to understand that the system of government that controlled me internally was similar to the systems of government in the world. It took a long while to admit that this was so—in part, because I was always projecting into the world the systems by which I was living. It was heartbreaking to realize that all the work I'd done in the world was undermined by the constant seepage of contrary values from my inner being. I could not be a democrat in the world or promote democracy while I was a tyrant within. Each day of my life, I had unwittingly reinforced and reseeded the world with what threatened it, myself, and everyone I knew: tyranny, slavery, militarism. I couldn't hope to accomplish change in the outside world until I changed the inner one.

This filled me with despair at first. I asked how was it possible to make any change if almost everyone had to change themselves internally.

Gradually despair was replaced by hope and confidence. I began to make some changes. I saw it was possible. No small measure of success or possible success was due to working on this through the imagination. Once I began to envision Zebra, to live with the realities of the Suns and Shades as within a novel, once I began to understand their dynamics as highly distinct from my own, as having their own lives and motivations, change, ironically, occurred in Deena. The efficacy and reality of the imagination convinced me that others could do it as well.

I began to see that the despair so many of us feel when confronting world conditions might also be alleviated. We can be effective, can make a real and substantial contribution. They can at the very least (which might turn out to be the very most) institute a government in their inner world that has integrity with their ideas and ideals. And in the very mundane living out of that system, they can project into the outer world some of the ways they hold dear—democracy, equality, equal access, respect for indigenous peoples, environmental protection, disarmament, and peaceful coexistence.

This new way of thinking was very humbling. I had to lay aside all glorious ambitions to save the world either by myself or in concert with a special cadre of beings. The task of change, the ant work of only one individual, was tedious, overwhelmingly absorbing, and took all my energy. Each individual had to do it for himself or herself. I could not be a hero, though I must confess the difficulty of doing it even for myself did at times make me feel heroic. Still I persisted, humbled and doggedly devoted. Why? Because I discovered I really cared for this little nation and for the world, and I did not want to continue to do them harm.

I began to develop a series of questions that I continue to pose to myself as rigorously as I can. I return to them again and again. Posing the questions, trying to understand the answers, and keeping the dynamics of Zebra in my awareness has been a way of clawing my way toward change. I try to be aware of the constant need to accord the inner reality of Zebra with my principles. I don't believe that because I've started this process it is automatically maintained. I do try to be vigilant. These are some of the questions I ask:

- What is the form of my internal government? Is it tyrannical, a dictatorship, an oligarchy? Is it a military government? Is it a police state? Is it a false theocracy?
- Who are my "beloved enemies"? Whom do I identify as the enemies within? The enemies without?
- What are my defense systems? What are the natures of my police force and armies?
- What weapons are in my arsenal? Do I stockpile? Am I in an arms race?
- What is the equivalent of my nuclear bomb?
- Will I sign a no-first-strike treaty?
- Do I have slaves?
- Whom do I imprison?
- Do I torture?
- Do I have an internal FBI and CIA, a secret police?
- What is the nature of my own propaganda and disinformation bureau?
- What territories do I seal off? Do people need passports or visas?
- Who are disadvantaged, exploited, oppressed, or disenfranchised in my country?
- Do I exploit, invade, colonize, or imperialize other countries?
- Do I pollute?
- Am I run by ideologues?
- Am I racist?
- Can I learn to tolerate and then praise diversity?
- Am I willing to disarm? To sign disarmament treaties? Am I willing to allow inspection? Am I willing to trust and be trustworthy?
- Do I really want peace? Can I teach peace to my inner populations?

Once, in a personal disarmament workshop, a man who'd been a peace activist had to confront the extremity of his distrust of others. Gently, I raised the analogy to the disarmament table. I suggested that the officials who sat at that table trying to reach agreements were as distrustful, suspicious, and injured as he was. He was broken by this realization and confessed that he couldn't in their place conscientiously advocate weakening the defense system; yet he had advocated disarmament all his life. Admittedly, if he were in their position, feeling the way he did, he would have to say, "More bombs." For a while, he lived with rage and humiliation. Then he began looking in himself for whatever was possible to allow him to trust. He found inner defenses that were not aggressive. He began to validate inner security so that he could come to the negotiating table in a wholehearted manner. He did not disregard potential dangers or fears, but he did develop confidence by reviewing his history and validating what sustained more than what undermined until he was willing to take a risk. When he returned to the ranks of peace activists, he had a new authority. He had found a way to test the sincerity of his political positions as well as a way to reconstruct his inner world so that it accorded with his principles. He was creating a dialogue between the two worlds.

In another personal disarmament class, a woman recounted that her house had just been broken into and her roommates raped at knife point. This woman had been raped and physically injured by a stranger on two other separate occasions and had herself been abused as a child. She was agonized about the effect of all this upon her adolescent daughter. Yet, as she spoke about her response to the incident, all of us were moved away from despair. As awful as the break-in had been, her courageous refusal to create an enemy and live in fear gave us enormous hope.

At the peace tent at the Non-Governmental Organizations–United Nations Conference on Women in Nairobi in July 1985, I asked an audience of African, American, and European women who it was that ruled their inner countries. The majority painfully acknowledged that they were ruled by tyrants. They agreed that nothing could change in the world until they also altered their inner conditions. The women had been saying similar things about foreign policy, that nothing would change internationally until domestic changes were instituted. Perhaps through the talk we'd managed to move the definition of the domestic closer to the heart and hearth. It wasn't that we thought we needed to stop efforts in the public world, but that there was other urgent work, also on the inner plane, which had to be pursued simultaneously. I didn't realize how much consensus we'd reached until I was approached later by the head of the Soviet women's delegation. There were tears in her eyes. She said, "We have been working so very hard, so very, very hard for peace, we didn't even begin to think how urgent it was to attend to ourselves. We didn't even consider that we have personal selves who need to be attended. Now the Soviet women have to begin this inner work." Yes, I thought, for all our sakes.

Epilogue

The Battle

by Peter Blue Cloud

They were so angry that they decided to have a battle. So terrible was their anger that they would not wait, but declared that the fight must be fought now, immediately, on this very spot. Fox blamed what he considered to be the crime on Badger. Badger in turn was all for placing the blame on Cougar.

Jackrabbit hopped in agitation, calling for Mole and for Mouse, and for Deer and Bear to fetch their sharpest arrows and their heaviest warclubs.

By the time Coyote arrived the sides had already been chosen, the battle lines formed, and the smell of hate and future bloodshed permeated the very air.

He, Coyote, listened to all the threats and promises of broken bodies to be. He walked out and stood between the enemies, declaring very solemnly, and in a very soft voice:

"No, I cannot allow this great fight to happen just yet. There has been no battle-preparation dance. There has been no pipe of cleansing. No, the Creation does not wish this battle to take place just yet."

And some say it was Bear, but strangely, no one actually remembers just who it was. Bear denied the accusation, but someone ran from one of the lines and struck Coyote dead!

And Coyote fell and indeed lay there, very dead. And the cry for immediate battle was resumed, and the menacing cries for blood again filled the air,

when, from the opposite end of the battle lines, Coyote again stepped out, dancing and brandishing a huge club.

He ran to his dead self and struck a tremendous blow upon the body, then turned to face the creatures, shouting: "Who killed this person? Who struck him down before I did? Was that person purified? Did he sweat himself and think of the children? Did he dance to assure that the life cycle continue?"

"Enough talking!" someone shouted and ran to Coyote and struck him dead.

And again, much later, no one remembered who or what struck the blow which killed Coyote for the second time.

Then from the left hand side of center, Coyote ran out swinging a great club and struck at his fallen selves until all that remained were two masses of fur and blood and broken bones and twisted sinew.

Then Coyote danced the dance of victory over his own fallen selves, pledging their death to his own great anger. Oh, he danced, he really danced.

"Now then," said Porcupine, "how is it that this one dances the victory in battle dance, when it was not himself who killed himselves? Is it within reason for him to claim this doubtful victory?"

"If I did not kill these two, then who did kill them?" demanded Coyote. "Let him step forward to claim these deaths, that I may kill him too in revenge."

When no one stepped forward, Coyote declared, motioning to his dead selves, "Then obviously, these kills are mine!"

"It seems to me," began Elk, who was interrupted by Skunk, who also began, "It's quite obvious to me that . . ." "Now hold on a moment," said Badger. And Coyote wheeled on Badger, shouting,

"Hah! Don't you know that you can't hold on to a moment, let alone a minute?"

And so they argued, all the animal creatures, about the finer points of who might or might not claim a kill.

And the women of these great warriors, at the urging of Coyote, prepared a great feast, so that these mighty warrior-debators might continue on full stomachs.

And soon, the recent anger was set aside for the more important battle of words leading to reason.

And by this time, everyone having forgotten all about Coyote,

he,
Coyote, took his fallen selves by their tails and dragged them away uphill.

Then he took a good hot sweat bath and then sang a song of renewal known only to himself, and soon his other selves revived. "Now," said one of them, "that's what I'd call making your point the hard way. You know, it really hurt when you killed me."

"Yes,"
said the other self, standing up and stretching, "the next time this happens, don't forget it'll be your turn to be killed."

"Hey, maybe this won't ever happen again, huh?"

"Oh, it will happen again." Coyote said, "Yes, it always seems to happen again."

Then he merged into himselves and walked away, far away.

Notes

Chapter 11

1. Uno Holmberg (Uno Harva), *Der Baum des Lebens* (Annales Academiae Scientiarum Fennicae, Ser. B, Tom. XVI, No. 3; Helsinki, 1923), pp. 57–59; from N. Gorochov, "Yryn Uolan" (*Izvestia Vostocno-Siberskago Otdela I. Russkago Geograficeskago Obscestva*, XV), pp. 43ff.
2. *Kalevala*, III, 295–300 (Everyman's Library nos. 259–60; trans. by W. F. Kirby).
3. I am here keeping the distinction between the earlier semi-animal, titan-hero (city founder, culture-giver) and the later, fully human type. The deeds of the latter frequently include the slaying of the former, the Pythons and Minotaurs who were the boon-givers of the past. (A god outgrown becomes immediately a life-destroying demon. The form has to be broken and the energies released.) Not frequently, deeds that belong to the earlier stages of the cycle are assigned to the human hero, or one of the earlier heroes may be humanized and carried on into a latter day; but such contaminations and variations do not alter the general formula.
4. Clark Wissler and D. C. Duvall, *Mythology of the Blackfeet Indians* (Anthropological papers of the American Museum of Natural History, Vol. II, Part I; New York, 1909), pp. 55–57. Quoted by Stith Thompson, *Tales of the North American Indians* (Cambridge, Mass., 1929), pp. 111–13.
5. Jacobus de Voragine, CIV, "Saint Martha, Virgin" (*The Golden Legend*).
6. One of a class of priests entrusted with the preparation and application of the sacred ointments.
7. Chief priest, governing as viceregent of the god.

Chapter 12

1. Cf. Millard C. Lind, *Yahweh Is a Warrior* (Scottdale, Pa.: Herald Press, 1980).
2. Compare Patton (*The Secret of Victory*, 1926): ". . . despite the impossibility of physically detecting the soul, its existence is proven by its tangible reflection in acts and thoughts. So with war, beyond its physical aspect of armed hosts there hovers an impalpable something which dominates the material . . . to understand this 'something' we should seek it in a manner analogous to our search for the soul."
3. Quoted in J. Glenn Gray, *The Warriors: Reflections on Men in Battle* (New York: Harper Colophon, 1959/1970), p. 52.
4. Ibid., p. 44.
5. Careful sociological research into the motivation of the American soldier (in World War II) shows that the factors which helped the combatman most "when

the going was tough" (as the quotation was phrased) were *not* hatred for the enemy or thoughts of home or the cause for which he was fighting. The emotions that did appear under battle duress—that is, when Mars was acutely constellated—were prayer and group fidelity. Piety and the love of fellows are what the God brings. (Samuel A. Stouffer et al., *The American Soldier: Combat and Its Aftermath,* vol. 2 [Princeton: Princeton University Press, 1949], pp. 165–86).

6. S. L. A. Marshall, *The River and the Gauntlet* (New York: Morrow, 1953), pp. 300–01.

7. "Tomorrow I shall have my new battle jacket. If I'm to fight I like to be well dressed" (attributed to General Patton, in C. M. Province, *The Unknown Patton* [New York: Hippocrene, 1983], p. 180).

8. Cf. Thomas J. Pressley, "Civil-Military Relations in the United States Civil War," in *War,* ed. L. L. Farrar (Santa Barbara: Clio, 1978), pp. 117–22; Otis A. Pease, "The American Experience with War," in *War,* pp. 197–203.

9. On the slapping incident, see: Brenton G. Wallace, *Patton and his Third Army* (Westport, Ct.: Greenwood, 1946), pp. 207–09; C. M. Province, *The Unknown Patton,* pp. 71–86, 191–92; H. Essame, *Patton: A Study in Command* (New York: Scribner's, 1974), pp. 103–17.

10. Gray, *The Warriors,* condensed.

11. *The Homeric Hymns,* trans. Charles Boer (Dallas: Spring Publications, 1979), pp. 60–61.

12. Gray, *The Warriors,* p. xii.

Contributors

Angeles Arrien, Ph.D., is an anthropologist and Basque folklorist. She is the author of *The Tarot Handbook* and *The Four-Fold Way: Walking the Paths of the Warrior, Teacher, Healer and Visionary.*

Peter Blue Cloud is the author of *Elderberry Flute Song: Contemporary Coyote Tales,* published by White Pine Press.

Robert Bly won the National Book Award for *The Light Around the Body.* He is also the author of the bestseller *Iron John: A Book About Men.* The most celebrated spokesman of the mythopoeic men's movement, he lives in Minneapolis, Minnesota.

Stewart Brand is a former infantry lieutenant and the founding publisher/editor of the *Whole Earth Review,* a co-founder of the Global Business Network, and author of *The Media Lab.*

Harris Breiman is a therapist at The Mustard Seed Center of Healing in Bearsville, New York.

Carlos Castaneda received a Ph.D. in anthropology from UCLA. His dissertation, published as *Don Juan: A Yaqui Way of Knowledge,* was a bestseller. Since then he has continued to publish books about his studies with Don Juan, most recently *The Art of Dreaming.*

James Channon is a retired lieutenant colonel in the U.S. Army and the founder of the First Earth Battalion.

Chagdud Tulku Rinpoche, who wrote "Bodhisattva Warrior," is a Tibetan Buddhist meditation master, poet, and artist who has taught extensively in the West for twelve years. His most recent book is *Gates to Buddhist Practice.*

Cheng Man-Ch'ing was one of the most influential teachers of T'ai chi in the West, and is an accomplished painter, calligrapher, poet, and physician. He is the author of *Master Cheng's New Method of Self-Study for T'ai-chi Ch'uan,* and *Master Cheng's Thirteen Chapters on T'ai Ch'i Ch'uan.*

Joseph Campbell taught comparative mythology at Sarah Lawrence College. His many books include *The Hero with a Thousand Faces; The Masks of God;* and *The Atlas of World Mythology.*

Charles A. Coulombe is the author of *Everyman Today Call Rome* and *The White Cockade*, as well as the forthcoming *Catholic Without Apology*. He is a regular contributor to the *National Catholic Register*.

Tom Crum is the founder of Aiki Works, a training group that brings aikido-based applications to businesses and other organizations. He is the author of *The Magic of Conflict* and lives in Aspen, Colorado.

Bill Devall teaches sociology and is the editor of *Deep Ecology*, and the author of *Simple in Means, Rich in Ends*.

Terry Dobson was a personal attendant and student of Ueshiba, the founder of aikido, and a pioneer in developing aikido applications to everyday life. He is the author of *Giving In to Get Your Way*.

Arthur Egendorff is a Vietnam vet, psychotherapist, and author of the prize-winning book *Healing From the War*.

Clarissa Pinkola Estés, a Jungian analyst in Denver, Colorado, is the author of the bestseller *Women Who Run With Wolves*.

Dennis Fitzinger is a founder of the Warrior Poets Society. He lives in Berkeley, California.

Dave Foreman is a cofounder of Earth First! and author of *Confessions of An Eco-Warrior*.

Robert Fuller is a former president of Oberlin College, and a founder of the Mo Tzu Project.

J. Glenn Gray taught philosophy at Colorado College after service as an intelligence officer in the Second World War. His book, *The Warriors: Reflections on Men in Battle*, was originally published in 1959.

Richard Strozzi Heckler is a psychologist and aikido teacher. He is editor of *Aikido and the New Warrior*, and the author of *In Search of the Warrior Spirit*. He lives in Petaluma, California.

James Hillman is a Jungian analyst and the founder of Archetypal Psychology. He is the former editor and publisher of the journal *Spring*, and the author of many books, including *Re-Visioning Psychology*; *The Myth of Analysis*; and *Blue Fire*.

Carl Gustave Jung (1875–1961) is one of the foremost founders of psychoanalysis. His *Collected Works* includes twenty volumes.

Bill Kauth is a founder of the New Warrior Training and the author of *Circle of Men*.

Sam Keen is a former editor and interviewer for *Psychology Today*. He is the author of many books, including *To A Dancing God*; *Faces of the Enemy*; and *Fire in the Belly: On Being a Man*.

Martin Luther King, Jr., was the leader of the Montgomery bus boycott in 1955–56, and thereafter of the nonviolent civil rights movement. He is the author of *Stride Toward Freedom*.

Maxine Hong Kingston is the author of the award-winning memoir *Woman Warrior*, as well as the novel *Tripmaster Monkey*.

George Leonard received his black belt in aikido at the age of fifty-two. A former staff writer for *Look* magazine, his many books include *The Transformation*; *Silent Pulse*; and *Mastery*. He is the founder of the aikido-based Leonard Energy Training (L.E.T.) and the inventor of the Samurai Game.

Audre Lorde's books include *The Black Unicorn*; *Sister Outsider*; and *Cancer Journals*. A black lesbian poet and essayist, and mother of two sons, she died in 1992.

Jarvis Masters is an African-American writer who lives in San Quentin Prison's Adjustment Center on Death Row. He is the recipient of a 1992 PEN Center Writing Award for Prisoners. He was given the Buddhist Precepts by Chagdud Rinpoche in 1991.

Deena Metzger is a poet, novelist, and teacher. Her books include *Writing For Your Life* and *Tree*. She lives in Topanga Canyon, California.

Ralph Metzner is the author of *Opening to the Inner Light*.

Milarepa was a Tibetan poet, yogi, and hermit. His songs have been collected as *The Hundred Thousand Songs of Milarepa*.

Dan Millman coached gymnastics at Stanford, Berkeley, and Oberlin. His *Way of the Peaceful Warrior* is an underground classic. He is also the author of *Warrior Athlete* and *No Ordinary Moments*, and conducts Peaceful Warrior Training Seminars in San Rafael, California.

Robert Moore and Douglas Gillette have written extensively on the masculine archetypes. They are coauthors of *King, Warrior, Magician, Lover: Rediscovering the Archetypes of the Mature Masculine*, as well as *The King Within* and *The Warrior Within*. Robert Moore is professor of psychology and religion at Chicago Theological Seminary. Douglas Gillette is a mythologist and co-founder of the Institute for World Spirituality.

M. R. Bawa Muhaiyaddeen was a Sufi master, and founder of the Bawa Muhaiyaddeen Fellowship in Philadelphia. He came to the United

States from Sri Lanka in 1971, and taught extensively until his death in 1986.

Carol Pearson is a psychologist and counselor. She is the author of *The Hero Within*.

Danaan Parry, a former physicist, is the founder of The Warrior of the Heart and the Earthstewards Network. He is the author of *Warriors of the Heart*. He lives and works on Bainbridge Island, Washington.

Ambrose Redmoon has written poetry, plays, and a military unit-tactic manual. He served as occult editor on the original staff of *Rolling Stone*.

Paul Shippee is managing editor of the *Men's Council Journal*. He lives in Boulder, Colorado.

Gloria Steinem is a former editor of *Ms.*, and author of *Revolution From Within*.

Chögyam Trungpa was one of the most influential teachers of Tibetan Buddhism in the West. He is the author of *Cutting Through Spiritual Materialism* and *Crazy Wisdom*, as well as of *Shambhala: The Sacred Path of the Warrior*. He was also the founder of the Shambhala Training Program.

Sallie Tisdale is a contributing editor to *Harper's*. She is the author of *The Long Search for Home in the Pacific Northwest*.

Mirtha Vega, born in Havana, Cuba, lectures in the U.S. and Europe and leads a workshop-retreat on "Becoming the Warrioress." She is based in Boulder, Colorado.

John Welwood, Ph.D., is a clinical psychologist in private practice and editor of *Challenge of the Heart: Love, Sex, and Intimacy in Changing Times* and *Ordinary Magic*, and author of *Journey of the Heart: Intimate Relationship and the Path of Love*. He lives in Mill Valley, California.

John White is an educator in consciousness research and higher human development. His most recent book is *The Meeting of Spirit and Science*.

Connie Zweig is former executive editor of *Brain/Mind Bulletin* and a former columnist for *Esquire*. As executive editor at Tarcher/Putnam, she founded the New Consciousness Reader Series, and is editor of *To Be a Woman* and *Meeting the Shadow*.

Permissions and Copyrights

Chapter 1 consists of an excerpt from the foreword by Chögyam Trungpa to *The Superhuman Life of Gesar of Ling*, by Alexandra David-Neel and Lama Yongden. Foreword 1981 by Chögyam Trungpa. Reprinted by arrangement with Shambhala Publications, Inc., 300 Massachusetts Ave., Boston, MA 02115.

Chapter 2 consists of an excerpt from "Sorcerer's Apprentice: A Conversation with Carlos Castaneda" by Sam Keen. Reprinted with permission from *Psychology Today* magazine. Copyright 1972, Sussex Publishers, Inc.

Chapter 3 is an original interview with Dan Millman by Rick Fields, conducted during a Peaceful Warrior Training in 1988.

Chapter 4 consists of an article, "No Peaceful Warriors!" by Ambrose Hollingworth Redmoon, which originally appeared in *Gnosis* magazine (P.O. Box 14217, San Francisco, CA 94114), Fall 1991. Reprinted by permission of the author.

Chapter 5 consists of an excerpt from *King, Warrior, Magician, Lover* by Robert Moore and Douglas Gillette. Reprinted by permission of Harper San Francisco.

Chapter 6 consists of an excerpt from *The Hero Within* by Carol Pearson. Reprinted by permission of HarperCollins.

Chapter 7 consists of an excerpt from *Rediscovering the Wild Woman: A New Age Journal Interview with Clarissa Pinkola Estés* by Peggy Taylor, pp. 121–124. Reprinted by permission of *New Age Journal*.

Chapter 8 consists of an excerpt from "Tales of a Reincarnated Amazon Princess: The Invincible Wonder Woman" by Gloria Steinem from *Wonder Woman/A Ms. Book*. Reprinted by permission of the author.

Chapter 9 consists of an excerpt from *The Woman Warrior* by Maxine Hong Kingston. Copyright 1975, 1976 by Maxine Hong Kingston. Reprinted with permission of Alfred A. Knopf, Inc.

Chapter 23 consists of an excerpt from *Cheng Man-Ch'ing's Advanced T'ai Chi Form Instructions* by Cheng Man-Ch'ing. The translation is by Douglas Wile. Reprinted by permission of Sweet Ch'i Press.

Chapter 24, "Aikido: The Art of Loving Combat," by George Leonard, originally appeared in the May 1985 issue of *Esquire* magazine. Reprinted by permission of the author.

Chapter 25, "Warrior Mind," by Sallie Tisdale, originally appeared in the Fall 1993 issue of *Tricycle: The Buddhist Review*. Reprinted by permission of the author.

Chapter 26, "War Games," by Rick Fields, is an excerpt from an article that appeared in the Fall 1987 issue of *Whole Earth Review*. Reprinted by permission of Riki Moss.

Chapter 27, "A Kind Word Turneth Away Wrath," originally appeared in The Lomi School Bulletin. Reprinted by permission of the author.

Chapter 28, "The Virtue of Moral Outrage," is excerpted from *Fire in the Belly* by Sam Keen. Copyright 1991 by Sam Keen. Used by permission of Bantam Books, a division of Bantam Doubleday Dell Group, Inc.

Chapter 29, "Bodhisattva Warriors," by Chagdud Tulku Rinpoche, first appeared in the Winter 1991 issue of *Turning Wheel, The Buddhist Peace Fellowship Newsletter*. Reprinted by permission of the author.

Chapter 30, "Transforming Warriors," by Arthur Egendorff, is an excerpt from *Healing From the War* by Arthur Egendorff. Reprinted by permission of Houghton Mifflin Company. All rights reserved.

Chapter 31, "They All Died in the War," by Bill Kauth, first appeared in *Wingspan: Journal of the Male Spirit*, PO Box 23550, Brightmoor Station, Detroit, MI 48223. This article also appears in his book *A Circle of Men*, St. Martin's Press.

Chapter 32, "The Awakened Soldier," by J. Glenn Gray, is excerpted from *The Warriors: Reflections of Men in Battle* (New York, Harcourt & Brace Co., 1959). Copyright 1959 by J. Glenn Gray. Copyright 1987 by Ursula A. Gray.

Chapter 33, "Combat and Consciousness," is excerpted from "Unleashing Special Forces in the Special Forces," by Richard Heckler, which first appeared in *Magical Blend* #28, October 1991. It was originally given as a talk at the New York Open Center. Reprinted by permission of the author. See *In Search of the Warrior Spirit*, North Atlantic Books, for Heckler's full-length memoir of his experience.

Chapter 45, "The Fight with the Shadow," is excerpted from C. G. Jung's *Essays on Contemporary Events — The Psychology of Nazism*, trans. by R. F. C. Hull. Copyright 1989 by Princeton University Press. Reprinted by permission of Princeton University Press.

Chapter 46, "Getting to Know One's Inner Enemy," by Ralph Metzner, is an excerpt from an article that appeared in *ReVision*, Summer/Fall 1985. It was also published in *Human Survival and Consciousness Evolution*, ed. Stanislaw Grof (State University Press, Albany, NY, 1988). Reprinted by permission of the author.

Chapter 47, "Personal Disarmament," by Deena Metzger, appeared in the Summer/Fall 1985 issue of *ReVision*. Reprinted by permission of the author.

The Epilogue is reprinted from *Elderberry Flute Song: Contemporary Coyote Tales* by Peter Blue Cloud (White Pine Press, 1989). Reprinted by permission of the author.

About the Editor

Rick Fields is co-author of *Chop Wood, Carry Water* and author of *How the Swans Came to the Lake: A Narrative History of Buddhism in America* and of *The Code of the Warrior*. He is co-translator of *Turquoise Bee: The Lovesongs of the Sixth Dalai Lama* and editor in chief of *Yoga Journal*. One of the leading experts on Buddhism in America, he lives in Berkeley, California.